THE BACK OF HIS HEAD

20,000 MILES THROUGH AFRICA AS A PILLION RIDER

BY

AUDREY FLEMING

Copyright © 2019 AUDREY FLEMING
All rights reserved.

THE BACK OF HIS HEAD

20,000 MILES THROUGH AFRICA AS A PILLION RIDER

BY

AUDREY FLEMING

COPYRIGHT AUDREY FLEMING 2019

COPYRIGHT:

All rights reserved. No part of this publication may be reproduced, distributed or transmitted in any form or by any means, including photocopying, recording, or other electronic or mechanical methods without the prior written permission of the author and publisher.

All the persons and events in this book are real and true. Some names of living persons have been changed but they may recognize themselves.

DEDICATION

This book is dedicated to Charles who masterminded the journey and to our children in the hope they will learn a little of who we were………….

CONTENTS

FOREWORD	1
APRIL 1991	7
MAY 1991	19
JUNE 1991	45
JULY 1991	87
AUGUST 1991	101
SEPTEMBER 1991	131
OCTOBER 1991	163
NOVEMBER 1991	199
DECEMBER 1991	237
JANUARY 1992	273
FEBRUARY 1992	319
MARCH 1992	367
AFTERWORD AND ACKNOWLEDGEMENTS	399

FOREWORD

I've travelled 20,000 miles on a motorcycle from Devon in England to Cape Town, South Africa. But, I can't ride a motorcycle. I'm a pillion. A very experienced pillion.

In the early days after I met Charles it became obvious, to me, that motorcycles were a big part of his life and I would have to accept them too. My first time on the back of his motorbike was nerve-wracking as I wondered what I was supposed to do: how would I know when and how much to lean over? The best news was that I didn't have to do anything. All I had to do was sit still and not lean. Additional instruction was not to hold on to Charles and not to crash into the back of him or his helmet when he braked. It all seemed simple enough!

But, I was soon to learn that being a good pillion rider is a skill. A skill I have honed to, almost, perfection over more than

30 years sitting behind my (then) boyfriend and (now) husband - Charles. To be fair, very little of my time is actually spent looking at the back of his head but his head is always there in my field of vision.

But, don't be deceived into thinking I just sit there. Oh no! There's much more to it than that – let me explain.

As a pillion rider I have to, basically, sit still and do absolutely nothing. I'm not supposed to lean or try and influence the bike in any way. I get on when I'm told and get off when I'm told. The rider has to be ready for the mount and dismount. He has to have his feet firmly planted on the ground and be ready to take the shift of weight. When we're going along I don't wiggle or wriggle, move quickly or move suddenly. And, we don't talk. But, I'm not really doing nothing. I take full responsibility for looking at the scenery and if I see something interesting I'll show Charles by a tap on his shoulder or thigh and point to it. I don't do this whilst he's overtaking, braking, accelerating or taking a fast bend – I don't want to distract him from the important task in hand.

Contrary to the popular image of a pillion rider I don't hang on to Charles around his waist either. I usually have my right arm behind me with my fingers loosely touching the bike frame or luggage rack – to be honest, I'm not exactly sure what it is as I can't see it. If the bike brakes suddenly or sharply my fingers will instinctively tighten on the metal and stop me being thrown forward too much. He hates me crashing into his back and my helmet hitting his although, to be fair, he has become more tolerant on the odd occasion it happens now. My left arm and hand rest on my knee and if the bike accelerates sharply or suddenly I can grab my knee, or him, and stop myself being thrown backwards – quite important, especially if there is no 'top box' behind to prevent me leaving the bike completely! This position also leaves my left hand free to wave at oncoming motorcycles.

Waving, or acknowledging other motorcycles, is a popular gesture when passing, meeting or seeing another bike – even if they are parked. Not scooters though. Definitely not scooters. Only bikes and, generally, large bikes and especially if they have luggage - panniers as they are known. Traditionally, we just acknowledge each other with a casual raising of the hand away from the bike – rider and/or pillion do this. If Charles is occupied with gears, braking, accelerating or manoeuvring and can't raise his hand I do the wave. Some of the, what we might call, 'cool' bikers will use a two fingered 'Peace' sign or a low key nod of the head. If a bike overtakes us or we overtake another the rider will generally extend his leg off the footpeg as an acknowledgement and I might raise my hand. The leg off the footpeg is also a 'thank you' gesture to a vehicle which has moved over to let us pass. It's all very complicated and a bit ritualistic but if you ever wondered about it all – now you know.

So, what else do I do back there? Well, I sing. I have quite a repertoire of songs and know quite a few of the words to them. Humming is a useful fill-in for lack of lyrical knowledge. I also daydream, think and talk to myself. Charles can't hear any of this, fortunately. If we do want to talk it's generally done at traffic lights but we don't bother with conversation much on the road – it gives us something to chat about in the lay-bys when we stretch our legs etc. Traffic lights are usually an opportunity to adjust our positions on the seat a little or I might lean forward and give him a cuddle if I'm happy with everything.

We can communicate though. He shakes his head if he disapproves of something happening on the road. If I do start to wiggle or wriggle he will know I'm getting stiff and need a break – or a wee. I can usually tell when he's getting ready to stop at the roadside or for a coffee.

If we're going too fast (in my view) I will squeeze my knees together and the pressure Charles feels on his thighs tells him to slow down. If he accelerates very sharply, or unexpectedly, I may grab him around the waist. He'll usually pat my knee reassuringly after either of these 'messages'.

And, if I get fed up or the scenery isn't good I do, occasionally, just look at the back of his head. I can see the reflection of my helmet in his helmet, clouds etc. behind us. And, when his hair is a certain length a little stray curl pops out between the bottom of his helmet and the top of his jacket collar. The little curl blows in the wind – I love that little curl as much as I love looking at the back of his head, or around it at the view.

So, this is the story of our journey ………… from my point of view. At the back. On the pillion seat, looking at the back of his head.

THE BACK OF HIS HEAD

APRIL 1991

DEVON, ENGLAND TO FUSINA, ITALY

SETTING OFF

As we stood beside our motorbike on a cold, dark and draughty English dockside waiting to board a cross-channel ferry the couple standing beside another bike made conversation.

"We're headed to Burgundy, what about you?"

"Cape Town", we replied casually.

It didn't seem at all ridiculous, to us, but the conversation died rather quickly. I suspect they didn't believe us – I'm not sure I did either.

Of course, the ridiculous appearance of our bike should have told them, anyone, that we weren't headed to Burgundy – or anywhere remotely within the bounds of a "normal" holiday destination.

Our bike was a blue and white 1989 BMW R100 GS. There were large, white wooden boxes on each side as home-made panniers. They were mounted on a custom-made frame which locked them and secured them to the bike. On top of each box was part of our camping gear (mattresses on one side, tent on the other) and the back luggage rack carried a bag with sleeping bags, liners, blow up pillows and pillowcases. Our camping gear might have seemed a bit over the top but we wanted to be as comfortable as possible so that we camped as much as possible. The wooden boxes had been built around plastic 1 litre ice cream tubs. Three would fit snugly in the bottom side by side. Each contained some important aspect of our luggage: spares and small tools, first aid, cooking essentials etc. Clothes filled the rest of one pannier and the other had a camping stove, pots, pans, plates etc. The panniers became known as 'the kitchen' and 'the bedroom'. When taken off the bike they provided seating. There was a large bag strapped to the petrol tank with cameras, paperwork and maps. Two jerry cans with water were mounted on the front engine guards. The whole thing was completed by a small rack at the front under the headlight with a folding spade strapped to it. I don't quite know why we had the folding spade but Charles said it would be useful. Charles was the planner, navigator, bookkeeper, cook, mechanic, rider and number one brains behind the expedition so if he said a folding spade on a rack was essential then it must be so. We never used that spade.

In the few months leading up to our arrival on the dockside we'd resigned our jobs, sold our house, put our belongings into storage, bought the bike, built the luggage and, as they say, put our affairs in order. We were ready to go - south, south, south.

On 14th April 1991 we set off from the Devon home of my parents-in-law where we had made our final preparations

The ferry crossing and our first few miles and hours in France had a very familiar feeling – so like our previous holidays. We had bought new jackets and (open face) helmets and mine hurt my ears. We wore jeans and sturdy walking boots. Our riding gear was, we hoped, going to be protective (to a point), practical and versatile enough for riding and general daily use. We had waterproofs but were hoping we wouldn't be using those too much.

Our first night was spent camping at Nevers in France. This was the first real test of our new tent and camping gear. After a visit to a supermarket we even decided to cook our own evening meal – all in the interest of economy and not so much like our French holidays.

As we went to bed I felt stiff, tired and weathered but it was good, at last, to be on our way. We were very aware of the mutterings in the family before we'd left – "They'll be back in a month." I was determined we would not be.

Two days later we had crossed France and were planning to 're-group' and relax for a few days with Charles' brother and girlfriend who had recently bought a house in the foothills of the Jura mountains. We'd made the trip there with them when they first moved in and were keen to see what progress they had made renovating it.

As it turned out, we stayed quite a few days and certainly longer than we'd planned. This was partly due to snow which we woke to on our first morning but after just a few days on the road we decided that a few things needed improving or fine tuning so took advantage of free board and lodgings, a workshop and a nearby town to sort matters out. We went shopping for electrical bits and pieces so that Charles could make a crude alarm system for the bike and luggage. It would be a long piece of wire we could wind around the bike and everything on it and plug into the bike's electrics. It would sound the horn if the circuit was broken by anyone interfering with it. It wouldn't deter a determined or clever thief but might discourage the casual opportunist – that was the theory, anyway.

(We didn't know it at the time but in Africa more than one interested passer-by dared not even touch the bike believing it would electrocute them if they did.)

Charles had also decided that the panniers needed some strengthening and, I believe, he wanted to have a general tinker with everything to see how it was working on the road. I passed my time reading and wondering when The Adventure, The Journey would really begin. Soon enough, though, it did and we were off again with fond farewells and no looking back. It was at this point that the bike was christened and F702 VEL became Flossie.

Flossie had been fairly standard when we bought her but we had beefed up the rear shock absorber by fitting a 'white power' system and she was going to be transport and home for whatever lay ahead.

Our next stop was La Plagne – a ski resort. I'm not sure, now, why we thought a diversion of two days for skiing (with no ski gear and the cost to the budget) was a good idea but we felt footloose and fancy-free and could do as we liked. So, we did. We rented a small apartment for as little as we could, hired some boots and skis, bought a day's ski pass and enjoyed ourselves on the slopes. Motorbike jackets, gloves and jeans are not ideal skiwear and we certainly felt the cold on the higher slopes but it was good fun and we felt it was time and money well spent.

Having rather indulged ourselves in France we felt ready for the next destination – Italy. We had decided our route would be over the Alps via the Col de Petit St. Bernard. We didn't know if the col was named after the dogs or vice versa but, as dog lovers, we rather liked the sound of it.

We set off and made good, if cold, progress higher and higher on twisting mountain roads with breathtaking views – and sheer drops to match. Slowly, slowly I counted down the miles to the col, the summit and Italy. As we rounded what we felt must, surely, be the last hairpin bend we saw it .... a barrier and a 'Route Barrée' sign. The road was closed. The sign said "Italy 8kms". We pulled up on good, dry tarmac and gazed across the barrier to the snow covered road stretching into the distance to Italy. We couldn't quite believe our eyes. We back-tracked to a café and asked when the road would open. "30th May" was the answer. We were still in April. Apparently, there had been signs about the road being closed and when it would open miles back in Albertville but we hadn't seen them.

Plan B was to backtrack to Albertville, eat and camp for the night. But, the camp site was closed. The hotel was closed. Plan C loomed up as riding on looking for other hotels and if we didn't find one to camp at the roadside. We had talked about 'bush camping' when we got to Africa but hadn't really considered having to do it in Europe. We drove out of Albertville in the general direction of Italy and after not too long we found a camp site which looked as though it might be open. There was no-one camping and no sign of anyone so we decided it would do as bush camping.

As we pulled in and got off Flossie a woman suddenly appeared. She was slightly confused about us wanting to camp and explained that although she was officially closed we were welcome to pitch our tent. We were offered the use of an apartment but we didn't want the expense of that and insisted we'd be fine in our tent. The woman said we could use the bathroom in the apartment in the morning and left us to our own, cold devices.

We were very glad of the offer of the apartment when we emerged from the tent in the morning. We had only just been warm enough in the night and the tent was crisp and white with frost. The water in our water containers was on the point of freezing and would take an age to boil on our camping stove and our milk was actually frozen. In the warmth and comfort of the apartment we both enjoyed a hot bath and leisurely breakfast before setting off to the Mont Blanc tunnel and Italy.

The road was a steady climb and quite chilly but the views were stunning and Mont Blanc itself was breathtaking in the clear, bright sky. On the other side lay Italy and we wound our way down the mountain road to Aosta. Aosta seemed to be closed. In fact, Italy seemed to be closed. Every shop and business was shut tight so we pushed on. We drove on until we found some life which appeared in the form of cars and bikes parked at the roadside and spectators watching karts whiz round a karting track just off the road.

We made a brief stop to watch the karts and then pressed on again. The scenery changed to miles and miles of flat fields of muddy water a few inches deep and just the odd ridge of piled mud or grass. It was quite a depressing scene and the possibility for roadside camping did not look promising.

We found an open petrol station, filled up and found out that today was a public holiday – the Festival of Liberation. The garage attendant said there were no camp sites locally but there was a hotel in town. As we'd been cold all day we opted for the hotel – and dinner in a restaurant.

Our first day in Italy had begun by seeing the BMW

Touring Club of Italy parked at the roadside as we emerged from the Mont Blanc tunnel but ever since then we'd only seen fast Japanese bikes which left us feeling 'odd man out'. As motorcyclists we were quite used to standing out from the cars and vans on the road but now we stood out amongst motorcyclists too. How much more odd would we be in Africa?

We pressed on to Genoa which was a big city and just one big traffic jam until we reached the open road again and could stop for a roadside snack overlooking the sea. The scenery had become very Mediterranean (even if the cool weather wasn't) and we passed the afternoon chugging up and down endless hills getting cooler and cooler until the sky darkened and threatened rain.

By now, predictably, we were quite keen to find a guest house or cheap hotel but a roadside sign for bungalows seemed worth investigating. It turned out to be a camp site entirely populated by large caravans but they did have 'chalets' on the hillside. We were offered a 'duomo picolo' (small house) which turned out to be a very secluded 3m x 3m wooden shed with a double bed. The cooking facilities boasted a fridge and there was a table and chairs outside under a porch and as it started to rain we decided this was all rather ideal. Our toilet was in a smaller wooden shed a few steps up the hill – just past the outdoor kitchen sink.

We cooked dinner and went to bed warm and comfortable to the sounds of small woodland animals snuffling around and over the roof of the little house.

The next morning we woke to birdsong, a blue sky and warm sun. At last! We left our little woodland retreat warm in body and content in our minds and spent most of the morning with more chugging up hill and down dale under a bright sky. Our destination today was Pisa.

Pisa had a good camp site with tents, camper vans, caravans and a good mix of nationalities. For the first time we were amongst other English vehicles but none were, of course, quite like ours. We got into conversation with other campers and found a spare table and chairs under some trees which made cooking and eating a very civilised matter.

The tent was very cosy but spacious enough for us, our riding clothes, helmets and shoes and as we settled down to sleep that night we were very smug about everything. We had a battery-operated short wave radio to listen to the news and music. We could run a light from Flossie's battery to the tent and had used petrol from her tank to fuel the camping stove. Flossie was really a part of the team now – home.

Venice was our next stop and we found a good camp site by

lunchtime so once we'd pitched the tent and eaten we headed off on public transport to see what Venice had to offer. I'd been to Venice before but it was a first visit for Charles. It was cleaner than I remembered but way too expensive for our budget so we just wandered around, took some photos and headed back to the camp site. By now it was raining so we headed to the only dry spot – the bar. We did go back to the tent to cook and eat but the mosquitoes and midges quickly drove us back to the bar.

The bar was buzzing as a group of 22 Australians doing their European tour on a double-decker bus had arrived. Their tour was 34 days long and their bus provided sleeping, cooking and eating space as well as being their transport. There was, apparently, a honeymoon couple on board and they seemed happy enough to be sharing such a small space with so many strangers.

The Australians and an English couple touring in a 2CV all talked to us about Yugoslavia which was our next destination. No-one seemed to have a good word to say about Yugoslavia but we were not deterred and determined to see for ourselves.

Mosquitoes and midges were still a problem so we sprayed the tent with lots of repellent before we went in for the night. As we lay there with our own thoughts and listening to the sounds of a camp site settling down for the night I wondered who would asphyxiate first, the mosquitoes or us.

MAY 1991

YUGOSLAVIA TO ISRAEL

RAIN, CIVIL WAR AND A SEA CRUISE

As May dawned we'd been on the road for two weeks. A good two weeks learning how we would 'live', learning to cope with the travelling and generally getting used to our new lifestyle – and Flossie.

Despite the liberal spraying of the tent before we went to bed we had been bitten mercilessly by mosquitoes and woke covered in itchy, red bumps. My left ear was so bitten it was swollen almost out of being ear-shaped and the prospect of putting a crash helmet on for the day was not a pleasant one. The weather was cool, the camp showers were cold and I felt generally very grumpy. But, we were heading off to pastures new so packed everything up and hit the road to Yugoslavia.

The morning was uneventful, the scenery unimpressive

and we arrived at the Yugoslavian border mid-afternoon. The border guard was very friendly and made very little fuss about our paperwork. He asked where we were heading and didn't seem at all surprised we were going to South Africa. He offered to stamp our passports as a 'souvenir' and we were quickly through the formalities.

This new country should have filled us both with excitement and expectation and the scenery was very attractive. But, it was raining. Raining hard. Motorcycling is best done on dry roads in dry weather – obviously.

As a pillion rider I can be quite protected from the weather (wind and rain) behind the rider. I can stay reasonably dry for quite a while in light rain although it does eventually begin to affect me. The spray from the road will hit my feet and although I can tuck my hands in my lap and keep my gloves fairly dry the water running off my coat will inevitably start to soak in. Our riding gear for this trip was a compromise and, inevitably, we were not as weather-proof as we might, ideally, have wanted to be.

As the rain looked to be set in for a while and conscious that camping would offer no way of drying anything we stopped to put on our waterproof suits. Whilst we did this we discussed the options of finding somewhere for the night and decided that a roadside bed and breakfast or small hotel would be our best choice for cost versus comfort and practicality.

Back on the road and despite our waterproofs we were quickly wet through. As (bad) luck would have it we didn't see any signs for 'Zimmer' or 'Chambres' or 'Rooms'. When, eventually, we did we stopped and I dismounted to knock on the door. The lady who answered took one look at me dripping on her doorstep and shook her head. I can't say I blamed her. I would probably have done the same. So, no option but to press on and she had helpfully indicated, with gestures, that there would be hotels in another six miles - Ilirska Bistrica.

We carried on at quite a slow pace taking account of the poor visibility and slippery roads caused by the heavy rain and sure enough we found the town and a tourist hotel. The receptionist thought we were German and was slightly puzzled we didn't understand her but we got a room which was more like a suite with a bathroom, bedroom and sitting room. We peeled off our waterproofs and wet clothing and soaked in the deep bath full to the brim with the hottest water we could bear.

Clean, dry clothing and out to eat – we deserved it!

The next morning most of our wet clothing had dried and we set off again for another very wet ride along the spectacular Dalmatian Coast. The road wound along under the cliffs on our left with the Adriatic Sea on our right. We were headed to Rijeka and were, again, soon wet and cold. The weather got wetter and colder and although our waterproofs helped to keep the worst out we were worried about poor old Flossie and the luggage which was very exposed.

The scenery continued to be beautiful and dramatic with a very rocky coastline and dramatic hills in the distance. The coastline itself was very green (thanks to all that rain, I suppose!) whilst the water was a very clear and clean blue.

The afternoon wore on and a hotel appeared. As the next town marked on our map was quite some distance further and it was still raining steadily we opted to stop for the night. The hotel was on the seafront of Karlobag and cheap enough for our budget. The hotel and our room were quite basic but the sun was, at last, beginning to show itself in a clearing sky.

The town was very quiet with not much to offer so we went back to the hotel for a beer and dinner. We seemed to be the only guests until two locals walked in. The owner/manager was very friendly and spoke good English but, hearing the locals talking amongst themselves was a stark reminder that Yugoslavian is a very different European language and we couldn't make any sense of it. All the Yugoslavians we met were very friendly and with a mixture of English, some French, a bit of Italian and one or two words of German we seemed to be managing to be understood by them. The written word offered no useful clues as the alphabet is Cyrillic which made pronouncing anything quite a test although I could actually read some of it thanks to my schoolgirl Russian.

I had spent five years learning Russian at secondary school. It wasn't a 'posh' school but it had a Russian member of staff and another language teacher who spoke Russian so it was offered as an alternative to French, German and Spanish. It always puzzled me why they thought it was a good idea because the USSR (as it was), at the time, was a very closed country and I still believe the school was just 'showing off'. However, although I hadn't enjoyed learning the language and couldn't remember much I had been fascinated by the alphabet and could remember enough to read a few words. This wasn't particularly helpful with menus etc. because although I could pronounce the words I had no idea what they meant. But, I did save the day a few times at road junctions as I could recognise the names of towns and could pick out the word for 'restaurant' on roadside signs.

We were quite reluctant to leave Karlobag. Not because it was a great place to stay but because the weather was still persistently wet with no sign of a break in the dark clouds.

When we set off through the town it was decidedly busier than the previous evening with quite a few people loitering in the square. The BBC World Service that morning had told us there had been 'some trouble' with the Serbo-Croat differences here in Yugoslavia and we thought that might be the cause of the people on the streets but it just seemed to be a lot of young men standing around with their hands in their pockets.

As we rode along the rain was very heavy and the strong winds coming in off the sea on the exposed bends were really not much fun and even an hour long coffee stop didn't cheer us up as we faced the inevitability of getting back on Flossie on the wet roads. We dragged ourselves back out and after not too long it did stop raining and the smallest amount of blue sky began to appear. As Charles drove Flossie on I watched the patch of blue grow bigger and bigger and soon the sun shone through and as we rode along we, and the luggage, began to dry off.

Under a brightening sky and welcome sunshine the scenery changed from a rocky coastline to a more flat, straight coastline with pretty bays. I could now enjoy the view and even felt like humming to myself.

We were heading for Zadar which seemed more touristy than any other town we'd seen but all the signs for rooms or accommodation seemed to be on half-built or half-derelict houses. It was hard to decide which was the better description and hard to know if the buildings were in the process of being built or falling down.

A lot of petrol stations, lunch stops etc. we saw advertised just didn't seem to exist and as we were now riding into a very strong headwind we were desperate for somewhere to take a break. We drove in to a small marina at Vodice. There were very few people around and most of Vodice seemed to be closed and the people we did see looked very miserable and poorly dressed and stopped to stare openly at us. There didn't seem to be anywhere serving food but someone buying food from the back of a van offered to show us to a restaurant and led us down several alleyways to a very modern, bright pizzeria. The only member of staff we saw seemed very nervous and shy but was very keen to please and dashed about to lay a table for us.

Two other men arrived and another member of staff rushed about fussing over them and their table. There seemed to be some problem in the kitchen and the two men who were being treated as VIP's seemed to make the waiting staff very nervous and edgy.

All four of them seemed to pay very careful attention to the radio when there were what we guessed were news broadcasts and the announcer spoke in very serious, measured tones. We could sense a real atmosphere which wasn't a relaxed one.

We were quite glad to leave the tense atmosphere of Vodice but the wind was blowing a gale and the sea was heaving and breaking over the promenade. We decided not to go too far before finding somewhere for the night but even this seemed, very quickly, to be a bad move. As we left town we had to cross an open bridge and the cross wind pushed Flossie violently sideways. Charles had quite a fight to keep Flossie in a straight line and had both feet off the footpegs and hovering over the ground to keep her upright. I was terrified we would be blown sideways into oncoming traffic although being blown the other way might take us over the barrier. Neither prospect was a good one and I could do nothing to help. I didn't know whether to hang on to Flossie or Charles.

We made it to more sheltered roads and a town - Sibenik. There was nowhere obvious to stay and the sky was black and lit with violent flashes of lightning. A few spots of rain sent everyone running for cover, the sky opened and we were instantly soaked through. Hail stones fell, thunder crashed and lightning lit up the scene. We abandoned Flossie and ran for an alleyway where we pressed ourselves against the wall for the little shelter it offered and watched the growing puddles creep towards us.

We sheltered (such as it was) for maybe 10 minutes and watched a lightening sky coming over behind the dark clouds. The rain eased and stopped and the sky brightened. People began to re-appear from shops and doorways. We returned to Flossie, who seemed none the worse for it all, and looked around for inspiration.

The Hotel Jadran was close by and although it was expensive there seemed to be no other hotels and as we were soaked through, dripping wet and they were willing to let us in we decided to check in. Although the hotel was quite smart with quite an international feel there was no heating in the room and the quickest way to dry our very wet jeans and shoes seemed to be to take a walk in the now bright, warm and breezy weather.

The town was very busy with lots of buzz and activity and we mingled with the cheerful crowds on the streets. The town square boasted a very official looking building and was packed with lots of cheerful young men – no women. There was an occasional loud cheer and applause and we could soon see this happened every time one of the younger men climbed up a statue of a woman holding the national flag and kissed her.

The only way to get up the statue to her face was by the other men forming a human ladder which they did very regularly. We weren't quite sure what to make of all this but it seemed good-humoured and the police seemed to be tolerating it and just keeping a watchful eye.

We found a phone box and decided to make a call home then bought a beer and went looking for something to eat. We were still struggling with the indecipherable words on menus so chose a tourist hotel where the menu was decorated with helpful photos of the food and we could just point and smile. The restaurant was just off the square and we could hear the mood had changed. We wandered out to the square and the crowd were now breaking windows in the official buildings which surrounded it. The police were moving crowds back. Everyone seemed to be waiting to see what would happen next. We were wondering what it was all about when a policeman grabbed us by the scruff of the neck and indicated we should leave. So, we did and went to bed.

The next morning we left Sibenik behind and I realised I now spent most of my time on Flossie watching the sky. This morning the sky was blue with grey patches but as we followed the coast around the endless bays with the high cliffs on our left and the sea on our right I could see that we were riding along the edge of very bad weather. Dark rain clouds hung heavily over the cliffs.

Our destination was Split and it came into view as a huge sprawl of tower blocks in the distance. We decided not to bother and to carry on to Dubrovnik for the night. As we rode the long straight road people in the fields cheerily waved to us. I was able to wave back but I sensed Charles was in no mood for pleasantries. The road had an appalling surface and we weren't entirely sure how Flossie's suspension would cope with it, us and the luggage. Charles was an experienced rider, an engineer by training and by nature and I had confidence in Flossie and him but couldn't help worrying as we bounced along the rough surface and weaved our way around potholes.

By late afternoon we arrived in Dubrovnik and started to look for somewhere to camp. The site we found which was close enough to the town that we could unload and walk in for the evening was not very enticing and was deserted. We spoke to the receptionist and checked the price for the night and while we stood looking at the depressing site and debating what to do he suggested we rent a room locally for 'the same price as camping'.

Our hesitation gave him the clue we were tempted and he immediately offered to phone someone for us. Very quickly a boy on a moped turned up and told us to follow him to his family's bed and breakfast. The room was pleasant and very clean but twice the price of camping although the landlady's English was good enough for her to understand we were not happy about this and she reduced the price – a little.

We headed out to Dubrovnik's old town for the evening and wandered around. The weather had warmed up enough for us to spend a few minutes admiring the view of the bay and the town's lights from our room's balcony. We felt quite at peace with the world. Our feeling of well-being was not spoilt the next morning and we woke to a bright, sunny morning and a good breakfast of salami, cheese and home-made fig jam.

As we left Dubrovnik behind the scenery changed little with high mountain walls to one side and the blue sea to the other. We stopped at the roadside for a picnic lunch in the warm weather and Charles took the chance to check Flossie's oil and generally see how things were bearing up.

During the afternoon we finally left the sea and coastline behind us and headed across a flat plain to Titograd. The road became a ledge along a deep gorge with endless spectacular, far- reaching views. When the road could not go round a lump of mountain it went through in a series of gallery tunnels. The tunnels were quite unnerving as they were unlit and, therefore, ranged from dark to pitch black. Flossie's headlight was practically useless. Finally, we left the last of the tunnels and got to Babljak which seemed to be the high point of the road and we began to descend towards Ivangrad and, we hoped, some camping.

Ivangrad (as it was called then) seemed to be very run down and sad and there didn't seem to be any camp site. We drove around town looking at graffiti covered walls and went down a few blind alleys before we saw a sign for a hotel which advertised an 'AutoKamp'. Two other bikes had arrived before us: two people and a tent. This looked promising. The bikes belonged to a Swiss couple who had spent two months in Israel and Egypt and were driving up through Greece and Yugoslavia to be home in a few weeks. We chatted and it became obvious we could share a lot of useful information so we pitched our tent alongside theirs and all headed off to town in search of something to eat.

Sunday night in Ivangrad was not a busy one and most places were shut tight. A young Yugoslav saw us and asked, in German, what we were looking for. Our new Swiss friends spoke good German and explained we were looking for something, somewhere to eat. The Yugoslav offered to help us but the first few places he suggested were closed which left him scratching his head until he met some friends who seemed to make a suggestion. We all set off again and were headed to the Sports Ground. This looked an unlikely option but inside the building there was a full-blown restaurant in full swing. Our Yugoslavian friend told the man on the door that we were visitors and he should speak German for us.

We were shown to four places on benches at long tables and food started to arrive in front of us. During dinner we learnt from our new Swiss friends that they had spent two months in England to learn English for this trip and that although they'd enjoyed their trip they were keen to get home. He was an electrician for a small domestic appliance repair company and his job was being held open for him whilst she was going back to temporary office work until they started a family together.

Well fed and having talked a lot about our differing experiences we returned to camp to find another tent had appeared. There was no obvious sign of how it had got there – no transport and no people but a woman's head popped out of the tent as soon as she heard our voices. The woman was Australian and explained that she and her husband were catching the 6.30 a.m bus to a local tourist spot. They were hitch-hiking and using local transport to get around Europe.

Their base was England for three years – he was working as a zoological vet and she was a small, domestic animal vet although they spent all their free time and money travelling Europe.

Charles fried eggs for our breakfast whilst I had a shower in the men's shower block. The facilities were not great and the women's block had no hot water, no mirrors, doors that wouldn't shut (let along lock) and no flat surfaces to put anything on.

The Swiss couple left and we weren't far behind going in the opposite direction. The road surfaces were particularly bad although part of it took us through a gorge so I, at least, had a pretty view to pass the time. Charles had no time for the view though as the road surface was very poor and in places it ran out altogether and was just gravel and mud.

Once down on the plain the road improved and we made steady progress. All the children and young men at the roadside waved at us. I presume the children were just excited and that the men recognised Flossie in some way. I spent most of the morning keeping up with returning the waves and felt rather pleased with myself. The area we were travelling through was very agricultural with elaborate haystacks arranged around a central pole and topped with greenery or a rag bow. The children were poorly dressed and leading cows and goats whilst men worked horse-drawn ploughs in the fields. Horse-drawn carts were on the road too amongst the fast, modern cars and, quite often, we all had to take avoiding action for cows, goats and chickens that wandered across the road. It all felt rather like a slice of the 20th century rushing through the middle of the 19th century. I wondered what the ploughmen and goat herding children thought of us on the road hurrying to a distant destination.

Despite these hazards we were actually making good time on a fast road and heading for the border to Greece.

In the early evening we crossed the border and carried on to Thessaloniki and the sea. We saw a sign for a camp site and followed it for 12 miles. The site was large, well-organised and half-empty so we picked a spot, pitched the tent and ate a quick meal before crawling in to our sleeping bags. Greece, at last. We planned to have a lazy few days and as we listened to the BBC World Service before sleep we heard the news that civil unrest in Yugoslavia was increasing and there was a strong possibility of civil war. It seemed we had left just in time.

After a few days looking around Thessaloniki, doing chores, shopping for basics etc. we set off again on fair to good roads in cool weather and unremarkable scenery. The horizon was just a line of distant hills – some snow-capped. As the hills grew nearer we could make out the 'special place' our Swiss friends had spoken about and recommended to us as worth a visit. I thought the hills were odd but will admit they had a certain mystery, an almost eerie quality about them. Their sides were almost sheer and dark in colour and most were flat topped – this was Meteora. We found a camp site which was well-organised, shady with smart, clean showers and loos. There were even large silk pot plants scattered about to give the place a homely feel. The site was full to bursting with huge Dutch camper vans and caravans but we found just enough space for Flossie and the tent.

Under a clear blue sky we visited the monasteries which topped the rocks. The spectacular views as we climbed up brought home the amazing feat involved to build these monasteries. The monasteries operated a strict dress code and as I was in trousers I was deemed unacceptable so we couldn't go inside. The rules were no shorts for men and no skirts above the knees or trousers for women who must also cover their arms. I was slightly peeved that Charles was perfectly acceptable in jeans but I was not and some girls were rather bending the rules by wearing a skirt over trousers. But, rules are rules and we back-tracked to the road and the camp site and settled to watch the Dutch cleaning and polishing their vans and cars.

Next day we were off again under a dull, overcast sky and most of my day on Flossie was spent gazing at the sky and rolling green scenery. The landscape was very agricultural and goat herds were very common. We found lunch at a BP station where Flossie had her own lunch of Super Unleaded. The scenery rolled on with snow-capped distant mountains and we finally stopped for the night in Delfi and pitched the tent in the rain. A run into town in the gentle but steady rain was depressing so we returned to the camp site and cooked under the lee of the tent and went to bed. We could hear the rain falling steadily all night long and listened to the sound of the ground getting wetter and wetter - a sound you know when you sleep in a tent on a rainy night. I laid there thinking about the prospect of a soggy tent to pack as the sound of rain on the tent kept me awake. About 5.30 a.m I must have dropped off to sleep because a noise woke me – a gentle crashing sound. Flossie had fallen over and so we were both up, dressed and rushing about in the dark and wet to get her upright and assess any damage. We thought the ground underneath her centre stand had got so soft she'd just gentle keeled over and there was, fortunately, no damage. We picked her up and put her on her side stand but by this time dawn was breaking so we decided to start packing up and be on our way.

Everything had to be washed as best we could to clear the red mud spattered on Flossie, the panniers, the tent and anything which touched the ground. As the fog and cloud rolled around the valley below us we caught glimpses of a view which is said to be breathtaking – we never really saw it.

That evening we rolled into Athens and the weather finally seemed to be improving which lifted our spirits. We found a camp site and the next morning dawned warm and sunny and marked one month since we'd left England.

Our main focus in Athens was to buy ferry tickets to North Africa. We quickly found out that this was not going to be quite as straightforward as we hoped. Ferries to Alexandria in Egypt did not start running until July. We were offered a cruise to Rhodes, Cyprus and Egypt or going directly to Port Said in Egypt or to Haifa in Israel. We asked around several agents and it seemed even the Crete to Egypt option was suspect and we might end up stranded on Crete.

The problem with the ferries seemed to be that this was not quite the Summer, tourist season and that most non-tourist services were still suspended in the aftermath of the

Gulf War. Eventually, we bought tickets with Poseidon Lines for 'Seawave' which would take us to Cyprus and everyone assured us we could go on from there "no problem".

We were determined to see Egypt and even though we weren't sure how or when we'd manage it we went to the Egyptian Embassy for visas where we were told to come back the next day. We used the rest of the day trailing round three different post offices looking for poste restante to see if there were any letters from home for us.

At this point in our journey we had decided to post our warmer clothing home. Jacket liners and heavy gloves were no longer needed so we made a parcel and posted it home before dashing to the port and arriving, by the skin of our teeth, just in time for boarding 'Seawave'. As it turned out we needn't have panicked as the dockside was chaotic with loading cars on to the ferry. The cars had to reverse on to 'Seawave' and we were the last to be loaded into a space only just big enough and already crowded with people and luggage.

Once we were happy Flossie was secured and we'd packed a small, overnight rucksack we made our way up to the deck. We met Nick (a Greek Cypriot from London), Suzanne (Australian) and Joel (a Canadian cyclist). We all fell into conversation and went to find what was described as a 'sleeping lounge' but which was, in reality, a large, airless and hot room crowded with rows of cheap, plastic seats. We were supposed to sleep here. We retired to the bar and met three British soldiers who said they were just back from the Gulf and had gone 'absent without leave' and a Greek couple we'd seen in passport control. The Greek couple were both on bikes and going to "do deserts" as he was a photo journalist writing freelance. He also had plans to do some trails, particularly Hadrian's Wall, in the UK. As we all settled down to get to know each other, swop stories and chat we hardly noticed our brief stop at Rhodes although we couldn't have got off anyway. To pass the time Charles joined a card game with the British lads, Nick and Joel whilst I read, chatted and wrote my journal. The three soldiers were clearly very close and very broke but they were also looking after a young Swiss hitch-hiker on her way to a kibbutz in Israel. She seemed to have even less money than the lads but they shared what they had with each other.

The card game only stopped for something to eat and some discussion about sleeping arrangements for our second night on board. The previous night had been very uncomfortable in the sleeping lounge and none of us were keen for a repeat performance so we decided to sleep on deck. We all had sleeping bags except two of the soldiers so the rest of us shared out anything we could and settled down for the night in a neat row under the stars.

We spent two days and a night on the boat to Cyprus. The time passed playing cards and exchanging stories and information. Three square, buffet-style meals were included in our ticket price and the food wasn't bad but, as fun and relaxing as it was, we were very pleased to get to Cyprus. We said our goodbyes to the group and headed for the nearest hotel which looked cheap enough. We checked in and fell into bed.

After a good night's sleep we faced the next problem which was still how to find onward travel to North Africa. And, it hadn't got any easier. There were ships going to Egypt but not to Alexandria until July and the ships to Port Said couldn't take vehicles. So, two options remained. We could stay and wait for the July sailing or go to Haifa in Israel.

Staying was a possibility, however vague, but we wanted to press on and booked a ticket for Haifa on 'Seawave' which would leave the next week. When we returned to the hotel the reception was jammed with luggage and people waiting to go to the airport. They were going home but we weren't – we had a ticket to Israel.

Accommodation was the next priority. The hotel was too expensive. Cyprus was in the early weeks of its tourist season and we decided to rent an apartment for a week, cook for ourselves and relax. Charles took the opportunity to change Flossie's oil and made some adjustments to the cylinder head whilst checking everything was in good order for whatever was to come.

A week later we were back on 'Seawave'. The sleeping lounge was just as unpleasant so without hesitation we opted for the deck again. We settled down to sleep to the sound of the waves, the gentle movement of the boat and the promise of a new country and, more importantly, a new continent tomorrow.

The next morning we watched as we approached the dock and enjoyed the last peaceful moments on board before officialdom and authority took over again and got us in its grip. We were right to be apprehensive as the Israeli passport and security controls were very thorough. Everything was checked, double-checked, copied and noted down. We were asked the same questions again and again. On the fourth round of questions we asked why and were told all our answers were carefully noted and any deviation on subsequent questioning would arouse suspicion. So, honesty or a good memory were essential requirements to avoid delays. We cleared Customs and had to buy vehicle insurance to allow us to drive on Israeli roads.

Our first stop out of the port was to buy a map and we headed for Tel Aviv to find somewhere for the night. The hotel we chose was not particularly cheap but we needed a hot shower and to find our feet so it seemed a necessary expense. We had a sea view and the view was beautiful with a very clean, deep yellow sandy beach and gentle breakers rolling in. The sky was clear and the promenade was dotted with marigolds and petunias of every vibrant colour.

We had been very happy with our world but woke after a hot, sticky and noisy night listening to constant traffic. I had woken several times in a confused state about where I was – not which town but which country.

The next day was the last one in May and we were headed through gentle green countryside to Jerusalem. We parked in the street and wandered off together to find a drink. After only a few minutes we returned to Flossie who was now surrounded by a small crowd and several policemen. We pushed through and the police asked who we were and what we were doing. They explained that Flossie was considered 'suspicious' and a tow truck was on its way to collect her. We gathered they were going to take her to a 'safe area' and blow her up! We explained who we were and it was our bike but the police were clearly nervous and unsure about it all. When the tow truck arrived Charles took action: repeated it was our bike, got on and fired up her engine. The crowd shuffled back a little, I got on and we edged forward out in to the traffic and away. A lesson learnt on Israeli security.

We opted to stay at the YMCA for the night and although it was expensive it was the cheapest we could find. We could only get a single room but there was a camp bed available so once we'd dumped our luggage we headed out to be tourists: The Wailing Wall, Dome of the Rock, Church of the Holy Sepulchre and endless offers of a tour guide. We eventually sought sanctuary in a Church where the guides were not allowed and sat quietly together enjoying the moment. It was all very different and very exciting.

THE BACK OF HIS HEAD

JUNE 1991

ISRAEL TO CYPRUS

A SEA CHANGE GOING BACKWARDS

After a reasonably comfortable night on my little camp bed we had a lie-in discussing a plan for the day. We felt we'd done enough tourism in Jerusalem and wanted to see more of the country before the question of how we were going to get out of Israel heading south needed our attention, again.

We wanted to visit the Dead Sea so that was the plan for the day. On the good, fast roads we came across a group of eight bikes travelling together. They went past us on the road and then slowed down and pulled to the side so that we had to go past them. They then came past us again and in this way we leapfrogged each other for quite a distance. It was clear they were trying to get a better look at us and Flossie and work out who we were and what we were doing. Eventually, we saw them far enough ahead for us to pull off the road and park amongst them. A young man approached and introduced himself as Gig - the 'leader' of the Israeli Motorcycle Club. Gig explained they were part of a group of 150 bikers going to a Water Park close to the Dead Sea and nearly 1,500 feet below sea level. The other riders came up and shook our hands, looked Flossie over and took quite a few photos of her. Nearly all of them were riding Suzuki bikes so our BMW rather stood out. Many of the group stood in the road to get the right shot and as more bikes rolled past on the road they were photographing us too. It was all rather surreal.

We were invited to join them for the day and formed part of their group. Lots of cars travelling together is 'rush hour' or a traffic jam but there is something quite different about travelling in a group of bikes. It is exciting and generates a real feeling of camaraderie.

The Water Park turned out to be a bustling oasis of recreation on the Dead Sea and we spent the day relaxing with the group and chatting. We sat quietly and watched them at play. Some of the bikers were quite shy but most were very happy to ask us questions about our lives, Flossie and our journey. They shared their own stories with us. Most of the group wore Israeli Motorcycle Club t-shirts and it seemed wrong not to join them so we bought one each. This, of course, qualifies us to honestly use the phrase – "Israeli Motorcycle Club? Met them, done that – and got the t-shirt."

During our brief time, so far, in Israel we had been struck by the number of soldiers around. Not soldiers on patrol or involved in security but just hitch-hiking or casually relaxing beside 'checkpoints'. This vision of Israel's army was not particularly threatening or reassuring (if it was meant to be either) as most of them were scruffy with machine guns dangling lazily over their shoulders or behind their knees banging carelessly against their legs, tables or anything they came close too. Soldiers were very much present at the Water Park too – relaxing with the rest of us even though they were in uniform and armed.

We left the Park and the bikers at the end of the afternoon and headed off. We had thought to get to the seaside resort of Elat but were quite keen to actually swim in the Dead Sea and so only drove a few miles to a camp site the bikers had recommended.

At the camp site we pitched the tent and headed into the Dead Sea to experience the very strange experience only it can provide. The seashore was rocky but the water was very warm and clear. The surface was oily and salt crystals stuck to our swimming costumes and bodies as we floated easily in water only knee-deep. When the novelty of it all had worn off we realised we were quite hungry so I headed to the showers to wash off the salt and rinse our costumes. The shower block was very open plan with no curtains or doors on the cubicles. The place was full of large, naked Russian women who were showering, gossiping and laughing amongst themselves with great enthusiasm. As a Brit I stood quietly, and politely, waiting for a cubicle to become free but this was clearly not the Russian way and they shuffled about and beckoned me to squeeze in beside them and share the shower. I could feel my Britishness and reluctance for communal nudity kicking in at this point but it seemed churlish to refuse so I took off my costume and edged in beside them – avoiding all body contact as much as possible. In practice, avoiding their huge thighs and large, bouncing bosoms was no easy feat and I was heartily glad when they got out and dried themselves, with equal enthusiasm and laughter.

Later in the evening we went to the bar for a drink and a huge television in the corner was blasting out an American comedy show which everyone seemed to be enjoying. Outside the air temperature was still warm and the tent was hotter still as we lay down to try and sleep. What a day!

The drive to Elat the next day was hot work. The headwind was warm so riding along was rather like moving towards a huge hairdryer. Although we were hot it was not particularly unpleasant but it did have a hidden danger.

We got to Elat and, with the help of a truculent tourist office who answered every question with a tone of voice which implied "Of course, isn't it obvious", we found a cheap hotel. The room had four bunk beds and as Charles was really not feeling well by this stage we just flung everything on the floor and he laid down to sleep for a few hours. A walk round town in the evening quickly proved too much for him and we had an early night. At this point it dawned on us that the dry, hot wind we had been riding into all day had dehydrated Charles and although I was not suffering quite as badly I had a persistent headache. The next day we only ventured out to buy something to eat and bottles of water and spent the day indoors, drinking plenty of water and resting. We ventured out in the cool of the evening for a dip in the sea only to find a large number of Israeli soldiers doing the same, in full uniform, on the same beach. It's hard to imagine the British Army being allowed to behave in such a way.

The next morning we both felt decidedly better and ready to travel. We'd certainly learnt a valuable lesson to avoid future dehydration problems. We were headed for Egypt with an early start to avoid riding in the hottest part of the day.

We got to Taba where we planned to cross the border to Egypt. There was a departure tax to be paid to leave Israel and then a short stretch of no-mans land before the Egyptian border.

Getting in to Egypt entailed endless checking of documents and various, different fees for the police, customs, a border tax, licence, insurance and many things we didn't understand or know we needed. This was more irritating than costly but the sight of the traffic official on his hands and knees and then lying under Flossie as he made brass rubbings of the engine and chassis numbers was worth every Egyptian pound he charged us. Eventually, we had all the necessary rubber stamps on all the necessary bits of paper and after two and a half hours we were in – Egypt. Everyone had been very polite and 'official' and we had a small pile of receipts for all our payments which had included a new identity for Flossie.

In Egypt Flossie had to have Egyptian number plates which had been fitted over her English ones. The new plates had an Arabic number and 'Taba' to identify her point of entry. Our first stop was for a cold drink and petrol for Flossie. A full tank cost us 16 Egyptian Pounds (slightly less than £3 sterling) which was incredibly cheap and marked a turning point in the cost of the trip.

We were funding our trip by living off the interest from the sale of our house in the UK. We had worked out that about £17 day would be the 'budget' for petrol, food, accommodation and anything else. The budget was arrived at by dividing our monthly 'income' by 30 days in a month – it wasn't any more sophisticated than that and probably not realistic. The ferry crossings had made a bit of a dent in our budget but we counted that as an exceptional and unavoidable cost. So far, through Europe and in Israel, we had failed miserably to keep to the budget but prices in Egypt suggested it would be very much easier to manage from now on. We anticipated being able to 'live' quite well and be well within budget.

Egypt was a change in so many ways. A very different culture and very different riding.

We rode all morning to St. Catherine's village and started asking around for accommodation. A bungalow in the tourist village was priced at US$105 for dinner, bed and breakfast. In the local village a room was 56 Egyptian Pounds so that's where we decided to stay. We took a walk around in the early evening when it was pleasantly cool. The sun had not set but had sunk behind the mountains. I relaxed on the veranda of our room and watched the yellow mountains around us fade in the setting sun to the background noise of prayers being chanted nearby and Charles huffing because he couldn't find his book.

We visited the monastery next morning and then left St. Catherine's. On the road we were soon stopped by a policeman at a checkpoint. He told us the road ahead was "no good" because it had "no black". The alternative he suggested was a long detour so we ignored him – how bad can it be? Well, we were about to find out.

After some miles the road became sand-dusted in places and then a short stretch of a rocky surface with no tarmac. Then, long stretches with no tarmac and patches of soft sand. Eventually, there was no tarmac at all. The 'road' was completely gone. Sometimes, the tarmac could be seen to the left or right of our track with great cavities and subsidence and we rode long distances on a track in the sand only marked by other tyre tracks. Yes, how bad can it be? This was my first experience of off-road riding and I didn't like it – not one bit.

Charles is a very experienced motorcyclist. He passed his test at the youngest age he could and has always had motorbikes – and ridden regularly. Over the years he has commuted to London for work and had a short spell, between jobs, as a motorcycle courier in London. Off-road riding has always been a hobby for Charles and he's ridden many miles on forest and mountain tracks in England, Wales, France and Spain. An off-road motorbike is designed for the purpose: light and manoeuvrable with knobbly tyres to cope with surfaces that don't offer the grip of tarmac. Flossie was a completely different motorbike. Flossie was large and heavy and her tyres were a compromise to cope with tarmac and an off-road element. Flossie, the luggage and us weighed in at a total of 450 kilos. Flossie was a handful and I don't think either Charles or Flossie had much experience of sand although that was rapidly changing. I sat on the back with just my faith in his riding skills and my safety in his hands. His riding skills and my faith would be sorely tested later in the trip.

I tried to distract myself from the lack of road as Charles, and Flossie, coped with keeping us going in roughly the right direction and picking the best route. To the sides of the tracks I could see small villages with derelict buildings nestling in flat areas between hills. Barefoot children ran about carelessly. After a while we stopped to drink some water and a car pulled up behind us. They asked to share our water but when they discovered it was warm they offered us their cold water to drink.

Our water containers sat on the bars just above the engine and whilst this was not a problem when we were on good roads the slow-going on rough roads would heat the water. On more than once occasion we used the warm water in the containers to have a pleasant, refreshing wash beside the road and it was sometimes very nearly hot enough to make a decent cup of tea.

After many hours of the road with "no black" we re-joined, with relief, the tarmac and saw the coast with a beautiful black ribbon of road winding along beside it. Roadside hotels looked smart and inviting and we felt we deserved some air-conditioning and a hot shower.

It soon became apparent that some of the hotels were closed but we found one that was open, clean, not too expensive and had parking we could see from our room. We even had a sea view. What we did not have was air-conditioning because it didn't work. Nor did we have a hot shower – or any sort of shower. There was no water. None. We were hot and sticky. Our hair was damp and matted and our clothes were soaked in sweat. We badly needed to cool down and get clean. The receptionist said the water would be on at 7.00 p.m. but it wasn't. We asked again and were told it would be running at 10.00 p.m. but when the receptionist saw

Charles' face darken angrily he changed his mind and said it would be on at 8.00 p.m. We had the distinct impression he really didn't know. We were the only occupants of the dining room so ate and went to bed. The next morning there was water and it was hot. We ate breakfast in the empty dining room, packed and left with Cairo in our sights.

If we'd thought (and we did) that Athens' traffic was chaos it was nothing compared to Cairo. No-one in Cairo obeyed any traffic lights, give way or stop signs. No-one really stopped for anything, anywhere. The whole place seemed to be perpetual motion to the sound of honking horns which were wired to the headlight flasher stalk to make it easier to keep up a constant barrage of noise.

At one road junction we approached the point where two roads joined (in an upside-down 'Y') to form one going forward. A policeman stood in the road holding back our line of traffic to let the traffic on the other road proceed. The beeping and honking and shouting in both lines grew until the policeman was so intimidated he waved both lines of traffic forward and leapt to the safety of the pavement whilst two lanes of traffic merged into one as a free for all.

Charles coped with the crowded roads of traffic and pedestrians as best he could and our aim was to find the pyramids and somewhere to stay. But, we seemed to be in the wrong end of town where the road was unmade, the buildings and people scruffy and run-down. Charles kept going until we found a slightly better part of town and pulled over to check the map for clues as to which direction we needed to go in.

A man came up and asked if we needed help. We said we wanted to get to the pyramids at Giza. He started to point the way but someone else came up and asked what we needed, could he help. He said he was waiting for his wife to come out of the hairdressers "in just a minute" and we could then follow him in his car. A woman appeared, they spoke briefly and then got in a car behind us and pulled out with a wave of a hand to indicate we should follow them.

We were able to keep up with the car and were soon in a huge traffic jam slowly progressing around a roundabout under a flyover with many exits. In the middle of the traffic the man in the car jumped out and told us this was as far as he could take us but he would find someone else. He then walked around the four lanes of slow-moving traffic and banged on windows to ask where they were going and could they guide us. We waited patiently as this was all clearly out of our hands now. A minibus driver said we could follow him but then a Japanese bike (a Honda CB500 Four) drove past us and promptly made a U-turn across the lanes of traffic to come back and pull up beside us. "What's the problem here?" "Looking for Giza," we replied. The bike did another U-turn, pulled in front and waved to us to follow.

At the time, this Honda was quite unusual in Egypt – an unusual model and much larger in engine size than most other bikes on the road.

The bike was a lot harder to follow than the car as it weaved and dodged between cars and lanes with ease. We had no choice but to do the same to keep up. We soon saw the very top of a pyramid towering over other buildings and the bike pulled over and stopped. Our guide got off and walked back to us. He asked where we were staying. We said we would look for a hotel but he said we should go home with him.

We set off again for a few minutes before pulling up outside a block of flats. We had arrived and introduced ourselves. Our new friend was called Mohammed.

We had to carry all the luggage from Flossie up to the fifth floor and were pretty hot and sweaty when we'd done so. Mohammed showed us to a bedroom where we could change and made us all a snack.

The flat had an open plan kitchen with a dining area and a comfortable seating area with a television and video player. It was all quite modern but slightly worn. The dining room had large doors to a balcony and a glass- fronted cupboard with display pieces of what was obviously the best china. The room boasted two large chandeliers. There were two bedrooms with huge furniture of very ornately inlaid wood. The bathroom had a loo which was leaking, a washbasin and bath. There were no curtains and some door handles were missing but it was homely. Mohammed explained that his wife was out working and that their son was staying with relatives. Mohammed told us proudly that he only had one wife because he was a modern Egyptian and that he allowed her to work as a masseuse although he didn't allow her to drive a car – he considered Cairo roads to be too dangerous.

As we sat and chatted Mohammed told us that he owned a video shop – Habib Film Video – and that he had come home for the afternoon and would be going back to the shop in the evening until quite late. He was very keen that we should not be on our own but come and see his shop.

So, early evening we got back on the bikes and followed Mohammed as best we could as he led us into the early evening traffic and the dusk. It was quite hair-raising and, almost inevitably, we lost his tail light in the mass of tail lights. We pulled over under a flyover and hoped Mohammed would realise we were no longer with him and re-trace his route back to us.

Almost immediately a young couple stopped to ask if we had a problem and could they help. The couple were well-dressed Egyptians, clearly well-educated and spoke good English. We explained what had happened and they listened with mounting disbelief and scepticism. They asked what Mohammed's full name was and did we know the address of his apartment or even roughly where it was. We had no answer to any of those questions. They said there was no problem and that we could go with them and stay the night. We then had to explain that all our luggage, passports etc. were at Mohammed's apartment. They asked us why we had gone with Mohammed and why we had trusted him. "Because he was riding a motorbike", we said. It sounded a bit thin when put like that but it had all seemed perfectly reasonable to us and we had confidence there was nothing sinister going on. The couple asked where we had been going with Mohammed and we told them about his shop and that we knew that was genuine because we had seen the stickers on the videos in his apartment. "The address?" they asked. "Don't know", we replied.

By now we had gathered quite a crowd of interested

onlookers who all wanted to help. We felt pretty stupid about it all by now but were still convinced Mohammed was genuine and all would be well – somehow.

The couple took charge and told us to drive a couple of hundred yards up the road to some shops and restaurants. They followed on foot but by the time they arrived they had to fight their way through another, new crowd of locals wanting to help. The couple asked the crowd if any of them knew Habib Film Video. Nobody did but someone was sent to fetch a phone book from a nearby restaurant and they looked it up. It was there with an address. By this time the restaurant owner was involved and said he knew how to find it. He shouted to a friend who had a taxi and asked him to lead us there. The couple said they would leave us with the taxi but gave us a slip of paper with a phone number on it "Any problems, anything you need phone us and we'll come to you." We thanked them and they left.

The restaurant owner gave us a small card from his restaurant and told us "Any problems, anything you need phone or come to me here and I'll help you." We thanked him and left following the taxi. After not too long we were driving down a bustling street lit with neon signs and could see Habib Film Video. The taxi pulled up and the driver got out. He said he would check this was the right place for us but he had no need as almost instantly people were coming to us calling our names. The taxi driver spoke to one or two and then explained to us that Mohammed had left instructions with everyone to watch for us and that he had gone back to find us. The taxi driver gave us his card with the now familiar phrase "Any problems, anything you need contact me and I will find you."

We thanked him and he left us to park Flossie. The gathering crowd made a big fuss of us and took us into the video shop. It wasn't long before Mohammed turned up – he had been very worried about us. He explained we would be in the shop until about 11 or midnight and then go back with him to the apartment adding "And don't get lost!"

We wandered around the local area looking at the shops and bustle of the street market before following Mohammed back to the apartment. By this time, his wife was home and she had collected their son and was cooking a meal. We suspected that their son had been brought home to meet the visitors from England and the meal was going to be something of an event.

Mohammed was 38 years old, his wife was 24 and their son was 10. 'Mrs. Mohammed' did her massages at the homes of her wealthy clients and travelled around Cairo by bus or taxi. Mohammed had bought his bike as new some months before and he was very proud of it. He also had a Fiat 128 car and used it as a part-time driver for Hertz. Mohammed had been in the Egyptian army and spent two years as an Israeli prisoner of war.

Dinner was served: meat, cucumber, tomatoes, pitta bread, cheese and a dip made from chicken stock and finely chopped dandelion leaf. The dip was very tasty but its colour and consistency of snot was a bit off-putting. I didn't know what the meat was but we had the distinct impression it was a special treat for the family. The first piece I ate was fine but the second was pure gristle and chew as I might I could not get it down to a small enough piece to risk swallowing without gagging on it. I couldn't chew it or swallow it and taking it out politely and setting it aside on my plate would, I was sure, have offended our hosts who were so keen to please us. Eventually, I excused myself to the loo and spat the meat out into the toilet. It didn't disappear with the first flush but floated persistently on the surface so I had to flush again and poked at it with the loo brush.

After pudding of fruit salad we returned to the comfortable seating and Mohammed suggested we watch a video before bed. We'd noticed in the shop that all the videos for sale and hire were either slushy, cheap romances, sickeningly violent or pornographic. Fortunately, Mohammed just wanted us to see a home movie of a family wedding.

Mohammed and his wife showed us to the master bedroom and found us some suitable nightwear. Charles had a rather fetching Arab robe and I was given a tight fitting jumpsuit. We all said goodnight.

During the night I had to visit the loo and saw Mohammed, his wife and son sleeping soundly laid out in a row on the living room floor with just a blanket between the three of them. It was clear we had been given the best they could provide. Our room was hot and stuffy and we tried to sleep despite the sound of mosquitoes buzzing around. We were woken by calls to prayer and although it was light outside our room was gloomy – and hot.

Mohammed made us breakfast of eggs, bread and jam and we were soon ready to leave.

Mohammed and his family had been incredibly welcoming, kind and generous with their time and hospitality and, of course, there was no question of insulting him with the offer of money. We promised to send a poster of a bike like Flossie for their son's bedroom wall when we got home and we left with more than a hint of sadness.

At the pyramids any thoughts of Mohammed were soon pushed to one side as we were overwhelmed by guides offering their services for anything we could want to see or do. We did use a guide to take us around the pyramids and he paid someone to look after Flossie while we did so. We managed to avoid being whisked off to visit a perfume house but just as we'd avoided that particular treat we were approached by a taxi driver who introduced himself as Mohammed.

Mohammed II wanted to take us to his home "for to stay" and as he offered us the use of his washing machine it was too good a chance to miss. We were introduced to his family and given tea before being shown to our room and the washing machine which was on the flat roof of the house. Over tea Mohammed II explained he worked at Cairo University but that it only paid E£150 a month (Mohammed's video shop took E£100 a day) so he worked as a guide, taxi driver or whatever he could offer as a service to tourists.

In the evening we wandered around town and found a pavement café to sit for a drink and watch the sun setting. A man approached us and declared Charles' legs to be "a shame". It was clear this chap disapproved of Charles' shorts (which were quite modest) and launched into a long and wordy explanation about how disgraceful it was to be dressed so immodestly. Interestingly, as the chap got into the swing of his explanation he was surrounded by several passers-by and hustled away. One of these men then came back to apologise and assure us that Charles' legs were perfectly acceptable and we should not be worried or frightened. We thanked him for his help and went off in search of the 'Sound and Light' show at the base of the Sphinx.

The next morning, after breakfast, Mohammed II was very sad to find out we were leaving as he'd been hoping to earn a week's rental on the room but we were ready for the road. Outside we were instantly stopped by someone who wanted to change our US dollars for us. He promised a good rate for $100 but when we told him we would only want to change $50 he scoffed at our meanness and poverty and stomped off to find other, richer, tourists.

It took us ages to find the right road out of Cairo to Alexandria and we were fairly desperate to find a bank and petrol. Riding along a good tarmac road we saw a sign for a bank. We followed the sign off the main road, through what seemed to be small housing estates until we found it. Charles went inside and I waited with Flossie until someone from the bank beckoned me inside. We were offered tea and cold water to refresh us before they even knew what banking service we might need. Having exchanged our US dollars for local currency the banking staff came outside to stand on the steps and wave us off. I've never had such service, before or since, in a bank.

In Alexandria we found a hotel. Our room was on the 7th floor with a sea view and although we couldn't see Flossie she was parked in an alley outside the hotel kitchen with the promise that the kitchen staff would always be able to see her and look after her for us.

The next morning marked eight weeks from home and as we looked at our breakfast of black tea, hard boiled egg and pitta bread we both felt a bit homesick. Not long after we were both actually sick which was a little worrying but we put it down to all the changes of diet we'd been through.

Today was the day we had to register with the Police although with the number of roadside police checks we'd been through, passports checked and documents looked at it seemed hard to think they couldn't know we were here. We found a minicab to take us to the nearest Police Station and the driver helped us deal with it all. We also needed to buy a few tools to make a repair to Flossie but it was Sunday and most shops were closed. Our driver agreed to pick us up again on Monday and take us somewhere that we could get everything we needed.

Our main reason for being in Alexandria was to visit the Commonwealth War Graves at El Alamein. Before out trip I had made efforts to find out where my Uncle Jim was buried as I knew he had died at El Alamein in 1942. The Commonwealth War Graves Commission had told me that although he had no known grave he was commemorated at the cemetery and that was where we were headed.

Heading out of town in the right direction was not easy and we covered 27 miles trying to do it. Other drivers were helpful and shouting at them through open windows soon became the norm. We followed one car for some distance until we lost him and then came across four Egyptians who didn't speak any English but with some pointing at our map we made ourselves understood and they drew us a simple map to the cemetery.

El Alamein's best features were, undoubtedly, the war memorials which stood calm, pristine and clinical in the face of surrounding noise, dilapidation and chaos. We found the cemetery we were searching for which commemorated 11,000 men and were staggered by its order and condition. There was a well-kept gravel path through gates to a memorial building and a sea of neat, white headstones set amongst trimmed green grass, flowers, trees and birdsong. We spent a quiet afternoon there before heading back to the real Egypt.

Back in Cairo again we headed for Giza hoping to find Mohammed II again and stay at his house but we were unlucky and the whole pyramid and sphinx area was remarkably quiet. 'Quiet' in the sense that within five minutes we were only offered money exchange, a cold drink, a camel ride, a visit to a perfume house and film for our camera. There was no sign of Mohammed II but we were directed to a local hotel – The Tiba House Hotel. This hotel was so well signposted it only took the help of four Egyptians to get us there!

The Tiba House Hotel was in a sand covered back street. Outside there was rubbish in the streets but the staff were welcoming and assured us Flossie would be safe with them. The hotel was run down, shabby and our room had a view of a brick wall, a shower with no shower head and rusty pipework. We spent a hot, sweaty night buzzed by mosquitoes and couldn't wait to leave for Suez.

In Suez we found a good, clean hotel and could relax with our list of 'things to do'. Top of the list was to send a fax to England and arrange to have a new cylinder head gasket sent out to us.

Flossie had developed an oil leak whilst we were in Israel

and although it hadn't been too serious at first it was not getting any better so something had to be done. As I understood it, there was a problem in the crank case and the cylinder head would have to come off and it would need a new gasket.

We also had to look for a shipping agent who could get us and Flossie to Kenya.

We could not drive south from Egypt because the route lay across Sudan and Ethiopia. Our research before we left England and application to their embassies for visas had made it clear we would not be welcome in either country. The Sudanese Embassy had been unequivocal: "There is very little fuel, water and food in Sudan. Large parts of the country are in the grip of a civil war. The roads are in poor condition. Daytime temperatures when you intend to visit will be in the region of 40+ degrees centigrade. In the circumstances, we do not recommend you visit Sudan on your motorcycle and are not prepared to grant you a visa to do so."

We went out to visit various shipping agents who had their offices overlooking the Suez Canal and although everyone was very polite and we drank a lot of tea we were told, by everyone, that it was impossible to get on a south bound ship to Kenya from Suez. It was suggested that we stood a better chance of finding a freighter in Port Said or might be able to catch a ferry to Jeddah or Aqaba.

Our time in Suez was quite a different experience from Cairo. Happy children played football in the local park and we joined the couples sitting on park benches or just enjoying an evening stroll. No-one tried to sell us anything and the children didn't pester us for money. Suez was greener and more relaxed than Cairo and Alexandria and we felt we were seeing a better representation of Egyptian people and daily life. There were more women on the streets and fewer men in Arabic costume. The streets were cleaner although they did still have a tendency to run out, become broken and finally disappear into sand.

The only real blot on our horizon was slight, but persistent, diarrhoea for both of us despite being very careful about not drinking local water. We'd given up ice in our drinks too since seeing a handcart being pushed past the hotel with a stack of green, slimy blocks of ice loaded on it.

We had to wait in Suez for four days for the parcel from England but once it arrived at the hotel we were packed and gone within the hour. Our destination was Port Said.

Port Said was much richer and cosmopolitan than Cairo and Alexandria. The shops were well stocked with all sorts of recognisable goodies and we found a clean and reasonably priced hotel. Most of the rooms and some of the stairwells had been recently painted and varnished and the lingering smell reminded me of school – fresh paint, varnish and creaking wood. We were only given a room for two days though because the big Moslem holiday was approaching and everything was fully booked. The receptionist was quite apologetic but explained it would be 'Christmas'.

'Christmas' required a lot of cleaning activity in the hotel with everyone fussing over it. We escaped the worst of it by visiting shipping agents who told us nothing goes to Mombasa more than a couple of times a year. We drank lots of tea in lots of offices with a spectacular view of the canal but it did no more than confirm that we could not sail around Sudan to Kenya. Air freight to fly from Cairo could only be organised in Cairo. We wondered about a yacht and went to the grandly named Port Said Yacht Club but it lacked two of the essentials - a clubhouse .... and yachts.

So, back to Cairo and our first stop was the cargo village at the airport. We were met at the gate and taken to an agent. The agent measured Flossie and told us the price of freighting her to Nairobi – 7 Egyptian pounds per kilo, in cash. Flossie's size and shape made her expensive so we pondered how much difference removing her panniers, mirrors and fairing (plastic trim etc.) would make to her overall size.

We drove back to central Cairo to check our finances and think it through properly. We were hot and sweaty and booked in to a hotel. We needed three things: to get cool, to get clean and to get out of Egypt – preferably south.

Once we were cool and clean we discussed our options. There were ships to Jeddah but we didn't particularly want to go to Jeddah. There were ships from Alexandria to Limassol. We couldn't really afford air freight and our own air tickets to Kenya unless we used our invested capital. If we decided on that option we weren't sure how quickly we could get money to Egypt. So, we seemed stuck in Egypt. What now? Back to Cyprus?

Going backwards was not an attractive option but we did think we might find work in Cyprus to cover at least some of the cost of air travel. Cyprus would also be an easier base from where we could organise our finances. Decision made. Back to Cyprus.

We found a shipping agent to book our passage on a boat but that wasn't so easy. There was only the Black Sea Shipping Company and we knew they couldn't take Flossie. The agent suggested we go to Alexandria and argue with them to get her on board. We decided to find another agent and asked about The Adriatica Line but found it would only go to Piraeus in Greece. We seemed to have fought so hard to get here and now we couldn't get out.

The only option seemed to be to backtrack to Israel and Haifa and catch 'Seawave' back to Cyprus.

We were both in foul moods by this point. The noise, chaos and constantly being accosted to buy a camel ride, go to a perfume house or whatever else was wearing us down. We had also changed £150 to buy a boat ticket which we didn't then buy and we couldn't change it back in a bank. At least, we could change it back but less $30 per night of our stay in Egypt which meant we wouldn't get any back. The hotel receptionist was friendly and asked how we were enjoying our stay. We decided to explain the problem of the money and he said he knew someone who could help us. A while later he tapped on our door with a bunch of US dollar bills for our Egyptian money which cheered us up considerably.

By now we had to check out of the hotel to make way for the guests arriving for Christmas. On Christmas morning the streets were quiet and I noticed a shop opposite our room. Several people were sitting around outside the shop with a sheep. I thought this might make a good photo so went to get my camera. When I got back to the window the shop front had been 'painted' bright red and the men at the shop were 'painting' it with their hands. I then noticed the sheep lying in the 'paint' in some distress and realised, with horror, that they had slit its throat and the 'paint' was blood. We left and decided to head to Fayoum which was said to be very green and pleasant.

As we headed out of Cairo to Fayoum we saw similar scenes of dead and bloody sheep. Fortunately, the road was a good one stretching like a curving black ribbon through the yellow desert and into the distance. The scenery was greener and lusher with trees and fields of sunflowers. We'd been told that Fayoum was very beautiful and where they grew the flowers to make the essence for the perfume shops and to export to French perfume houses.

Suddenly, we saw a dirty brown lake which seemed oddly out of place. Small boys and young men were playing on the lakeshore but we sped past to find Auberge Fayoum which, we'd been told, was the only hotel on the lakeside. The Auberge was modern and clean but priced in US dollars and, consequently, out of our price range. We drove on but Fayoum was a grubby, run down town with nothing much of interest – nothing except the road out.

Typically, the road out was not so obvious and we had to make several circuits of the town before we found our way. During our tour we saw a good many sheep had met a bloody end and there were lots of small boys on bicycles with sheepskins and bloodied carcasses slung over their crossbars, behind their saddles or, even more gruesomely, over their shoulders or around their necks.

We didn't find another hotel so headed back to Auberge Fayoum and stopped at a small group of huts and shacks selling cold drinks. A smiling man and three small, dirty boys came over and offered us a choice of drinks and began asking for 'backsheesh' and pens. This was something we were quite used to by now but it felt slightly different here and we drank our drinks as fast as we could but, even so, by the time we'd finished the group of three had swollen to a dozen or more older, bigger boys. We were surrounded and they became quite insistent. Their dirty, bloody hands were everywhere on us, Flossie and the luggage. We got ready to leave and they sensed this and that we were not going to give them anything. Their demeanour and tone changed. Their hands were more pressing and their interference with Flossie, the luggage, water carriers and our clothing became more obvious and searching. As I climbed onto Flossie the small rucksack I was wearing was pulled at several times and the small hands turned to fists. The man just stood smiling while we felt we were being mugged. Charles fired up Flossie and revved the engine meaningfully. The children stepped back just enough and we pulled away fast. Once out of their sight we stopped to check everything and, glancing at each other, take a few deep breaths.

By now the Auberge Fayoum was coming back into view and the price of a room seemed a small price for the peace and safety we now felt we needed. Once we'd checked in we had no desire to leave its cool, calm confines so had lunch and a siesta. The hotel did have a pool which might have tempted us outside but it was the same dirty brown colour as the lake.

The next day we headed to Ismailia on a long, hot desert road. I could see nothing for miles except sand and, oddly, most of the traffic on the road was lorries loaded with sand. The logic of moving sand from one place to another in a desert failed me.

In Ismailia itself we found yet another series of gloomy, dilapidated hotels to choose for the night. The one we chose was the best of the bunch. Our dark room was three floors up a dark stairway. When we got to the room we flopped down on the bed and decided we would immediately go out and find something to eat. At this point we realised we could not find the wallet we used for our passports and daily cash needs. We'd handed our passports in to reception and Charles remembered dropping the wallet down on to our pile of luggage before going out to park Flossie. I had waited by the luggage. Two porters had gathered up the luggage and led me up to the room. Halfway up we had met another porter who helped us get to the room with everything. We left the luggage in the room and all went back to reception where we met Charles on his way up. We both clearly remembered all this and searched the room for the wallet. We went back down the stairs looking for the wallet and asked reception if it had been found. The receptionist called the two porters who said they hadn't seen the wallet. We searched the room again, checked the cupboards, under the bed and pulled every bag apart. After all this we agreed it was not in the room.

We tried to think calmly about what might have happened and came up with two possible explanations. Either the porters took it or it was dropped and picked up by someone else. Either way it was gone. Fortunately, the wallet only had Egyptian £80 in it. This was a loss but not the end of the world to us although to an Egyptian it would be half or more of a month's salary. I didn't think the porters had taken it because it looked and felt empty and they didn't have the opportunity to look inside. But, if they had dropped it or passed it to someone else they could have looked inside and seen the money.

The loss of the money aside we decided we should report it and get a police report for our insurance.

We went back to reception and told them we could not find one of our bags with our money and couldn't pay the bill. We asked for the police to be called. The receptionist summoned a man in a blue shirt and we repeated our story. Both men seemed to understand the problem but denied any knowledge of the bag. We asked them to call the police. Nothing happened. I asked them to phone the police so that I could speak to them myself. Time passed and we asked what the delay was and they said we should wait until 6.00 p.m. when the third porter would come back to work and could be asked if he had seen the wallet.

At 6.30 p.m. the porter had been spoken to, denied seeing the wallet and they seemed to think that was the matter closed. We became a little more insistent that we needed to contact the police and the receptionist smiled, held out his open palms and shrugged ever so slightly. This did nothing to improve our mood and we asked, again, for the police. The receptionist then said he was not 'authorised' to call the police and the manager would have to do it.

The manager appeared and was told about it all. He wanted to search our room, the luggage and Flossie. Then, he wanted us to wait for the owner of the hotel. At this point we decided to go to the police ourselves and off we went.

In the police station we sat and waited our turn and got into conversation with a UN employee who was also reporting a theft. His report was laboriously being written out and we got chatting. He'd been in Egypt for some time and spoke good Arabic. He liked the country and the people but kept a small, local apartment to get away from things from time to time. Once he'd been dealt with and left Charles and I were ushered into a smart, large and airy office with a huge desk dominating the room and a row of visitors' chairs lined up in front of it but at a distance. A well-dressed Egyptian came in, shook our hands and introduced himself as Brigadier Ibrahim. He listened to our story and phoned the hotel. He seemed to speak to several people and then hung up. The Brigadier said we should return to the hotel and speak to Mohammed Unis who was the owner and that we could have our report in the morning if the wallet had not been found.

Back at the hotel we asked to see Mr. Unis who was very disagreeable and suggested we had delayed reporting our loss to him to embarrass him and that we were mistaken. He called a porter and they had a long, long conversation in Arabic. Mr. Unis wanted to search our room and luggage. We all trooped upstairs and they had a quick look around. We explained exactly what had happened with lots of actions and arm gestures and finally managed to persuade the manager that we were not blaming the hotel but needed the police report. The manager explained all this to Mr. Unis who then seemed to calm down and we all set off back to the police station.

By now it was nearly 10.00 p.m. We hadn't eaten all day and were hot, tired and hungry. Fortunately, the Brigadier saw us straight away and he gave us some paper to write our report. The Brigadier was a very polite, charming man who obviously enjoyed his position and the respect of his men who were very much in awe of him. Whilst we sat at his desk and wrote our story he phoned the hotel and asked for our passports to be brought to the station. What followed next made up for the events of the whole day.

The senior porter from the hotel appeared clutching our passports and was shown into the Brigadier's office. The porter saluted and stood rigidly in front of the Brigadier. He was clearly over-awed by the size and décor of the office, the desk and all the phones. He seemed almost incapable of moving but his eyes darted around the room taking everything in until the Brigadier dismissed him and he backed out bowing.

By the time we left the police station and found something to eat it was past midnight. What a day - exasperating and exhausting.

It took us ages to pack up the luggage which had been scattered all around the room during various searches but once it was all back on Flossie we were ready to leave. Charles said we would have to pay with our credit card but the receptionist said they could only take cash and directed us to the bank. I was on the point of saying we were on our way to Cairo to report to the British Embassy and ready to invoke the Brigadier's name but Charles persuaded the manager to find Mohammed Unis and word quickly came back that, in the circumstances, there would be "no charge".

We'd now had enough of Egypt and were headed, without delay, to Israel.

At the border we surrendered Flossie's Egyptian plates and she became British again. We trailed patiently through all the border formalities including one official who took our passports and examined each page carefully until he got to the front, saw the photo and realised he had them upside down.

Without changing his expression he very carefully turned the passport the right way up and then went back through it page by page. I think we were supposed to be intimidated. We weren't.

Leaving Egypt involved all sorts of officials checking things and asking for miscellaneous payments and taxes. We had been warned about this and advised to get a receipt for everything to be sure it was 'official'. Official or not every uniformed man gave us a receipt but we were running out of Egyptian cash with all these unexpected taxes and payments.

We told one official we would have to pay in UK Sterling or US Dollars and he carefully made the conversion on his calculator. The figure he came up with was so ridiculous that Charles questioned it. He re-did the calculation. It was still ridiculous so Charles asked to use the calculator and found the number '5' button was not working. "I know," replied the official. "I have to use it a lot and it is broken." We did the sum on our calculator, paid the money and donated our calculator to him. His need seemed greater than ours.

Formalities to get into Israel were no less tedious with extensive security needing everything to be searched, X-rayed and, in some cases, unpacked. It took three hours to get through the whole process but we were eventually free and struck by how green and clean Israel seemed to be after the grime and chaos of Egypt.

We were headed to Tel Aviv and Haifa but didn't realise the road would take us through the notorious Gaza Strip until we were stopped at a checkpoint. Soldiers casually lounging by the road told us vehicles were often stoned and sent us on a long detour. When we got to Haifa we booked into the first decent hotel we found and asked about parking for Flossie. We were told to park her in reception. Charles queried what, exactly, they meant but they were insistent she should be in reception so he drove her up the steps, through the front doors and parked her beside the reception desk.

The next morning our one and only thought was to get tickets for 'Seawave' to Limassol on Cyprus. We were disappointed to be back-tracking so far but looking forward to Cyprus and our next attempt to get further south.

I was also looking forward to being a person again. In Egypt everyone was polite to me but they deferred to Charles, spoke to Charles and expected Charles to speak on my behalf. The Egyptians understood, of course, that European culture recognises women but I'm not sure I was ever really approved of by being there. The Brigadier was charmingly polite and old-fashioned in his courtesy but he was only interested in anything Charles had to say and only wanted Charles' passport and version of events. I had been very much a by-stander in everything. In Israel, by contrast, I had been included in tasting wine at the table and treated as an equal. Is that because Israeli women fight in their Army?

At the port we waited patiently in the melee of 5,000 US sailors on shore leave and an awful lot of Russians with lots of dollars, lots of luggage and no real idea of what was going on.

Security for an Israeli bike going to Greece on holiday was swift. But, the officer who dealt with us was very suspicious and asked endless questions and then called another officer. Fortunately, the second officer remembered us and waved us through to the departure area. We sat in the crowded waiting area and surveyed the scene. Very soon a man who had been sitting opposite got up and walked away. He left his bags behind and I watched him go to the small shop and out of sight. The patrolling security people who were making regular circuits, checking bins etc. came round and I pointed out the bag and that the man had left it there. "We know. We're watching him. Don't worry." was the reply which was reassuring – and quite impressive. It seemed second nature to them.

The Israelis seemed quietly aggressive and security

conscious in a way we hoped we would never need to be. When we were chatting to Gig of the Israeli Motorcycle Club he had described lying in his apartment listening to Saudi missiles fall in nearby streets. He said he had felt helpless but not defenceless. He was ready, willing and able to go to war if required and although younger than us he had already fought in two wars.

Once Flossie was loaded and secure on 'Seawave' we went up on deck to take a last look at Israel. The port was crowded with warships and a fellow passenger pointed them out and advised us to keep our cameras well out of sight and not show too much interest in anything vaguely military. I think, by now, we had got the message that Israeli national security was not to be under-estimated.

We were very glad to be back on 'Seawave' and quickly settled to sleep on deck. When we landed on Cyprus we headed to the hotel we stayed in before which was now more expensive because the main tourist season had started.

It had been one month since we left Cyprus for Israel and now we were back with a determination not to waste any more time and energy. We started scouring newspapers to get a feel for jobs, prices of apartments, etc.

THE BACK OF HIS HEAD

JULY 1991

CYPRUS

PLAN A v PLAN B

Our early good intentions to get things done in Cyprus took several knocks.

Any and all forms of freight from the island were going to cost about £1,000 and we needed to make some repairs to Flossie. Flossie was now badly spraying oil and repairing it had revealed she needed a new piston ring. We asked local dealers but they couldn't help so we had to send to England for the part and wait for it to arrive.

We lazed around for quite a few days doing nothing much but then decided to hire a bike and, at least, see a bit of the island. We drove along the coast to a lighthouse and a wonderfully rocky coastline creeping down to the water's edge. There were lots of rock pools lapped by small waves rolling in.

We drove on to Coral Bay and from a high vantage point looked down to a sandy bay laid out with pairs of sun loungers in neat rows equally spaced from each other in every direction.

We found a bar in town for a quiet beer but whilst we were relaxing the bike was knocked over. We had parked outside a shop and when we returned it was lying on its side in a pool of petrol. We looked around for the culprit who had been watching for us and turned out to be the Chairman/Managing Director of BMW on Cyprus. He gave us his business card and seemed very unconcerned as he drove off. The owner of the shop came out and said he'd seen everything and knew the bike rental place. He said he would phone them to explain any damage was not down to us. The driver of the car had already insisted there would be no problem and seemed to regard the whole thing as inconsequential but the bike's clutch lever was broken and the petrol tank was dented. When we took the damaged bike back to the rental company with the BMW business card and our explanation the owner seemed reasonably happy to deal with it all and we walked away relieved and happy. We were relieved there was no cost to us and happy it hadn't happened to Flossie.

Days passed as we waited for the piston ring to arrive. Once we knew it had left we went to the local post office who said it could take 12 days to arrive. They seemed rather pleased and proud with how long it would take and how complicated it all was for us.

It was now three months since we'd left England and we couldn't quite believe we were still in Europe and, seemingly, marooned on Cyprus with holidaymakers and waiting for a spare part. We decided to try and contact Nick – the chap we'd met on our first trip on 'Seawave'.

It would be good to see a familiar face and cheer ourselves up. We were depressed at the prospect of another week or more on Cyprus and all the news was full of cuts in interest rates in the UK which was not good for us as it would seriously affect our monthly income.

It was mid-July before the postman delivered the piston ring and Charles got to work to install it and clean Flossie up to be ready for the road again. But, although we'd solved one problem we still had the problem of how we were going to get over or around Sudan and Ethiopia and into Kenya.

Whilst we waited for the piston ring we'd tried to explore every possible means and route off the island to Kenya. A container company said they could help but their quote of $1,000 for space in a container on a very indirect route was the best they could do. We decided that an 'indirect route' meant a long route and there was no knowing how long we'd be separated from Flossie.

Knowing we were stuck on Cyprus for at last a couple of weeks we had committed to renting a small studio attached to a private house. Our studio was fairly newly refurbished with a modern kitchen and comfortable seating although the beds and linen were quite well-used. One wall of the studio was all glass with large patio doors and Flossie was parked right outside so was secure and close to us.

After we'd settled in we were invited to our landlady's terrace for a coffee and chat. We talked about our lives in England, explained our travel plans and how frustrated we were about getting to Kenya. Our landlady suggested that we might find work on Cyprus. Apparently, there was a shortage of trained engineers on the Island and a lot of new radio and TV stations were opening and struggling to find staff. Charles worked in television broadcast in England for some years and thought he should be employable here. Our landlady's husband joined us and offered to talk to Radio Paphos for us. He got Charles an interview for 'a chat' with Mr. Fotis at the radio station for 3.00 p.m. the next day.

The landlady's husband also suggested a shipping agent we might try.

The next day we found the shipping agent and he agreed he could ship Flossie to Kenya for Cyprus £260. He said he needed to check the price and timing (seven weeks in transit) with another agent but was sure Flossie could be crated here and shipped via Rotterdam. We chatted around the logistics and it became apparent the price related to a crate measuring one cubic metre. We explained that Flossie was quite a bit larger than a cubic metre. The agent said we had better make a very careful measurement for a made-to-measure crate.

We went away with a tape measure and returned to tell him that Flossie was 8 foot long, just over a three foot tall and about the same in width. The agent listened with growing disbelief and after a few moments shaking his head in denial he said he "must see this bike for myself." We took him outside to the street but by now a van had parked between the front door and Flossie so she was obscured from his view. As we beckoned him around the van and Flossie was revealed in all her glory he stopped in his tracks. "Jesus wept" was all he could think to say. We laughed but only briefly because it became obvious that Flossie's size was going to affect the shipping price – upwards, naturally.

In the afternoon Charles spent half an hour talking to Mr. Fotis at Radio Paphos who explained that the station was not actually making any money and didn't need any engineers. Charles decided to ask around some of the other local radio and television stations for work.

My background was secretarial and I'd worked for Rank Xerox/Xerox Corporation so we decided I would approach the local Xerox agent and other offices in search of work.

We also got interviews with a couple of local employment agencies and they suggested various options. Although everything they had were permanent positions they had no qualms suggesting we should take anything offered and just leave when we were ready.

We sat for hours in our studio apartment discussing all the various possibilities and options and eventually decided to head off to the Troodos Mountains for cooler, fresher air which might clear our thoughts and cheer us up.

We camped for two nights in the mountains and it was good to be under canvas again although the evening mountain air was quite chilly and we were usually in bed by 8.00 p.m. just to get warm. The mountain air did focus our minds though and we made plans: Plan A and Plan B.

Plan A was to find work, rent a cheap apartment, save money and catch 'Seawave' back to Athens for air freight and flights to Nairobi. Plan B was not to find work or rent an apartment and catch 'Seawave' back to Athens immediately for air freight and flights to Nairobi.

Plan A and Plan B were both based on us having found out that air freight and flights from Athens were much cheaper than from Cyprus.

By now we'd ridden quite a few miles around the Island and Charles decided that Flossie ought to have new brake pads and tyres and that it would be better to get it done here and now.

The brake pads were ordered from the BMW dealer in Nicosia but we found the right tyres in stock at the local Cagiva/Ducati dealer. We took Flossie and the tyres to a tyre fitter next door. The fitting of the front tyre proved to be quite difficult. Various banging and pushing failed to produce a seal so the wheel was laid aside and the back one fitted. Returning to the front tyre it proved just as obstinate and the fitter tried forcing the tyre onto the wheel by means of a rope bracelet tightened tourniquet-fashion whilst inflating it. The fitter's wife had arrived with his lunch by now and was included in the struggle – to no avail. Next, they tried fitting a tube and inflating the tyre. Then they removed the tube and tried to re-inflate the tyre. By now an hour had passed and, finally, with the aid of a mechanic from the dealer next door it sealed. We were mobile again.

With new tyres we decided to see some more of the island and Nicosia whilst collecting the brake pads. We bought a loaf of bread, some ham and cheese and had a picnic at Governor's Beach before heading inland to the capital. The road was pleasant and cool and turned into flat, agricultural plains with barbed wire in the distance – the result of the Turkish occupation of the Island.

In Nicosia we found a flat to rent for a week and went out in the early evening to explore.

The main square was buzzing with people. Earlier in the afternoon we'd seen them hanging Greek and Cypriot flags everywhere and testing a sound system. This all seemed to be something to do with the July 1974 invasion of the Island by Turkish troops. There was a lot of general milling around with people carrying flags and a large police and military presence.

Trying to get back to our apartment we found the roads were being closed and had to plead ignorance and persuade the police to let us through. It seemed that the Cypriot President was going to speak to the people after President Bush's recent visits to Athens and Ankara and his efforts to solve 'the Cypriot problem'. The rally going on outside was to show support and protest and included lots of speeches and the lighting of 1,619 candles to mark the number of Cypriots who disappeared in the wake of the invasion. There was a concert by a Greek singing star visiting the island and the lights were scheduled to go out at 9.00 p.m. with the whole event broadcast live on local television and radio.

The following morning I was woken at 5.30 a.m. by air-raid sirens. Deafened and terrified I wondered, for a moment, if the Turkish were invading again. However, it was just another marking of the invasion of the island – the marking of the precise time the Turkish Army landed on Cyprus on that July day in 1974.

During our time on Cyprus we had been able to talk to Nick who we'd met on 'Seawave' months before and as we were now in Nicosia where he was based we had arranged to meet up. We wondered if Nick would have some local knowledge to help us decide between Plan A and Plan B.

We met Nick and caught up with his news and told him ours. Nick was working for a family of farmers helping them make the best use of technology they had but didn't really understand. Nick seemed surprised we couldn't find sea freight for Flossie and passage for ourselves and offered to ask the family if there would be work for us on the farm or in the related cheese and yoghurt making businesses. He explained that work would, almost certainly, include basic board and lodgings. We rounded the evening off by going back to Nick's apartment which was large but barely furnished although he had basic cooking facilities. Nick had chosen not to live out at the farm where he worked as he'd found himself fighting off all the local farmers with jobs and houses – and daughters thrown into the deal!

We did a bit more job hunting in Nicosia. Charles had an hour and a half interview with one company but emerged empty-handed. The managing director was not keen on employing locals and said he would have jobs for both of us – but not until December. I had an interview at a local Employment Bureau which occupied a rather seedy office and the man in charge was a slightly creepy Cypriot with wandering hands. He wanted me to register with his bureau for Cyprus £3 and explained he would take 35% of my first month's salary as his fee. He thought I could earn Cyprus £300 a month in a permanent job and invited Charles in to discuss what he could do for him. We told him we would think about his offer.

So far, we'd been working to Plan A which was to find jobs and cheap accommodation and earn some money. But, after many phone calls and various interviews it became obvious that all the promises of work were too vague to be taken seriously. Plan B was now looking a better option.

We decided that we must get moving and would release the necessary money from our invested capital to make it happen. We wrote a letter to our UK building society and sent it to Charles' mum to forward on with the instruction to send the cheque to her. Mum would receive cheque and pay it in to our bank so that we could draw on it.

Plan A and Plan B both involved returning to Athens because air freight to Nairobi, Kenya would be much cheaper from there and we could probably get cheap air tickets for ourselves using the many, competitive bucket shops in Athens.

Just as we'd made this decision Nick got in touch to say he had spoken to his father who, according to Nick, owned a Greek shipping line. Nick said his father would put Flossie, crated, on a ship going to Kenya. The ship would take us as passengers for £100 each. The ship wouldn't be in Cyprus until mid to late August. So, we now had another option to throw into the mix.

We were slightly sceptical about Nick's offer. It seemed too good to be true. We couldn't really understand how, or why, Nick's father could divert a ship so easily.

So, we were still in limbo as to what to do and as a

diversion we sorted though clothes and paperwork to decide what we no longer needed and post it back to Charles's mum. 'Surplus' clothing included the liners of our jackets, winter gloves and warmer clothing. We kept some long trousers and one long-sleeved top each and now rode in light-weight gloves.

We arranged to meet Nick again and find out a bit more about his father's offer. Nick told us his father was quite a wealthy, influential man and the ship being suggested for us would divert here from Thessaloniki in Greece to collect us and any other cargo it could find. The ship would be English with an English crew and often carried passengers in the form of Lloyds' agents who dealt with the cargo in Kenya. Nick told us the ship's costs are mainly covered by the northbound trip so anything carried south is extra profit. Nick was very convincing and suggested the whole experience would be a good one for us as we would be under the protection of the shipping line and not parted from Flossie at all.

Nick also said he would ask the family again about employing us and we went away wondering whether this could all be relied upon. But, it was too late to do anything else this week as 'Seawave' had sailed and there was nothing for us to do but sit it out for another seven days.

We decided to have another change of scenery and go to

Limassol for what might be our last week on Cyprus. We were determined to make a decision one way or another: get a commitment for a job or onward passage or book ourselves on to 'Seawave' for Athens.

We were quite familiar with Limassol and finding cheap accommodation by now and it wasn't long before we got settled in for Cyprus £10 a night.

We spoke to Nick again and he said there was a ship leaving Piraeus in Greece on 17th August which would be here on the 20th. This ship would take us and Flossie to Mombasa. We had to wait for further, confirmed details.

The next day was Charles' 36th birthday but there was no pile of cards or birthday present of a job although he did have an appointment to speak to the local Sony agent and I'd made him a birthday card.

At the Sony agent's office I waited outside minding Flossie while Charles went in. It was a good job I was there as a local man seemed to think Flossie was in his way and wanted to move her. I left my shade of the building and walked over. The man asked if it was my bike. "My husband's", I said. The man asked me to move Flossie but I said I couldn't. "It's too heavy", I said. The man said he'd move her. Well, Flossie was a big bike and heavy – even without her luggage. I suggested moving her would not be a good idea. I said if he dropped her he would have to pay us a lot of money. "The helmets will fall and they cost £100 each. This piece here might break and that is another £100, and this piece here might be bent or damaged and will cost at least another £100". I rambled on pointing at various parts of Flossie and eventually the man gave up and moved away to find somewhere else to park. At least, he persuaded another local to move his vehicle.

Charles re-appeared and told me the agent said there might be some work but not until October. We hope to be long gone by then .... one way or another.

And so we ended the month where we'd started it – stuck on Cyprus.

AUGUST 1991

CYPRUS TO KENYA

A NEW CONTIENENT

Another month and we were still on Cyprus. We were still working out the best way south but, to be honest, we were rather enjoying the sunshine and not having very much to do. Cyprus was 'easy'.

We collected the brake pads and Charles fitted them to Flossie but other than that our daily routine settled in to a morning of 'chores' and an afternoon at the beach. I still kept my daily journal but there wasn't that much new to write on any day although I did realise I had stopped counting the days and weeks since we'd left home.

We phoned Charles' mum who said she had received our parcel and paid our cheque from our invested capital into our bank. This had happened more quickly than we hoped and

Charles gave her our address to post a new eurocheque book to us.

We were using eurocheques from our UK bank to get local cash and would continue to use them when (if?) we ever got to Africa. We had a little book from our bank which listed all the countries and banks which would accept or cash eurocheques. These cheques were a security, back up measure in the event of us losing our cards or them not being accepted.

With the brake pads and the money sorted we began to feel that things were slowly coming together. When Charles spoke to his mum he made the point, firmly, that we would not be back in September as had been suggested to us, by many, and before we'd even left the UK!

Charles' mum also passed on news that our cat, Oscar, was still in their care and now, apparently, spending more time around the house or, at least, closer to the house. Oscar lived in their holiday flat attached to the house when no-one was there which is where we had stayed, with him, before we left. When visitors arrived Oscar moved to the barn but Charles and I were both relieved Oscar was still there and, probably, waiting for us to come home. Poor cat!

After the conversation with Charles' mum I decided that before we left Cyprus I would write one letter to both mothers to outline timescales etc.

Before we left the UK we had made an informal arrangement with my own and Charles' mum that we would try and make regular contact with one of them – taking it in turns. When one received a call or card/letter from us she would contact the other mother and pass on the news. This would mean they were both reassured and kept up to date without us having to repeat ourselves to both of them.

We were going to phone Nick that evening to find out what was going on but had committed to another week here. Tourists on Cyprus seemed obsessed with phoning home and there was always a queue for the public phones and that evening there were eight or 10 people patiently waiting to use the one nearest to us.

When we did get through Nick explained that he had not contacted us because he had no new information for us. His father was in Rotterdam and expected to phone any day. Nick promised to contact us as soon as his father had sorted out the details and there was news for us. We felt quite confident about leaving on the 20th.

The days went by with no news from Nick but we continued to think about how and when it would all come together. When we did phone Nick and could speak to him we found out the boat was still on schedule for the 20th. Apparently, a captain and crew had been found. Nick was coming to Limassol for the weekend and we would meet him at a flat (belonging to his father, of course) that he had for the weekend. We arranged to meet at 8.00 a.m. on Saturday morning and go together to the agent to arrange the details regarding crates and fares etc. Nick said he had to negotiate a contract on behalf of his father and that had been the delay in confirming everything to us. We invited Nick to come to dinner on Saturday.

On Saturday morning we were up early to go to Nick's flat as arranged. Flossie's front tyre was flat which caused a slight delay but we rang Nick's doorbell just a few minutes past eight. There was no answer. I'm not sure we were surprised but we were frustrated. What do we do now? We went off to find a phone box to try and call Nick. There was no answer. We went back to the flat to try again. Still no answer. We went back to our flat.

Neither of us knew what to think but we knew that, because of the date, we could be on 'Seawave' next Friday. We decided if we hadn't heard more positive news by next Thursday, a few days before our 'D day' of 20th, we would have to be on the weekly 'Seawave' sailing on Friday.

We spent the afternoon at the beach but after a shower we decided to try and find Nick one last time. We were just about to leave when our landlord caught us to say Nick had phoned that morning and left a message he would come over to us here tomorrow at 11.30 a.m. Nick had spoken to our landlady whose English was not very good and we hadn't got the message in time. By way of an apology then invited us to their part of the house for coffee.

Over coffee we learnt our landlord had a home in Famagusta in the north of the island but when the Turks invaded they came to Limassol and bought a field, surrounded by other fields. They built this house on the field, fourteen years ago, and had since watched the surrounding fields be taken over for hotels, apartments, bars etc. They were now enclosed by tourist nightlife and had lost their view of the sea and mountains over the years. The whole house belonged to them: a three bedroom house at ground level with another in the other half which, though empty now, they hoped to rent. The below ground level was our studio apartment, a one bedroom flat next to us and an apartment in the other half where another family lived.

Nick came at about midday on Sunday bearing two bottles of wine as a 'peace offering'. He was very bright and cheerful and armed with various bits of information for us. The new arrangement was for him to see the agent on Monday morning and call us to go there too.

The ship, 'Antonia', would leave on 19th or 20th, sail direct to Mombassa and Nick would be there when everything (including Flossie and us) was loaded to ease any problems. There would be other passengers on board and our fare would be UK £100 each.

We were so pleased with all this information we went out to lunch which lasted all afternoon. A bottle of wine and some beers later we finally left the restaurant as the sun set and went in search of a curry. Nick left at 1.00 p.m. The more we talked to him the more reassured we were but the less we knew about him.

On Monday morning we waited for Nick's phone call – in vain, again. There was no word from him all day.

Tuesday morning dawned and we were woken just before 8.00 a.m. by our landlady telling us we had a phone call. It was Nick. When Charles returned he said Nick had told him he had been breathalysed when he left here Sunday night and detained at the police station until 3.00 p.m. on Monday.

Despite this Nick did meet with the agent who had, apparently, done none of the required paperwork. This meant the cargo could not leave on the 'Antonia' which would not, therefore, come to Limassol. Nick said he would call his father and ask if the 'Antonia' could wait at Piraeus for us. "Some hope," we thought.

So, after all this time and finally believing it might just happen for us we were let down. We were both very disappointed. We now knew we had no option but to go back to Piraeus and air freight Flossie and fly to Nairobi. We spent the rest of the day in a bad mood but re-planning and re-thinking. We spent some time wondering about Nick. Had it all been an elaborate charade, some sort of ego trip he was on and spinning us a tale?

It was now mid-August and very hot. Doing anything in the heat of the day was exhausting. On the way back from a cooling dip in the sea we noticed a very small sign on a supermarket declaring that tomorrow was a public holiday. This meant we would have to get our 'Seawave' ticket today but we just couldn't face going out on Flossie in the midday heat so phoned Amathus Navigation and arranged our ticket to be collected on Friday morning at their offices.

The price was Cyprus £69. We'd paid our rent until Friday and were eating our way through the store of food we'd accumulated during our many weeks here. We both got a haircut and were ready to leave Cyprus but with a feeling of resignation that we were again, still, backtracking. Our last night on Cyprus was a strange one of mixed feelings – we'd never intended to come here and at first we only reluctantly decided to stay a week!

Friday, 16th August dawned and we were up and at the Amathus office to collect our tickets before going back to our flat to pack everything. We were at the port in good time only to find a two hour delay on 'Seawave's' departure. When we did board we found three other large bikes on board – one German and two Italian. The rear deck area was full of all manner of rucksacks, sleeping rolls and people. We laid out our 'area' and settled down to read and pass the time. It was all very familiar.

On deck we got into conversation with an Australian girl (Karen) on her way back from some time in Africa. Karen told us Kenya and everywhere south of there was "hard work" but we couldn't wait to find out for ourselves.

The part of the deck we were occupying, along with many other travellers, was very sooty and the deck, us and everything was quickly covered in black, sooty deposits. We passed the day reading, talking and relaxing with the passing scene. Charles had a tendency to seasickness but seemed fine, so far. The ship stopped at Rhodes around lunchtime and we had a picnic of cheese, biscuits and crisps followed by melon and grapes.

Back at sea and towards dusk the wind picked up, the air temperature dropped and as the sea became a bit choppy Charles did not feel too good. After dinner, which Charles didn't really want (he must be feeling unwell!) we very quickly tucked down to sleep.

During the night the boat began to rise and fall with the growing swell of the sea and the wind picked up significantly. The deck was noisy and the corrugated plastic roofing over our heads began to hammer and flap against its fixings. Plastic chairs slid around the deck until a seaman came along and made a neat stack of them. Sometime later he came back and lashed the chairs to the railings of the deck. I wondered, at that point, whether he would return a third time to lash us down too!

Our sleeping bags fluttered and flapped in the wind but I tucked right down into mine and wasn't cold. I went off to sleep and was surprised to find I had when I awoke at midnight. The wind had got worse, abated after a couple of hours and got worse again towards dawn. We woke with the dawn and although I doubted anyone slept much during the night everyone and everything seemed to be in one piece. As we emerged from our sleeping bags most people were doing the same and packing everything back into bags and rucksacks. Charles and I sat quietly watching the passing islands and around mid-morning the Greek mainland coast came into view.

On dry land and back on mainland Europe we found a hotel with Karen from the boat. In our room we saw the first bath we'd seen in many weeks and soon turned it and the bathwater black with the soot from our hair and bodies. We still had some clean clothes and feeling quite presentable we went to the pool and met Karen and another Australian (Robert) she had met there. Karen and Robert had met an Englishman (John) who was a truck driver and told us he regularly parked his truck behind the hotel and slept in it but quietly used the hotel pool and toilets.

We started to ask around about air freight and airfares for ourselves. Flossie's air freight price was quoted at UK £700. A lot! But, our airfare of UK £296 each pitched us into deeper depression.

We decided to go out to the cargo village and see if we could negotiate something better for ourselves. Without too much difficulty we found Olympic Airways' cargo department who quoted 336 Drachmas per kilo (as expected) and then suggested we use a forwarder to make a crate so we set off again.

The forwarder quoted 336 Drachmas per kilo plus 50,000 Drachmas to make a crate and another 10,000 Drachmas for the paperwork. After much discussion and talking about other African destinations it appeared that Kenya was the cheapest. Next, we discussed dismantling Flossie for crating and talked through the procedure. We agreed to go to the forwarder's warehouse the next day.

We were given a photocopy of a map to find the warehouse but it took another hour, three people and much argument amongst them to do this. Eventually, we left with a map and instructions and were resigned to the cost being more than we had hoped. But, we really wanted to go to Kenya and now felt we should go at any price. Not going would be something we'd always regret and would be such a waste of everything we'd done so far. What was the alternative? We couldn't give up now.

An early breakfast and we went in search of the company who would be making our crate. We had a little trouble but after some backtracking we found their warehouse. They seemed very relaxed and confident about what we wanted to do and the carpenter measured Flossie for a base. Charles began stripping off the wing mirrors and fairing. The front wheel came out and then the forks. Several men gathered to lift her onto her pallet and steady her while Charles took out the back wheel spring and settled her down on to her engine. She effectively sat down! The carpenter braced her in position with various blocks of wood and Charles fussed around – but not too much! Once Charles and the carpenter were happy we wrapped all the loose parts in bubble wrap and stacked them around Flossie on the pallet. Charles drained the petrol and disconnected the battery. The loose, small parts went in the panniers with our jackets and the helmets sat on top of them. We took a final look at her 'squatting' on her pallet taking up as little room as she practically could and left her in, we hoped, good hands.

Now we were temporary pedestrians and our next job was to book our own flights. The first agent we found told us that Athens to Nairobi on Alitalia was 84,000 Drachmas. Next, we asked about Egyptair flights. Athens to Cairo to Nairobi was 81,000 Drachmas and involved a one hour stop in Cairo and a night flight landing in Nairobi in the early hours of daylight. We asked around a couple of other agents but the story, and price, was the same so we settled with the first one. We booked for Athens to Cairo but had to be waitlisted for Cairo to Nairobi. The price was UK £255 each and we still didn't know how much Flossie would cost until we contacted the agent again.

We contacted the air freighter but there was no news so we took a taxi to Camping Voula. The camp site had filled up considerably since we we'd been here in May but we found a shady corner and pitched the tent.

In Voula there were lots of Italian and German bikes and a fair number of tourists from the Eastern block countries – Czechoslovakia and Hungary mainly. We had lunch in the camp café/supermarket which wasn't open last time and then went off into Athens to see the travel agent. Our flights were confirmed so we rushed over to the bank to cash 170,000 Drachmas, paid and got our tickets. Now we had to get Flossie moving too.

A night in the tent was warm but not unpleasant. We both had a hot shower and bought breakfast at the camp site shop. We found two chairs and a table abandoned by previous campers and felt quite comfortably settled. It was very strange not to have Flossie beside us though because she was, by now, very much part of the team in so many ways.

Flossie was our transport and carried us and all our

luggage. When we were camping Charles used her mirrors to shave in and I used her seat as a shelf to put my contact lenses in, brush my hair etc. The bars which kept the panniers secure could be folded out and used for drying our towel. The panniers, when taken off Flossie, made good seats. After dark Flossie's battery powered a light in the tent and our radio. Flossie was vital, integral – and so much more than a motorbike.

We phoned the freight office and got the price - 199,000 Drachmas. We went to Glyfada for the money and then on to the freight office. We were given all the information we needed and a waybill and paid the money. It actually came to just over 201,000 Drachmas with everything. The charge for the crate and administration had been reduced but Flossie was still measured by volume at 430 kilos and she weighed 375 kilos – more than Charles had thought.

Flossie would leave via Olympic Airways the next day and we were given a lift to the Olympic Airways warehouse to deal with the Customs there. We saw our crate and it was a lot larger and taller that we'd imagined but there was not a label in sight on it. The agent stuck Charles' name on with the address "Nairobi – Kenya". We asked for a few 'Fragile' and 'This Way Up' signs and these were stuck on too. At least now our crate looked as though it belonged to someone. The paperwork was stamped and Charles' passport checked and stamped and suddenly it was all done. We got a taxi back to the camp site.

When we woke up in camp on 23rd August we thought of Flossie and that she would be on her way today. So, we had to get ourselves organised for our flight. We were ready to leave late afternoon and got a taxi to the airport. We had time to phone home so I called my mum. Unfortunately, she was out so I talked to my brother. He only wanted to know one thing "When are you going to Africa?" A good question and one we knew a lot of family and friends had been asking. I was so pleased to finally be able to say "We're going today, now."

The Egyptair desk opened just before 7.00 p.m. and we got ourselves fairly near the front of the queue although behind several Egyptian families with a mountain of large suitcases. Our luggage was given a fairly cursory check and security tagged. Then it was weighed and tagged for 'Cairo'. Charles told them we were going to Nairobi. The desk clerk paused and said we couldn't go to Nairobi – only to Cairo. After much indignant questioning the clerk explained that the Cairo flight had not yet even arrived from Cairo and would leave at 1.00 a.m. tomorrow morning. This would mean we would miss the connection and so we couldn't get to Nairobi. We were told we'd have to go to the Egyptair office in Athens tomorrow. We protested and were referred to the supervisor who checked alternative routing for us but said that as we were the only two passengers in Athens going on to Nairobi they would not hold the connecting flight. He said the best thing we could do was go to the office on Monday morning. My disappointment, frustration and anger boiled over into tears. After everything we'd got so close only to fail, again. So close – we couldn't believe it.

We caught a taxi back to Athens. The driver didn't speak any English but he understood we wanted a cheap hotel and took us to one. At 8,000 Drachmas for one night and 6,000 for other nights it would do. It was scruffy but clean and we were hungry and tired. We'd planned to eat and sleep on the flight but instead here we were – still in Athens with the prospect of having, yet again, to sort out how to get to Nairobi and who would pay for this further delay. I suspected it would be us!

Monday morning and we woke up depressed not to be in Nairobi and went directly to the offices of the travel agent. The man we'd dealt with for money and tickets recognised us and asked "Are you still here? What happened?" Two good questions!

We explained what had happened and he said we should have got on the flight and Egyptair would have dealt with us in Cairo. A bit late for that now. He rang Egyptair who agreed to re-book our flight but it wouldn't go until next Thursday. We were a bit nervous of the same thing happening a second time so he suggested an Athens to Cairo morning flight and Cairo to Nairobi evening flight. But, the Cairo to Nairobi flight was full. Other airlines were much more expensive.

We decided to take matters into our own hands and left to speak to Egyptair in person. They apologised and said the flight delay was "most unusual" and we could be waitlisted for Thursday's Cairo to Nairobi flight and we "should be OK". We asked about expenses for our night in a hotel and the clerk said we'd have to come back later to talk to a manager.

We kicked our heels for most of the rest of the morning and went back. Confirmation for Cairo to Nairobi had still not come through but the manager was available. A security guard took our passports and showed us to a pleasant woman who took our tickets and told us to wait. We were shown into an office with two women sitting at computer terminals. One of the women asked us to sit down and said she was checking the next available flight on any airline to Nairobi for us. The first flight was Ethiopia Airlines to Addis Ababa that evening and

Kenyan Airways to Nairobi tomorrow but it was full. The next option was a Kenyan Airways direct flight on Wednesday morning. Full. Next choice was Olympic Airways direct to Nairobi on Wednesday evening. Available. The woman confirmed us on this flight and went off to get the tickets. Once we had the tickets in our hands she took us through to Accounts and said she'd arranged for us to see Mr. Abdala who would deal with our hotel expenses.

In Accounts everything went from being very Greek to very Egyptian. We might really have been in Cairo. A man we assumed was Mr. Abdala took us into his office where his wife and a small child sat in the corner. A prayer mat was draped over the back of a visitor's chair. We handed over our Egyptair tickets and asked for money to cover our hotel. Mr. Abdala didn't seem to understand and asked what language we were speaking. This struck us as odd (to say the least) because the Greek clerk who'd spoken to him on the phone had spoken English to him and told him to expect us.

We persisted and waited while Mr. Abdala referred to several weighty books and made numerous calculations. He then proudly declared that we owed him 13,000 Drachmas! Charles said "no" and crossed his arms petulantly. There was obviously a misunderstanding here.

We were invited next door to another office – Mr. Abdala! He invited us to sit down, looked at our tickets and offered us 5,000 Drachmas. Each? No. Charles said this was not enough and Mr. Abdala explained that our cut-price ticket would not normally be endorsed, i.e. transferred to another airline. We had been told this by the clerk downstairs and when we'd argued that the ticket didn't say that she said the agent should have told us. He didn't. I told Mr. Abdala of the 1,000 drachma taxi ride to the hotel and after a call to a General Manager we agreed on 6,000 Drachmas. I think we were all dis-satisfied with this but it was agreed. A subordinate was summoned and dispatched to do the paperwork and get the cash while we settled back to discuss the city and international travel with Mr. Abdala. Very Egyptian – but no tea. We left clutching our money and tickets.

This experience underlined what we'd learnt in the four months since we'd left home. We'd learnt a lot about travelling. We'd learnt not to trust anything, any information unless it was written down and not to believe that what was written down was all we needed to know. We'd learnt that if we kicked up enough fuss we could get some of what we thought we deserved and should settle for it.

At the hotel we booked ourselves in until our flight for

Nairobi. The receptionist gave us a business card for the hotel and urged us to take it with us whenever we went out. We were puzzled but she explained that they had recently had an English couple staying who had refused such a card and spent a night in the police station because they went out and couldn't then remember where they were staying. So, another lesson learnt: make a note of where you're staying and take it with you! We wondered how long our compatriots had spent looking for the hotel when they didn't know the name or address.

28th August and we thought "This time tomorrow we'll be in Kenya!" We indulged ourselves with a long lie-in on the basis we wouldn't have a bed for the night – just an airline seat. Basically, we spent the rest of the day waiting for our flight and checked out early evening to go to the airport. This time we had our fingers crossed.

Our crossed fingers did the trick and with no further problems we were woken just before 5.00 a.m. with news that we were on the final approach to land at Nairobi. Kenya at last. Africa. We hardly believed it after all the to-ing and fro-ing. Kenya!

We stepped off the plane into an international airport which looked much like any other. We filled in our immigration card and currency declaration form and were through the formalities to a waiting line of taxi drivers offering their services. The flight was probably the worst possible time to arrive – the airport being deserted and the town asleep. However, we agreed a taxi fare to town and, slightly confused, climbed into a London black cab.

We asked the driver to take us to a "nice, but not expensive" hotel and were taken to the Parsonic Hotel which had a very dubious entrance of corrugated sheeting and scaffolding. The driver assured us it was "good, all good" and by now we were so tired we didn't argue. We just wanted to go to bed – any bed.

We checked in and were shown to our room via what seemed just stairs and long winding corridors. The room was basic but clean with a bathroom. A sign on the bathroom door boasted hot water 24 hours a day but that turned out to be a slight exaggeration.

We undressed and fell into bed. The early morning was quiet and cool and we settled down to sleep.

We woke at nearly midday and I felt wide-awake and ready for anything. I looked out of the window to see the day outside in full swing with people and the city going about its noisy business. Our room overlooked a large, dirt covered area crowded with people, ramshackle stalls and shops. There were hand carts and vehicles coming and going and a general air of trade being done.

We washed, dressed and went for a walk to explore and find something to eat. We found a small shop selling meat samosas and our first impressions were of a friendly people who had places to go and things to do. We drifted around trying to decide on our next move. Reclaiming Flossie and getting mobile again was obviously a priority but we decided we couldn't do much about it today.

That evening we went out for a beer at a very local bar. The Modern Green Day & Night Bar was full of people and European music. The room was dimly lit and the bar and barman were locked behind a heavy grill with a gap just large enough to pass drinks through. Most people were speaking English although it was occasionally difficult to tell because of the way they spoke. Their accents were unfamiliar to us.

We wandered along to The Norfolk Hotel which was very posh so we opted to eat in a local vegetarian restaurant which was busy with locals and tourists. When we got back to the hotel we asked about parking for Flossie and they seemed sure they could take care of her. They were very helpful and reassuring nothing could possibly be a problem.

Breakfast was very European with cereal, sausages and scrambled egg and toast and then we were off to be reunited with Flossie. We caught a taxi to the cargo terminal at the airport. Once we'd stepped out and the taxi left we were approached by a man who introduced himself as an agent who would look after us. He took our waybill and led us to the import enquiries desk. He took complete charge and confirmed Flossie had arrived but that there would be a lot of paperwork to do. "No problem," he assured us. He would take care of it all for us. I sat down in the Customs Hall because it looked like being a long wait while Charles was busy signing forms and proving who he was and that Flossie belonged to him. Our agent hovered and stepped in at what he thought were appropriate moments. He explained that the Customs would close at 12.30 p.m. and that he would speed things along so that we didn't have to wait through lunch. He seemed rather pleased to tell us that no less than seven different people and departments would have to see Charles and his passport but that he could help us through all this - "no problem".

As I sat and waited Charles was ushered from person to person and desk to desk and our agent busied himself on our behalf. Eventually Charles was taken past the barrier and into the warehouse itself to see Flossie. He came back out, gave me the thumbs up and Flossie's crate followed him out of the warehouse and on to the loading dock. The shutters firmly shut behind her – 12.30 p.m.

A small crowd of onlookers gathered and willing hands started to open the crate with crowbars, hammers and bare hands. Flossie had been well packed and the only damage seemed to be a bent indicator which could easily be straightened with pliers. The crate was dismantled and removed – every part of it was of value and carried away eagerly. Flossie sat on her pallet and Charles set to work rebuilding her whilst the crowd of silent onlookers slowly grew in size. More willing hands lifted Flossie for Charles to put the back wheel in and then she was lifted clear of the pallet and stood on her own two wheels as the last of the pallet disappeared into the crowd.

Charles worked quickly and Flossie was slowly put back together. When everything was done our agent re-appeared and beckoned Charles to one side, away from the crowd, to negotiate his fee. He asked for 5,000 Kenyan Shillings (UK£100) but eventually settled for US$80.

Charles got on Flossie and she started first time. The small crowd clapped. I got on and as we drove off with a wave the crowd dispersed to get back to whatever it was they'd been doing when we turned up and provided an interesting diversion to their day.

At the Parsonic Hotel we were shown where to park. Behind the corrugated sheeting we now saw the 'real' entrance. They were renovating the hotel but Flossie could be left behind the corrugated screen and no-one would know she was there. That evening we went out to see some more of the city as tomorrow we'd be moving out to cheaper accommodation in the suburbs.

First stop was The Pub in the 680 Hotel which was supposed to be a well-known meeting point for travellers. Next stop was The Thorn Tree restaurant which was even more famous. The Thorn Tree was part of the New Stanley Hotel which was built in 1902 when the railway line arrived in Nairobi from Uganda. When the railway line arrived Nairobi was just a watering hole and the hotel was the first to be built and had since become a meeting point for tourists and travellers. In the 1960s the hotel was re-built and an acacia (or thorn) tree was planted and became a message point for travellers who would pin letters and messages to the tree for friends and fellow travellers to find when they passed. The café and its tree became popular and famous although by the time we got there a more formal message board surrounded the tree for messages and notices etc.

One of the notices pinned up was a warning about a local scam known as the 'police trick'. Tourists would be approached by a reasonably well dressed local man who would engage the tourist in conversation. He would be friendly and pleasant and not ask for anything. He might order a drink and the tourist might offer to pay for it – it didn't matter either way. After a while the friendly local would shake hands with the tourists and leave them. Once he'd left two very well-dressed local men would arrive and approach the tourists. These two men would introduce themselves as the police and say they had seen the tourists 'consorting' with a known villain, a trouble-maker, a drug dealer – it varied, apparently. One of the 'policemen' would say that the tourists would have to go to the police station to explain what sort of deal they had made with the man. Then, the other 'policeman' would persuade his colleague that this would be a lot of time and trouble for everyone, these tourists probably didn't mean any harm and surely it could all be sorted out quietly. The first 'policeman' would appear to relent but only if the tourists made it worth his while to "make the problem go away". There were obviously variations on this scheme but that was the gist of it. Unknowing, frightened tourists and travellers were said to have parted with hundreds of US dollars and UK pounds.

We'd been warned about this scam by Karen in Greece and thought we'd already had it tried on us. In a café a local chap had sat down at our table and made conversation. When he got up to go we did too and when we got to the door he said he was going to the left but that our hotel lay to the right. We said we weren't going back to our hotel but going the same way as him. We did see two other men in suits hanging around but as we followed the man from the café they didn't follow us.

The next morning was the last day of August and we were headed out of the city to the suburbs and a camp site.

The camp site was owned by an elderly Polish lady known, affectionately, as Ma Roche who welcomed travellers of all nationalities. There were backpackers, cyclists, Land Rovers and other 4-wheel drive vehicles alongside converted military vehicles and a few motorcyclists. The camp site was actually the lady's house set in its own grounds with flowering bougainvillea, roses, poinsettia and magnolia trees. There was a dormitory for those without a tent, a storage room where things could be left securely, toilets, a shower block and a large concrete slab with cold water taps where clothes, dishes etc. could be washed. In every corner of the garden, in every available space was a vehicle or a tent. The site was legendary amongst travellers and Ma Roche was, herself, a legend.

The story was that Mrs. Roche had moved to Nairobi many years before with her husband and children but that after he died she became nervous of living alone and needed to make a living. So, she opened her garden to travellers and had been doing so as long as anyone could remember. Mrs. Roche became known, affectionately, as Ma Roche and she and her camp site became a destination, a haven in Nairobi.

Ma Roche's gardens were surrounded by a high concrete wall and there was only one way in and out – large metal gates. A local chap, Stephen, worked as gardener and handyman and there were two guard dogs. The dogs were quite friendly and spent most of their time following Stephen about or lazing in the sun. The dogs were quiet and docile until a local, black face dared to appear over the wall or around the open gates and then they went absolutely berserk – rushing about, barking and snarling. Things would only quieten down when the 'intruder' disappeared or Stephen escorted him in. Anyone European or in Stephen's presence was welcomed but the locals knew not to attempt to enter the camp site unescorted. I never knew whether the dogs had been trained or whether it was a natural protective instinct of Ma Roche and her residents. Either way, they were very effective.

When we arrived the sky was grey and overcast and the camp site did not look very appealing but we found somewhere to park Flossie and pitched the tent. We soon got into conversation with our neighbour, Crispin, who was English and travelling around Africa on his bicycle. We met an American couple who had just bought a Hanomag truck from some Germans and were planning on touring Africa in it.

Hanomag's were originally German 4-wheel drive military vehicles dating from the 1950s and 1960s but since then many had been bought and converted for off road 'touring'. They were big, heavy and slow vehicles but very popular and we saw several throughout our travels in Africa.

As we settled in Ma Roche's was everything we had hoped for in terms of meeting others travelling to and from all points of the compass. There were people here coming from the west, north and south and Nairobi (Ma Roche's in particular) seemed to be a 'melting pot', a meeting place for us all. The gardens were quiet and home to many travellers and all sorts of coloured birds who sang and chirruped all day.

We found the local supermarket and bought sausages and beans to cook. We treated ourselves to some Kenyan red wine but decided we wouldn't bother with it again and stuck to the local beer. The evening was cool and it was dark by 6.30 p.m. so we were glad to have cooked and eaten early and settled in the tent for an early night. With Flossie close by and the sounds of the camp site settling for the night we had a new country on a new continent, a new day and a new month to look forward to tomorrow.

SEPTEMBER 1991

KENYA

ONWARDS AND UPWARDS

At Ma Roche's simple, everyday chores seemed to take ages because everything involved long conversations with anyone who happened to be doing the same chore: washing clothes, showering, queuing for the loo. And, it was great! Any and all information was useful or just plain interesting.

Overnight a tour truck had pulled in to Ma Roche's and we got into conversation with the driver as they had come from the south. The driver told us the 'gun run' through Mozambique was really not safe and Zambia would be a much better alternative route. The 'gun run' was travelling in convoy through Mozambique in a narrow corridor with armed, local troops providing protection. We (that is, Charles) had been considering it. I had never liked the sound of it and this new information seemed to back me up.

One of the first things we had to deal with in Kenya was getting vehicle insurance for Flossie. This gave us our first experience of a matatu. Matatus were the local, cheap transport which ran around Nairobi and the suburbs. They were mostly 12 seater Nissan minibuses although they always carried many more than 12 people and the most we ever saw was 27 including us and a mother breastfeeding her baby. We waited outside the gates of Ma Roche's and one of the matatus making constant circuits stopped and although there didn't look as though there was any room for us the 'conductor' insisted there was and we squeezed in. Everybody shuffled up. The bench seat at the front designed for the driver and two passengers already had the driver and three people and we were in the row behind them. The conductor stood in the footwell, slammed the door shut behind him and leant over the seated passengers. The cost of a matatu was 5 Kenyan Shillings each and the stereo blared loud, rhythmic African music. We made the short journey to Nairobi centre and went off to arrange insurance. It took most of the afternoon but we left with a month's cover for 1,000 Kenyan Shillings.

We had planned to go north to Uganda the next day but

the tour truck driver said we needed visas so that meant another trip to Nairobi centre. Charles also decided to change Flossie's oil and thought we should get a jerry can to carry spare petrol before setting off anywhere.

Whilst Charles dealt with Flossie's oil I sat around watching camp life. The camp site was full of people of all nationalities travelling in one direction or another on almost every type of vehicle. Everyone's day was occupied with vehicle maintenance, organising equipment, washing clothes or just generally chatting and exchanging information with others. An Australian/German couple in a Land Rover had a pet chicken which they had bought for fresh eggs and, eventually, meat but had become so fond of it they couldn't kill it. The chicken roamed happily and freely around the camp with the two dogs.

Our Ugandan visas cost US$34 each and we bought a jerry can, tyre valves and some dried and tinned food. The water was off in camp when we got back so we couldn't have a shower and spent the evening sorting through things we didn't think we would need for our short trip and putting them into the storage room. Next day we set off on a route which would take us to Lake Naivasha on a good road with green, rolling scenery. We made steady progress gaining height until we saw the full spread of the Rift Valley below us with stunning views and the hills in the distance.

At Lake Naivasha we found camping at the YMCA just as grey clouds rolled in and it started to rain. We waited in the communal hall for the rain to pass and were joined by a couple of lads: a Scotsman and an Australian who had met here and teamed up for walking in the National Park. They suggested we rent a banda rather than camp and given the weather we decided to take their advice and negotiated a good price for a couple of nights.

A banda was a round, windowless building with a thatched roof. The door was about 5' high and inside there were seven beds – bunks – and we had it all to ourselves. It was dry and warm and once settled we went back to the communal room to make tea. The two lads came back in with some fresh milk still warm from the resident cow they had just milked.

The next morning we were up early and found the Scotsman milking the cow again so had warm milk for our tea – in contrast to the freezing water for washing.

Our early start was part of the plan to walk to Hell's Gate and the gorge in the National Park. We paid our entrance fee and set off with an eye out for any game which might be around. We saw antelopes and zebras quite close to the path and lots of brightly coloured birds. There were animals in the distance which might have been wild boar. Walking was hot work and we stopped in the shade of the cliff for the picnic lunch we'd brought. On the walk back our water supply was running low and we were parched under the hot sun. We'd walked 18 miles by the time we got back to the YMCA.

The YMCA had new arrivals. A tour truck had pulled in complete with staff in an advance party who had arrived ahead of the truck to cook the evening meal. The people on the tour truck itself were a miserable, unfriendly bunch except for one couple on honeymoon. We met the new husband in the communal kitchen – he was at the sink scrubbing his new wife's knickers. We nodded a 'hello' and he raised his eyes. "If you're travelling too let me give you some advice," he said "don't wear white on safari!" Good advice but it hardly seemed necessary to us.

We had an early night and slept off our exhaustion. Next day the weather was warm and the scenery as we left was very easy on the eyes – a gently rolling green landscape dotted with people and small, neat communities. The afternoon clouded over and the sky was very threatening but the road was good and the roadside ditches were draining the water from earlier rain. We pressed on to Kisumu on Lake Victoria and found Dunga Refreshments to camp for the night.

The main attraction here was hippo that would cross the field beside the restaurant to reach the lake's edge. The field was the camp site and after pitching the tent and eating we watched the sun set across the lake. But, by now the mosquitoes and flies were too much for us and we opted for the sealed sanctuary of the tent. We laid there listening to slight rustlings in the night wondering if it was hippos.

We were awake just after 6.00 a.m. and got up in the cool morning fresh breeze and boiled water for a wash and for Charles to shave. Once we were ready for the road we made good progress to the border for Uganda.

The Kenya/Uganda border formalities were fairly straightforward although we were charged 300 Kenyan Shillings for 'overtime' as it was Sunday. We didn't have enough Kenyan cash and there was no bank and after some arguing and persuasion the Kenyans backed down on the charge and waved us through to Uganda where there was no fuss and no money to pay to anyone.

Uganda was noticeably poorer than Kenya and the roadside villages were very shabby and the washing lay out on the dry, red mud to dry. We did notice that every village had at least two, and often three, 'beauty salons'. It was hard to imagine what went on in these salons and one was actually, optimistically, called 'The Hope For The Best Beauty Salon'. All the people we saw looked very poor and ragged. Everyone was on foot or on a bicycle but the road to Jinja was a good, fast one and we soon found somewhere to stay.

The Victoria View Inn was arranged around a courtyard with secure parking for Flossie in the courtyard behind gates. We looked at several rooms and picked the cleanest with a double bed. The price was 5,500 Ugandan Shillings.

The room was simple and basic and we ordered hot water which arrived in jerry cans carried by a local woman. We'd only changed US$10 at the border so once we'd paid for the room we were very short of cash. We went for a walk around town in the hope of finding the local black market money changers who, in Africa, usually found us with little effort on our part. Not so on this occasion, so we went back to the hotel to eat.

The hotel restaurant boasted an extensive menu but in reality only meat and matoke was available. Matoke was fried banana and although it sounded quite tasty it was, more often, a tasteless sludge with the consistency of mashed potato. There wasn't much meat on offer but it was tasty and tender.

We slept well and were offered tea, eggs and bread for breakfast. We checked out and went to find a Bureau de

Change and post office. Charles came out of the Bureau de Change with an enormous pile of notes. Cash rich again we bought petrol and left on the road to Kampala. We were stopped at several toll stations but they couldn't deal with bikes like ours so we were waved through for free. Police patrols were also a frequent sight but, similarly, not interested in us and we were usually waved past.

The capital of Kampala was very green and although shabbier than Nairobi it was clearly better than any of the other towns we'd seen in Uganda. In a small café we got chatting with a well-spoken, polite young local man – probably in his early 20's. He asked if we were English and when we said we were he asked if we could help him get into an English University. He explained that he didn't have any of the necessary connections to apply to a Ugandan University and so hoped "a kind visitor" would help him get to England. We said we were sorry but could do nothing and that it would be very expensive for him in England. The young man explained he had a plan. He would persuade the University to let him sleep in the corridors or classrooms and he would, in exchange, clean everywhere for them. It was so hard to explain that it just wouldn't, couldn't, work like that for him. We said we were very sorry, wished him luck, made our excuses and left.

We were genuinely sorry to have shattered his illusions and plans and often wondered what became of him.

The tour truck driver at Ma Roche's had recommended the Athina Club House as a camp site. There was a bar and a restaurant and the car park was given over to camping and fairly secure. The Club House doubled as the Consulate of Cyprus. We decided to see what the YMCA had to offer before deciding where to stay but as it turned out to be a very seedy building near an even seedier housing estate we went back to the Athina and pitched the tent. The restaurant offered sausage, bacon, egg and hot buttered toast for breakfast which set us up for a day which threatened to be grey and overcast and soon turned to rain.

Buying petrol in Uganda was a challenge. The locals we met were sullen and unhelpful and paying took ages as we counted out piles of notes from even bigger wads of notes. A UK £1 was worth 1,459 Ugandan Shillings. The largest Ugandan bank note available was 100 Ugandan Shillings so any sort of purchase involved large numbers of bank notes.

The weather by now had also taken a turn for the worst with thunder and lightning as we followed signs to the Pelikan Hotel. We never found the hotel and when the storm passed carried on to Kasese. We rode on through another storm and took shelter in a small roadside collection of huts and buildings where we bought mugs of hot, milky, sweet tea. A small, quiet crowd of people gathered to watch us drink our tea, climb back on Flossie and leave. I turned to wave but only one solitary hand was raised uncertainly to wave back.

We carried on miserably through rain and wind and by the time we got to Kasese we were wet, cold, hungry and very fed up. A guide book had recommended the Saad Hotel and described it in glowing terms so we headed there. The parking was secure, the staff were friendly and the room was clean and hot water arrived in a large steaming bucket. The woman who delivered the water asked if we had any laundry she could do. We told her to come back in half an hour. We stripped, showered, put on our slightly cleaner clothes and handed the rest of everything we had over for washing. The woman promised to bring it all back, dry, in the morning.

The next day was dry and sunny and we relaxed over breakfast with an American couple we'd met at Ma Roche's and some more who had arrived from working for the Peace Corps in Zaire. Breakfast itself was not very relaxing. We had noticed that the staff were very keen to clear any plates, cutlery, mugs etc. away from the table as soon as we appeared to have finished. We lost quite a few mugs with a last mouthful of tea and on one occasion my plate disappeared while I was still chewing on the last bite with my knife and fork still raised. It paid to hang on to anything if you wanted to keep it!

Our cash crisis was now becoming a persistent nuisance. We had US$9 and some Ugandan Shillings to our names. We walked around town to see if we could get cash on a eurocheque or against our credit card but had no luck. So, with little cash we packed up and left under a hot sun in a clear blue sky.

The road took us over the equator where we stopped for some photos and to get petrol. We used the last of our 10,000 Ugandan Shillings. The petrol we bought was probably not going to be enough to get us back to Kampala but we still had the US dollars and stopped in Masaka hoping to find a foreign exchange. There was one but it was shut and a local directed us to a garage but he wasn't interested in the paltry sum of US$9. The woman in the shop next door saw us and called us over to say she would change the money for us.

Retracing our route back to Kampala and the Athina Club House we pitched the tent before dark and were still, amazingly, on the main tank of petrol we'd bought with the last of our local cash. We heated up some soup and ate bananas. The sleeping bags were damp and the tent and grass were wet with the heavy rain. We fell asleep listening to the radio rambling to itself.

The next morning and getting some cash was a pressing priority. Barclays Bank in town wouldn't cash a eurocheque so we decided to try the Uganda Commercial Bank. This bank had long queues snaking across its large, palatial banking hall, out of the main doors, down the steps and out onto the pavement. We walked past the queues and straight to the Information Desk which had a small crowd of locals gathered in front of it. We stood at the back and wondered what we should do when the man behind the desk saw us, pointed at us over everyone else's heads and said "Next." He meant us and the crowd parted to let us through. We were sent upstairs to the first floor to see a manager who would decide what, if anything, could be done.

After some time, negotiation and explanation the manager wrote a note to the Forex Department and sent us off. In the Forex Department we had to see another manager and then wait while a clerk did the paperwork and we were given UK Sterling traveller's cheques. This wasn't ideal but meant we were solvent again and it had only taken an hour and a half.

The next job was to find a welder to re-weld the front rack which had fallen off the front of Flossie the day before. Charles supervised the work whilst I sat on a bench with four local little boys who seemed very excited to be sitting next to me. Once the welding was finished and Charles was happy we headed out of Kampala and back to the border for Kenya. We'd had enough of Uganda.

We didn't get to the border until mid-afternoon and it was early evening before we actually got through to Kenya with only an hour of daylight left. The road was very poor and we had to ride slowly and negotiate various diversions off the road and on to dirt tracks. The sky darkened as the sun set and we knew it would be too dangerous to drive after dark so started to look for a likely place to camp.

We drove in to a field with some empty buildings and stopped under a tree. Immediately, half a dozen boys appeared and when they understood we wanted to camp in what was their school playing field they explained we'd have to ask the headmaster's permission. One of the older boys offered to take Charles to the headmaster. I waited with Flossie and the other boys.

One of the older boys introduced himself, very formally "Madam, my name is Patrick", and wanted to show me their school. The school was a roughly built building with a concrete floor and a dozen or so desks and chairs of various shapes and sizes. Patrick offered me a chair and then proceeded to fire questions: "Where in England do you live?" "What countries border England?" "What mountains do you have?" "What continent is England?" What do you eat?" Every answer I gave was received with an "OK" and nod of the head before he moved on to the next.

Before Patrick ran out of endless questions the headmaster appeared, rescued me and took me into his office. The office was furnished with a rough wooden desk and several wooden chairs and piles of books and papers. Dusk was really on us now and it was quite hard to see in the dark room which seemed to have no light. The headmaster (Morris) explained he had 371 pupils and added it wouldn't rain tonight. We then heard engines and two English Land Rovers we'd seen at the border bumped off the road and into the field. Charles got out of one. It seemed he'd walked quite a way to find the headmaster was out (he was with me!) but Charles had met the headmaster's three wives before being picked up by the Land Rovers also looking for somewhere to camp. The headmaster seemed delighted to have us all stay and appointed a watchman to look after us through the night. Patrick was still hovering and said he wanted his photograph taken. I explained it was too late and too dark but he could come back in the morning. Patrick also wanted a Bible to be sent from England and we said we'd deal with it all in the morning.

Patrick hung around with a small, but growing, crowd of onlookers as we all pitched our tents and gathered under the tarpaulin spread between the roofs of the two Land Rovers. The group of two girls and three boys had been on the road for three months overlanding from Algeria and they quickly organised tea and vegetable stew for us all. The crowd of spectators watched every move we made. They murmured, muttered and pointed and while some eventually got bored, or hungry, and drifted off one lad actually only went to fetch a stool to be make himself more comfortable. The watchman arrived and introduced himself by snapping smartly to attention and saluting before he settled himself a discreet distance away to, as he said, "watch for you".

Next morning the sound of the gathering crowd woke us up at dawn. They watched silently as I crawled out of our tent, crossed the field to the loo, walked back and got back in the tent. Once we were all up and about the watchman came for his money and the headmaster appeared and asked Charles to go to the office and sign the visitor's book. The Land Rover group tidied up and pulled out whilst we only stayed long enough after them to take the promised photo of Patrick and the group. Once Flossie was loaded and ready to go Charles got on and started the engine. Some of the smaller boys ran away but the main group waved us off until we were out of sight.

On our return to England we sent the photo of the boys and a bible to the school. Hopefully, both arrived.

We spent the morning on very poor roads and stopped by the roadside to brew some tea. Instantly, three children were beside us. They quickly disappeared and came back with two more to watch us. Four of the five little girls came slowly closer and were eventually close enough to offer their outstretched hands and we all solemnly shook hands. They retreated to a polite distance and watched us drink our tea before drifting back off in to the surrounding countryside.

The long, winding road led down to the Rift Valley and we headed for Lake Baringo. We had hardly any cash and not enough petrol but we made it to Roberts Camping on the lake shore and went in search of Mrs. Roberts, the owner, to ask about cashing travellers' cheques or finding a bank. Before we could do either we found three very well-spoken English people who had heard us talking. They told us there was no bank until Nakuru and that the lodge next door would only change money for residents. One of the three was going home the next day though and would be happy to give us their unwanted Kenyan money in exchange for a UK cheque. Problem solved – if a little unconventionally.

Solvent again we pitched the tent surrounded by sweet smelling eucalyptus and acacia bushes. A quick shower and we went to the next door lodge to eat. As dusk was falling we almost walked into a hippo just a few yards away in bushes making its way back to the lake. I'm not sure which of the three of us was more surprised but the hippo seemed less perturbed than us about it all as he ambled on his way.

During the night we heard hippos grunting and munching the grass. We had been told that they would not generally bother anyone although had been known to knock into guy ropes in the night. A large notice told us the only real danger was in the mating season when fights might break out between rival males. These fights could be violent and the battling beasts would have no thought for their surroundings and campers were advised to take shelter in their vehicles. I wasn't entirely convinced that Flossie would offer any protection and might, perhaps, even be mistaken for a threat. I fell asleep hoping it wasn't the mating season for hippos.

The next morning we did our chores of washing and cleaning surrounding by brightly coloured birds and in the late afternoon wandered down to the water's edge to see six or seven hippos wallowing in the muddy water. On the way back to the tent we met a 70 year old giant tortoise snuffling along. Again, in the night, we could hear the hippos grazing very close to the tent and feel the earth shaking gently under them as they moved.

Lake Bogoria was our next destination on a fairly good road for about five miles which then became a rough stone and rock track until we reached the lakeside and a pink mist of flamingos came into view on the water. They were a delicate pink with darker salmon pink under their wings and a streak of black and created a carpet of pink across the lake.

We drove on past hot springs on the rough track which seemed to go on and on and on and we were both soaked in sweat before we reached a sharp downhill section and a sign told us it was another mile to Fig Tree Camp. I got off Flossie to walk and watched Charles and Flossie disappear round the bend as I trudged on in the silence. I surprised a couple of monkeys and some baboons and a few antelopes but was otherwise alone until a final bend and I was at the camp site. Flossie was parked and Charles had stripped to cool off in the stream running through the camp to the lake.

We pitched the tent under shady trees on the lake shore with monkeys and baboons shrieking and leaping through the green canopy above us. Our guide book had described them as "loutish hooligans" and advised campers to lock anything and everything away from their mischief. As we settled down to cook and eat several kidu appeared from the bush to look at us before moving slowly and gracefully away to drink at the lake.

Several other vehicles arrived during the evening and the occupants of one let out a loud cheer as they rounded the corner after dark and our campfires came into view – I knew the feeling. The other excitement was when a baboon got into an unlocked Land Rover and let off the handbrake. The vehicle started to roll slowly down to the lake's edge and the baboon leapt out as the owners gave chase. Fortunately, the vehicle slowed and came to a stop just before it hit the water.

During the night we heard the sounds of baboons screaming and screeching above us and the soft patter of them peeing etc. on the tent. In the morning we found Flossie was similarly 'spattered' but everything was otherwise intact. We washed in the stream, boiled some eggs for breakfast and left to negotiate the seemingly endless miles of rough, stony track. There were several times when Flossie fought for grip and only just found enough to stay upright. I got off again for a short time but eventually the track improved to a good dirt track and then tarmac.

Once on the tarmac we made good progress to the town of Nakuru where we changed some money with a plan to go on to Naro Moru and Nairobi. But, we'd heard that Nyehururu and Thomson Falls Lodge had hot showers and such a promise seemed worth a detour.

The lodge had a camp site where we pitched and were told hot water would be available after 6.00 p.m. We wandered off to look at the Falls. A long cascade of water powered over a rocky edge onto a shelf and swirled on down into a deep ravine. It was quite a spectacle which held our attention until it was time for the promised, long awaited hot shower. We took our time enjoying the novelty and with clean bodies, clean hair and clean clothes we headed into the bar for what we felt was a well-deserved beer.

Clean and refreshed we were now fairly focussed on our next challenge – Mount Kenya. We left the Falls to go to Naro Moru River Lodge where we camped and checked out prices for hiring equipment for our assault on the mountain. We had good, sturdy walking shoes but needed rucksacks, warmer clothing and blankets to supplement our lightweight sleeping bags. We could see Mount Kenya in the distance with a cap of clouds – it looked forbidding but we couldn't wait to get closer.

We went back to Nairobi and Ma Roche's where we met up

again with the Land Rovers from the Uganda/Kenya border. We pitched the tent and spent the evening catching up with everyone's news and meeting new arrivals, particularly another English rider (Peter) on a Tenere (christened Dobbin) with a similar route to our own.

Peter was a tall, slim and good-humoured motorcyclist and we travelled together on occasions and met him in many more places in Africa. We kept in touch after our return to England and he is still a friend today.

The next day was damp and gloomy and we finally met Ma Roche herself. Ma Roche was a large, friendly woman who had become famous amongst locals and travellers and clearly enjoyed having so many people around her – an ever changing scene. We also, of course, provided an income for her.

We spent the next few days doing chores and chatting. The English Land Rovers pulled out to Tanzania where they hoped to sell the vehicles to fund their flights home. Charles checked Flossie's brakes and back suspension and we sorted the panniers out to post things home and leave other things in storage whilst we tackled Mount Kenya.

We ate most of our meals in camp or at the local Everest Hotel which served a very good curry. Breakfast was a short walk from Ma Roche's to a local street restaurant – the Stop

'N' Eat. They served good, sweet tea and roasted toast. 'Toast' was plain sliced bread but roasted toast was toasted bread - toast. We took our own marmalade to spread on it. The building was a metal shack with a dirt floor and some basic chairs and tables. The men did all the cooking over open fires and used their bare hands to pick up the hottest toast and pans of boiling milk or water. They never flinched – even when they occasionally spilt some hot liquid on themselves.

Eventually, we felt ready to set off to Naro Moru for Mount Kenya. It was a straight, boring road for a couple of hours until we turned off to a road being re-graded which meant a load of earth and clumps of grass had been dumped on the surface. This made for a very hard and uncomfortable ride and we fell a few times but no damage was done and letting some air out of the tyres helped a bit. At the hostel we met Joseph who ran the camp site and said we could use the kitchen and that the showers were hot. We arranged to hire some equipment from Joseph: extra socks, sweaters and blankets although he only had one large rucksack available.

The next morning we left some of our gear with Joseph and set off back down the dirt road to Chagoria. I was wearing the large rucksack and Charles had a smaller one on his chest. The tent was strapped to one side of the pannier frame with the mattresses etc. on the other. We had a journey of nearly 100 miles around the mountain to Chagoria village where we planned to buy bread, milk and vegetables. The first 12 miles on the rough, wet, rutted dirt road was very difficult and the weight of the heavy rucksack threatened, several times, to pull me off the back of Flossie.

The road got wetter and boggier and I got off to walk several times. Flossie fell and got stuck and Charles' temper got shorter and we even considered turning back. But, instead, we re-organised ourselves. We put the tent and mattresses on one side of Flossie and strapped the larger rucksack to the other side. I then wore the smaller rucksack. This worked much better – less weight on my back and Charles was more comfortable to ride and control Flossie as she struggled. Even so, as the road got wetter and slippery Flossie began to slide backwards down the hill. Charles managed to hold her long enough for me to get off and he tried her again. After a few attempts the tyres found just enough grip and I followed on foot as they disappeared ahead. After not too long a Dutch Land Rover coming down stopped and told me they had seen Charles who was leaving the luggage at the Park Gate and coming back for me. I plodded on and found firmer, drier, flatter ground and then heard the sound of Flossie approaching.

At the Park Gate we pitched the tent and cooked a meal. We were at nearly 10,000 feet and sat for a while watching walkers come down off the mountain before it became too chilly and an early night seemed a good idea.

We woke early and as we packed up got chatting to an English couple (Andy and Jill) who were waiting for their porter to arrive. We set off on Flossie and the road wasn't too bad for a way and I only got off when Flossie had to cross a stream. We didn't want to risk either or both of us getting wet feet with a long day of walking ahead of us. We passed several groups of walkers and nearly four miles later we arrived at the end of the road at nearly 11,000 feet and parked Flossie in some bushes more or less out of sight of a casual glance.

We loaded the small rucksack with warm clothing and set off across the stream to start a steady climb. I was immediately breathless and struggling. Charles took my rucksack and I just carried our coats for about an hour and settled into a rhythm of 50 paces and a short rest to get my breath back. I'd thought I was pretty fit but Charles was doing much better than I.

We did, however, catch up with Andy and Jill and there was some comfort that Jill was doing little better than me with nothing at all to carry. We walked along together with frequent stops for water, peanuts, chocolate and rests. The scenery changed from grassy slopes to sparse, strange vegetation as we climbed higher and higher through the morning.

At about midday clouds rolled in and the temperature dropped. It started to rain on and off. In between showers we dried off but all four of us were now wondering, out loud, how much further and how much higher before we reached our scheduled overnight stop.

We climbed on and reached a crater to walk down and across a moonscape. A daunting climb faced us but Andy and Jill's porter urged us on that Minto's Hut (our overnight stop) was just the other side. It was now raining steadily and much colder.

The sight of the hut quickened our pace as we went down the path, past the hut, to the lake and camping ground beyond. Charles and I got the tent up almost instantly after so much practice and we rolled out the sleeping bags and blankets just as fast. Once inside the tent we changed into dry, warm clothing, lit our little stove and made hot tea listening to the sleet falling and other walkers struggling with their unfamiliar, 'bought for the trek tents'. We had a meal of hot corned beef and cold boiled eggs and snuggled down to sleep. We had walked for six hours and reached 14,000 feet.

We were up early, dressed and made breakfast of muesli with hot milk. The morning was crisp, cool and clear with a heavy frost which made it difficult to roll the tent up and froze our hands in the attempt but we were soon ready for another day's walking. The first half hour or so was fairly flat across a grassy plain threaded with small rivulets of water but then the vegetation thinned and disappeared and we were climbing steeply on rock and snow. We scrambled across a slope and over a ridge to see down to the Austrian hut which was our next overnight stop.

Warm from walking and tired from climbing we reached the hut at nearly 16,000 feet by midday and tumbled inside. The wooden hut was fairly clean and as we had walked almost all the way with Andy and Jill we decided to share the four berth sleeping bunk (more of a shelf) with them.

Jill and I decided to investigate the toilet which was some way from the hut up a steep, rocky slope whipped by icy blasts of wind. The two of us then went down to the tarn to get some water which meant breaking the ice and filling our containers from the icy waters whilst balanced precariously on slippery rocks. We cooked baked beans, made tea and ate hot pineapple chunks before settling down for the night.

We were quite warm in the hut but the altitude was

affecting us all. We all seemed to wake and sit up around 11.00 p.m. We couldn't believe the time and all complained of an almighty headache. I didn't expect to get back to sleep but must have done so because we were all rudely woken again at 4.30 a.m in the dark when walkers from another hut on the other route burst in on their way to Point Lenana to see the sunrise. They crashed about the hut for a while and then left so we got up, made tea and set off ourselves into the dark and cold to climb the path to Point Lenana.

Point Lenana was the 'walking summit' at 600 feet above the Austrian hut and we walked towards it under a bright moon. We separated from Andy and Jill and were soon high above them climbing steadily and watching for signs of the sunrise we'd come to see.

As the sky lightened Charles heaved himself up the final few feet to the top and I followed. The group of noisy Englishmen from the hut were already there posing for photos and very pleased with themselves. They told us they were training for an ascent of Mount Kilimanjaro in Tanzania and took a photo of Charles and I to record our success for posterity. In conversation we mentioned our shortage of Kenyan cash and one of the group said he had more than he needed for the rest of his trip so there, on the top of Mount

Kenya in the early morning light, we exchanged US Dollars for Kenyan Shillings.

We didn't linger much longer than it took to take a few more photographs and left just as Andy and Jill came over the edge but by now the sun was up and the sunrise was over for another 24 hours. We scrabbled down the rocky path and back to the hut for a hot drink and breakfast and were packed and ready to start the long descent just before 8.00 a.m. The sky was now clear and the sun was shining on spectacular views of the mountain. We walked steadily down retracing every hard won step of the previous day but my pack was lighter than before as I'd been carrying most of the food which we had now eaten.

Walking down was easier than the ascent but in places the ground underfoot was loose scree which took some care to negotiate. But, I had time to think about our achievement and that Charles was my hero. He carried the heavier pack, led me, encouraged me on, cooked and generally took care of me. He always looked after me – on and off Flossie – but here on the mountain he had risen to another challenge: strong and reliable.

The walk back from Minto's Hut was quick and almost a pleasure as we met other walkers struggling up and in the distance, along the ridge, we saw the glint of vehicles. Just after 2.00 p.m. we crossed the stream and dropped our packs at Flossie's side. We'd done it. We'd climbed Mount Kenya – and, more importantly, Flossie had come too.

We drove back to the Park Gate and booked ourselves in to a hut for the night. We bought beer and eggs from the handyman who also gave us armfuls of teak to burn on our open fire in the hut. He told us he would light the fire under the outside water tank which would soon provide a hot shower. We settled down to enjoy the luxury of a kitchen, sitting room and bedroom with a proper loo in a proper bathroom and a hot shower. We lit the fire and showered and were just settling down when we heard a commotion outside.

There were shouts and a girl rushed out from a neighbouring hut with her feet and lower legs ablaze with flames. She dropped to the ground and began beating at her feet while her boyfriend flung something flaming from the hut and on to the ground before rushing back into the smoking hut. Charles grabbed our fire extinguisher and ran outside but by now the girl had managed to smother the flames and seemed unharmed. Charles went to the hut but the fire there was out too and although the fire extinguisher pin was rusted in place I think he was a bit disappointed not to have had the change to try and use the extinguisher!

The couple were Israeli and, apparently, their camp stove had a rubber tube connecting it to the fuel supply. A poor connection had come undone and it had exploded into the open fire and flung flaming fuel on the girl's walking boots and trousers. The hut was very damaged but no-one was injured and as Charles came back to our hut we saw the woman next door going over to the girl with tea in a china cup and saucer. I'm not sure what the girl thought of the rather motherly looking woman in her flowery cotton frock, cardigan and walking boots, nor whether she appreciated the tea but the excitement was over and we all soon retreated to our huts. We opened the beer and cooked sardines and rice before going wearily to bed. We'd been told the electricity would go off at 10.00 p.m. promptly and it wasn't long after that I woke up. I was cold so climbed into bed with Charles and we snuggled down together.

I fell asleep again very quickly and satisfied with our success. We had climbed Mount Kenya on the recommended route, walked the recommended distance, ate the recommended food and stayed the recommended number of nights in the recommended places. We'd even had the 'recommended' altitude symptoms.

OCTOBER 1991
KENYA TO TANZANIA
CASHFLOW, WILDLIFE AND SPICE

We rolled back into Nairobi and Ma Roche's around lunchtime. Some old faces were still there, others had moved on. After cleaning the tent, our clothes and ourselves we settled down and felt exceptionally relaxed and lazy with no desire to go anywhere or do anything.

We chatted with fellow Brit and biker, Peter, until we were interrupted by a rather strange character wanting help to get his old, beat up motorbike going. He (Damien) was a young lad and had just bought a Honda 125 but had no mechanical aptitude to get it going. This challenge provided an interesting diversion for Peter and Charles – especially when they noticed the front forks had been replaced by broom handles. One of the more interesting innovations of African engineering!

The mechanical challenge of the Honda lasted until it was time for a curry and beers at the Everest Hotel which was a favourite haunt of most of Ma Roche's residents – and the lady herself. Charles and I and Peter were joined by another English couple and Ma Roche who seemed to have taken quite a shine to Peter. As the evening wore on Ma Roche became very 'merry' with the drink flowing and offered us all a lift back to the camp site. We all piled into her very small car with Peter in the front. Peter had helped Ma Roche with some documents and licences and was clearly now her favourite.

Ma Roche started the car without problems but it took four or five attempts to get it moving as she had her foot on the brake rather than the accelerator and it wasn't until Peter pointed this out that we finally got going. Fortunately, the Everest Hotel to the camp site was a short drive and Ma Roche knew the straight road well enough so there were no further incidents or mishaps – we all arrived safely and went happily to bed.

The next day several vehicles and occupants were planning to move on. A German Hanomag left and we said goodbye to Peter and Dobbin as they were headed north to Masarbit.

Our plan for the day was to visit the Nairobi Show and the Karen Blixen Museum but having acquired a couple of deckchairs instead of sitting on our wooden panniers we were so comfortable we lazed around all morning and decided to just visit the Nairobi Show in the afternoon. Karen Blixen could wait for another day. On the point of heading out to the Show we discovered Flossie's back tyre was flat and pumping that up caused a further delay.

The Show was very like an English County Show with stands by local manufacturers and producers alongside larger stands representing countries: Great Britain, Italy, Zambia and Tanzania. There was also a large contingent from Pakistan selling attractive wooden furniture.

Back at Ma Roche's a young English couple (Simon and Belinda) who had a Land Rover (christened Sidney) we'd seen parked had returned from Mount Kenya to get a ticking off from Ma Roche who maintained they left their vehicle without permission. Simon and Belinda argued that they had paid parking in advance but Ma Roche was clearly on the warpath and charged a very small, red camper van more than the Land Rovers despite the protests of the owners claiming the Land Rovers also had tents. Ma Roche would have none of it and stomped around in a bad mood.

Simon and Belinda were a young couple not long out of University together and had overlanded from West Africa with the same eventual destination as most of us – Cape Town. We would meet them later in many different places and share adventures and beer and food. We have kept in touch across the miles and years and they are now settled in New Zealand.

Given the atmosphere at camp we caught a matatu into town with Simon and Belinda. We exchanged stories about Mount Kenya and were pleased to find that we'd done it quicker than they had. A few beers later and we were in a bar throbbing with live reggae music and the sight of happy locals dancing and relaxing. Quite a few of Ma Roche's residents were in the bar and it was the early hours of the morning before we made it back to the tent – stony broke, again.

We had to make do with bananas and cold milk for breakfast before heading off into town and the bank where we had a familiar problem getting cash. We had to buy Kenyan Shillings with our sterling and then buy US dollars with the Shillings – two lots of commission. We argued but there was no way around it and one bank even said we could not buy US dollars or UK sterling unless we had an air ticket. Flossie didn't count.

Our next task was to update our cholera vaccination which proved quite straightforward and we were soon back at Ma Roche's to see Dobbin (Peter's bike) parked up. We found

Peter and heard he had fallen off on a dirt road and although he was OK the pannier frame mounting was cracked and he had decided not to risk carrying on without a repair or replacement.

The next day and Peter was set on phoning Motorcycle City in the UK to ask about parts for his pannier frame and we were headed into Nairobi to phone home and do some souvenir shopping. The phone call to my mum went well and she had second guessed that we would not be home for Christmas which saved me having to break the news to her. After that and lunch we tackled the City Market and to the familiar sounds of "Jambo customer" and "Come inside customer – free to look" we haggled and bargained until we'd got some soapstone carvings to our liking.

The deal had left us out of cash – again. We went to the Zanzibar Curio Shop which was a popular black market haunt but the manager would not be there until late afternoon so with no cash for a drink or a matatu we headed for The Hilton Hotel and sat in their reception watching the comings and goings until we could change our money on the black market and get back to Ma Roche's.

Back at camp Charles and Peter got involved with Damien and his Honda problems again while I did some washing and other chores until approached by our new Namibian neighbour who offered to give me details and information about Tanzania and Malawi. We spent a long time with his map, log and notebook and I made as many notes as I could about petrol, camp sites and road conditions. Charles meanwhile gave Flossie some attention and found the slow puncture in the back tyre was around the valve.

We were both keen now to be on our way in the next few days and made a short list of the things we needed to do before we moved on. We had to visit the BMW dealer, change Flossie's oil, post a parcel home and visit the Karen Blixen Museum.

First task, as ever, was money. Barclays Bank presented us with the usual challenge by saying they would have no US dollars to sell until the afternoon. We tried the Kenya Commercial Bank and were recognised and greeted with a smile and a handshake by the friendly teller. He told us the best thing to do was have US dollars or UK sterling traveller cheques to the nearest round number and the rest in Kenyan Shillings. We would pay the difference in exchange rates for buy and sell and 1% commission in Kenyan Shillings. We agreed and left him to sort it out while we checked Grindlays and another Barclays Bank to see if we could get US dollars.

We couldn't so headed back to the Kenya Commercial Bank to finish the deal. While Charles waited I went back to the first Barclays but they now said there would be no US dollars for days and we couldn't order or reserve any. Charles had finished by now though and we had £90 in travellers' cheques and $11 in local cash.

Back at the camp site Peter said we should try the airport so we went with him and drew $500 on a credit card – no delay, no fuss, no questions.

Cash rich we drove out to the Karen Blixen Museum which was her house set in beautiful, peaceful grounds. The house was a low, sturdy building with lots of windows and a veranda which offered views of the garden and distant Ngong Hills. The inside of the house was bright, cool and simply but elegantly furnished. Karen's bedroom was very feminine and softly draped. We sat in the garden for some time just enjoying the beauty and the peace and as dusk approached we drove back to camp and headed up to the Everest Hotel for dinner.

Ma Roche was at the Everest Hotel and had clearly been there for a while. She was incoherent and almost incapable of standing. Ma Roche was very upset about disturbances at the camp site. One of the Hanomag's had a dog in heat on board and Wolfie (one of her dogs) had become quite unmanageable, noisy and aggressive as a result. He was keeping everyone awake at night with his howling and had attempted to bite several people within the camp site. Ma Roche didn't know what to do and had had several loud disagreements with campers. Ma Roche's friend, Mollie, who worked as a radiologist at the nearby Aga Khan Hospital was with Ma Roche but didn't seem to be able to help much. Mollie was genuinely concerned about Ma Roche and her main aim in life seemed to be to curb, or at least limit, Ma Roche's drinking and, when that wasn't possible, to make sure she didn't buy drinks for everyone in the bar. Ma Roche was a difficult woman – especially when drunk – and it was impossible to reason with her but fortunately everything was quiet when we got back to camp.

The next day the camp was still quiet and after Charles and Peter had spent some time fixing a puncture on the Honda of the still mechanically inept Damien we headed off to town to change some money. We gave up in Barclays Bank as all the staff were too busy with paperwork to even make eye contact with customers and we had to get to the post office to post a parcel home. The parcel was inspected by Customs and then weighed. It was going to cost nearly 700 Kenyan Shillings so Charles headed off to the Zanzibar Curio Shop for cash. The parcel had to be inspected by Customs and then we were allowed to finish wrapping it, tie it with string (regulations) and stuck on 647 Kenyan Shillings' worth of 5 Kenyan Shilling stamps which covered every available space and threatened to obscure the address. We left the clerk laboriously franking every single stamp.

It was now 14th October which put us exactly six months from home. I wasn't sure where we had hoped, expected, to be after six months but it spurred us on to make plans for travelling south. These plans were made, obviously, over a curry and some beers in the Everest Hotel and on the walk back to Ma Roche's with Peter we saw an eerie, small orange light approaching us in the dark African night. We stopped and watched as the light crept towards us until we could make out it was Damien on his Honda – with just one non-blinking, orange indicator lighting his way!

The next morning Charles enthusiastically put the dirty washing into soak whilst we had breakfast and it was mid-morning before I discovered he'd picked up the clean washing by mistake so every stitch we owned was either dirty or wet. Once we'd sorted it all out we headed off to the local BMW dealer to get an oil filter, oil and gear oil. It was early afternoon before we'd packed and were ready to leave. We said farewell to Ma Roche and drove off with Peter waving from the gate.

Our first stop was the airport to stock up with US dollars although by now the sky was heavily overcast with ominously gathering storm clouds. The storm broke with heavy rain, thunder and lightning. We waited for the worst of it to pass and then put our waterproofs on and set off – south.

The rain continued in showers as the scenery changed to a flat plain with dark hills in the near distance. The people changed too and became less ''European' in dress. Tall, long legged men draped in blankets carried spears and were adorned with necklaces and earrings. The road was good tarmac and fairly straight but, even so, we knew we wouldn't make it through the border that day so stopped on the Kenyan side of the Namanga border crossing and pitched the tent. Tomorrow Tanzania!

We were heading towards the border early next morning and spent the last of our Kenyan cash on breakfast. It took no time at all to leave Kenya and change some of our US dollars into Tanzanian Shillings before starting with the border formalities for Tanzania. We had expected to have to pay a road tax but it seemed this did not apply to bikes and we were soon through the border and trying out the Tanzanian roads.

The road from the border was fairly narrow but well

maintained and the scenery had changed little from Kenya although the few people we saw waved happily and the roadside houses were much more African in style – made of straw and mud with no corrugated iron in sight.

We drove steadily on towards Arusha which would be halfway between Cairo in the north and our destination of the Cape in South Africa. We passed the Arusha Abbatoir which boasted being 'The Home of the Happy Sausage'. Another road sign told us that "Power is Knowledge" which was an interesting twist on a well-known saying. We arrived in Arusha itself mid morning for a drink and snack of ndazi - a sort of jamless doughnut.

Arusha was the start point for safaris into the Ngorogoro crater which we wanted to visit and as we sat and ate a man came up and introduced himself as Richard. He gave us his card with details of a safari company on one side and a hotel on the back. He assured us the hotel had secure parking and that a two day/one night safari into the crater would only cost £180. He felt this was a very reasonable price.

We had been told, by other travellers, to look for safaris at the Arusha International Conference Centre but had no real need as anyone selling a hotel or safari soon found us. The Namibian couple we'd met in Ma Roche's had told us that a safari would be cheaper if we could find another two people to join us and that we should look at Pelican Safaris and shop around before making any decision. We wandered around collecting 'helpers' and offers and eventually met a couple of men (Scandinavian business men with some free time) who had booked a safari and were looking for another two people to go with them. We discussed their offer against offers we'd had and decided they had the best deal. One of the local men (named, appropriately, 'Black') who had been trying to help us was still lingering and knowing we'd now done a deal for a safari offered to help us with a hotel.

Black took us to the Safari Guest House which was basic but clean and after much discussion it was agreed we could park Flossie inside the hotel in a room with luggage which would be kept locked. We settled in, secured Flossie and headed out for some food. When we got back we decided on a final check on Flossie to find that the 'watchmen' (boys really) had been fiddling with her and whilst they'd done no harm Charles gave them a ticking off and they promised they would look after her and "no touch".

Next morning we had a good, English breakfast at the New Arusha Lodge where our safari partners, Tor and Gustav, were staying. Tor's English was very good and although Gustav seemed to follow our conversations he said very little. By 8.00 a.m. we were all ready and our driver, Somi, arrived to take us off. Being driven was quite a novel, long forgotten, experience for Charles but the road was new and smooth and we relaxed until the turn off to Lake Manyara which was a dusty, dirt road. However, our speed hardly slackened and we rattled and bounced along until Mto Wa Mbu where there was a short stop for a drink and we bought some fruit which would be lunch.

At the park gate there were some formalities with paperwork and quite a bit of money changed hands but once on our way again we were distracted by lots of baboons, many with their young. We saw a lone elephant and a group of hippos bathing in shallow mud with flamingos on their backs. The flamingos made a far reaching pink wave stretching from the shore which seemed to billow and drift as we approached. Impala, pelican, cormorant and stork were all pointed out to us and we saw larger game of waterbuck, zebra and giraffe before our lunch stop at a picnic site crowded with other safari vehicles.

Leaving the park we were driven along the ascending dirt road and as we drove up the weather became wetter and we bounced along until we reached Rhino Lodge where Tor and Gustav were going to stay. At this point Somi admitted that the 'near' camp site he had told us about was actually nearly four miles away and it wasn't practical for him to take us there, bring us back for dinner and then take us back there for the night so we agreed to wait around until dinner and he could come back for us after dinner.

With everything agreed the four of us settled down for tea beside a huge fireplace with a pile of smouldering coals. Tor fanned it into a blaze and we watched time tick away towards dinner.

At 8.30 p.m. Somi arrived and took us on the short drive to the camp site which was uneventful except for seeing a lioness standing in the road. When we caught her in the headlights she slowly walked off into the bush. The camp site was fairly well populated and we picked a spot and dropped into our well practiced routine of pitching the tent using the headlights of the vehicle before saying goodnight to Somi who would be back at 6.30 a.m. for us.

We quickly settled to sleep but were woken in the early hours by the sound of munching just outside the tent and when we dared to look out we found the bananas we had bought for breakfast were gone. The munching resumed at a distance and probably carried on through the night but we fell asleep until 5.30 a.m. When we washed and packed up ready for Somi.

The early morning was cool but began to warm up and we enjoyed the view into the Ngorogoro crater as we slowly drove down the rough track. The crater is over 12 miles wide and over 2,000 feet deep and the view down and across the flat plains to the lake was, to say the least, impressive. Once on the plain we began to see birdlife which Somi identified for us. There was larger, four-legged, wildlife and we managed to get very close to wallowing hippos, a line of zebras and ostrich. Somi pointed out a rhino lying in the long grass but to us it looked just like a rock until we noticed the occasional, lazy flick of ears.

As the morning wore on we began to overdose on so much game until we came across a group of lionesses with two five month old cubs. The group were obviously full after the morning's kill which lay nearby and none of them seemed very bothered by us and the other vehicles crowding around watching and taking photographs. One lioness did become a little concerned and moved away from the group with the kill but she only went as far as necessary to lie in the shade being cast by one of the safari vans. The morning safari improved with sightings of a white rhino and a small group of elephants.

Somi reminded us that we had to be out of the Park by mid

afternoon or pay for another day and as he was quite anxious about the time we agreed to head off and slowly ascended to the rim of the crater and bounced back along the dirt road to Mto Wa Mbu and the tarmac beyond.

Charles and I had hardly eaten all day and by the time we got back to Arusha it was early evening. At The Safari Guest House we checked on Flossie and planned to have a shower before heading out for food. But, there was no water available so we went in search of dinner and fell into bed exhausted.

We slept late into the next morning but there was still no water in the taps so had breakfast, re-arranged the luggage and were soon ready to leave and headed for Moshi.

The ride to Moshi was uneventful on a good road and the town was enjoying a quiet Sunday. The town was not so quiet that we didn't attract the keener money changers though who couldn't resist the arrival of a tourist. But, we just needed information to find somewhere to camp. We were sent to the Golden Shower Restaurant just out of town which was a very smart restaurant with a small, neat patch of grass for us to camp on. We parked Flossie, pitched the tent and washed ourselves by the tent using the jerry can of water which was pleasantly warm from the heat of the engine and the sun. We lazed about for the afternoon talking and had a very good dinner in the restaurant.

Our next destination was the capital – Dar Es Salaam and the road was said to be some tarmac and some dirt so we set off with a slow day in mind. The first half hour or so was fairly good tarmac but we missed a turning and had to backtrack and then found the tarmac became graded dirt. We made good progress, filled up with petrol and did more than 60 miles on good, fast tarmac before we hit another section of dirt road which was quite deep and fine mud in places.

The mud road was very difficult for Flossie and there were several times when she threatened to lose her grip completely and throw us off. Herds of cows and goats wandering across the road aimlessly and unattended did nothing to help matters. Eventually, Charles decided to let the tyres down a little and although this helped and the road surface improved a little it was still a very rough and uncomfortable ride.

With such slow progress we soon had one eye on the road surface immediately ahead and the other eye on the sun which was sinking fast. It was an unwritten and golden rule not to drive after dark in Africa so we were hoping for a small town to come into view and keeping a lookout for a good roadside spot for camping.

Korogwe came into view and we found a Lodge with a

clean room, a fan, a mosquito net for one of the beds and a screen at the window. The showers worked. Flossie was parked right outside the bedroom window with an askari for protection so we relaxed and headed for the bar.

Askari was a local word for a night watchman and he would keep an eye on Flossie overnight in return for a small payment from us. We'd made use of askaris quite a bit in Africa and their quiet presence gave us great peace of mind. During the trip Flossie had been referred to as a 'moto' in Europe and a 'motosickle' in Egypt but in Tanzania they called her a 'bik bik'. Whatever next, we wondered.

Despite settling down for the night, well-fed and confident in the presence of Flossie's askari, we were woken at 10.30 p.m. by the hotel owner knocking on the door and rattling the handle. It seemed he wanted to be paid and was not easily put off. He was yelling about passports and money and police. Charles was fairly insistent we could deal with it all in the morning but it wasn't until another guest told the owner to "shut up and bugger off" that he gave up and we settled back down to sleep. Sleep didn't last long though and I was woken again at 4.00 a.m. by Charles brushing and beating at his bed. He was being bitten and close inspection showed that the room was actually infested with mosquitoes. We sprayed our repellent on the walls and Charles came to my bed which had the net. We'd thought, wrongly we now knew, the room was OK with the fan and good screen at the window and hadn't been too concerned about the lack of a net for both beds.

We were woken again at 7.00 a.m. by the polite knocking of the askari who told us he was going home. Charles paid him, we had breakfast, filled Flossie and were ready to set off again for a day which was already warming up.

The tarmac road continued to be interrupted by sections of mud and progress was slow and steady until we came to silky smooth tarmac which gave us the distinct impression of floating. We floated for mile after wonderful mile until we came to the part where the roadworks started and the surface was changeable for the rest of the day as we drove through and over the various stages of Tanzanian roads under construction.

As we got closer to Dar Es Salaam the tarmac became obviously poorer and more patched and repaired but the city itself was not as run down as that suggested and we had our first sight of the Indian Ocean looking very blue and appealing. We drove around for a while hoping to find, by chance, The Salvation Army which had been recommended to us as a good place to stay.

With no sign of The Salvation Army we headed for the YWCA

which had a secure looking car park and a room for 2,200 Tanzanian Shillings. As this was a women's hostel I had to go in and book the room (men were only allowed in if they were in the company of a woman) and when I went back to the car park to help with the luggage I found Charles negotiating with the local black market for cash. The rate was not good so we settled to let the man wash Flossie – it would be nice to see her clean again.

Back in reception with our bags Matron read the rule book: prompt for breakfast, no visitors, no alcohol, no smoking and no revealing clothing for either of us. Apparently, in her view, guests would wander around "half naked" unless told not to do so. The room was exactly as we expected given Matron's tight grip on the place: spotlessly clean, netted and with a fan. The room had obviously once been a large room for four beds but had lately been divided by a three-quarter height wooden partition which made each room long and narrow where it had once been square and spacious. The toilets and showers were similarly pristine but had also recently been divided to cope with the modern phenomenon of male guests!

We showered, found our cleanest clothes and set off to buy some washing powder so that we could wash the worst of them. We ate that evening in the canteen which was modelled on the very best of English institutional cooking with roast chicken, cabbage and mashed potato on the menu. The large room was furnished with plastic or chipped formica tables and sensible chairs – practical and long-lasting. It was all very wholesome and institutional and we settled down for the night in our respective, and very narrow, single beds.

The morning was hot and sticky and we spent a pleasant and lazy hour watching the children of the nursery school attached to the YWCA rushing around at play. They were all neat and clean and happy and totalling absorbed in their games with no interest in us or offering outstretched hands to foreign visitors.

We took a walk around town looking for the black market but no-one approached us and when we eventually plucked up courage to broach the subject in several likely looking places we were firmly referred to the bank. We conceded defeat and it took a very hot and sweaty hour in the bank to change £30. After lunch we were besieged by loud, enthusiastic money-changers on every corner but refused to do business on the open street. One chap said he had an office so we followed him (with six or seven others in tow at a not very discreet distance) but the 'office' turned out to be the dark doorway of a building so we turned right round and left him there. We were offered taxi and car rides but refused all these offers and headed to what we hoped would be the peaceful inside of a coffee shop. At this point a lone money changer sidled up to us and suggested we meet him outside and that we could do a deal in the post office which was next to the YWCA. We arranged to meet him there.

We killed some time finding out about fares and sailings to the island of Zanzibar and after we'd booked a second class sailing for later in the week we went to the post office and found our man in the area reserved for private mailboxes. He showed us a wad of Tanzanian Shillings and we asked to count them. We counted bundles of 10,000 Tanzanian Shillings, handed over $100 and hurriedly left. Back in the room we re-counted the money and found it 4,000 Tanzanian Shillings short. We didn't know if we'd counted wrongly or whether there had been some sleight of hand swopping the piles and kicked ourselves for not knowing better. The only, small, consolation was that it could have been a lot worse.

We spent a second night at the YWCA and then approached Matron to ask if she would keep Flossie and some luggage while we went to Zanzibar for a couple of days' sightseeing. Matron would not help so we checked out and went in search, again, of The Salvation Army.

The Salvation Army compound provided neat, clean, spacious and well-furnished stone huts with a bathroom and Flossie could be safely parked right outside the door. The receptionist was more than happy to store some of our luggage and Flossie could stay in their vehicle compound in our absence.

Although our hut was very comfortable the water supply was sporadic so we showered with buckets and jugs, re-packed the panniers into a small bag and a rucksack and put everything we didn't need into a storeroom. Flossie was taken to the compound and to a 'cage' within it where she was locked up, chained and very secure. There would also be an askari keeping watch all night.

We hopped on a bus to the harbour and boarded the boat to Zanzibar. The boat was quite modern and smart and the deck area was furnished with large 1950-style three piece suites and rows of plastic chairs. We were amongst the first to board so had our pick and settled down to enjoy the journey as the boat moved out of the harbour and into the gentle swells of the Indian Ocean.

The island of Zanzibar lay 30 or so miles off the east coast of Tanzania and the three and a half hour trip passed pleasantly with a cool sea breeze. As Zanzibar came into view we were given immigration cards to complete. We were also told we would have to show our health cards. We hadn't bought those with us – just our passports for safe-keeping. Tanzania and Zanzibar were the same country so we thought we'd only need our passports but we were soon to find out that the health card 'requirement' was a bit of a perk for the harbour and Customs officials on Zanzibar.

On the dockside we disembarked and followed the crowd through the harbour. At the health office we were called aside and an official explained to us and an Australian that we needed to show our Yellow Fever certificates. Charles explained we didn't have ours and we all three tried to persuade the official that we had the certificates because they were, of course, a requirement to get into Tanzania but that we hadn't brought them with us to Zanzibar. The ticket office had not said we needed them. We argued on and although the official said he was sympathetic we realised what was really going on when we were split up and the Australian was taken to another room - splitting us up made the matter of a bribe easier.

On our own with the official he continued to be sympathetic and explained that he took the regulations very seriously and what did we think he could do to settle the matter with no embarrassment for anyone. At this point we offered him money and he thanked us politely for helping him to help us!

When we emerged from the grip of the formalities a small crowd of locals was waiting to offer us help to find a hotel. We re-grouped with the Australian to compare notes on the size of the bribe paid and found somewhere for a drink together. Whilst most of the crowd drifted away one of them followed us and apologised for our 'problems' at the port. He paid for our drinks which rather restored our faith in human nature.

We took directions to a guest house and down a narrow alley we found the Warere Guest House with clean, netted rooms with a fan, running water, friendly staff and breakfast all in for $10.

We left our bags and strolled out into the hot day to take a proper look at Zanzibar. The streets of Stone Town were all narrow, some were even too narrow to turn a bicycle, and scruffy with dark, mysterious doorways. There were shops selling the usual, and by now familiar, African paraphernalia of Omo, soap, Blue Band margarine, Hedex tablets and Vick's vapour rub. Some of the dark openings housed carpenters' workshops where ornate furniture and carved chests were being made. The Arab doors on many of the buildings were testimony to their skill and the standard of woodwork was much greater than that required for the average building.

We walked for miles in the hot sun taking in all the new, strange sights. We passed the People's Palace and the Fort and the market and found ourselves at the waterfront. That evening we ate from the various stalls gathered there which offered peanuts, barbeque meat, corn, sugar cane juice and vegetables in hot, spicy sauces. Everything was washed down with bongo juice (a local fruit drink) and we finished with ice cream. A feast!

The next day we left town on a crowded Land Rover and headed across the island. We bumped along on rough roads for an hour and a half until we reached Jambiani Beach and a small, humble building with the enticing name of The Horizontal Inn. We decided we'd arrived and checked in to a very simply furnished room. We met our four fellow guests: two couples – three New Zealanders and a Canadian. The New Zealand/Canadian couple were Stephen and Linda and our paths would cross with them later and many times. More than 25 years on we are still in touch across many miles.

The hotel's owner was a young man named Mbarak. Mbarak was 18 years old and he and his brother had taken over the building and made it into a hotel when their father died. Mbarak's brother was in hospital with malaria in Zanzibar town but Mbarak assured us there were no mosquitoes to trouble us on this side of the island.

The view from the covered veranda of the hotel was of a strip of perfect white beach fringed by palm trees and the Indian Ocean lapped gently in the distance to complete the scene of a tropical paradise. Paradise with no running water or electricity which didn't bother us at all.

Lunch was included in our $5 for the room and we relaxed over fresh coconut. Everyone was relaxed, friendly, cheerful and undemanding and there was the promise of fresh lobster for dinner.

We wandered along the silky, smooth white sand to the water's edge and found the water pleasantly warm – certainly warmer than a lot of the showers we'd had recently. We picked up shells and watched local men harvesting seaweed and bringing in their fishing boats. As the sun set the lamps were lit and we tucked into dinner under a clear sky crowded with stars. We went to bed and the gentle sound of the sea and the breeze through the palms was all we could hear as we drifted off to sleep.

The next day Mbarak arranged for one of the local fishermen to take us out to the reef so we had a day on the ocean to look forward to. At least, Charles was looking forward to it. I'm not a strong swimmer and don't really like to be out of my depth. I hate being unexpectedly in the water and being underwater is only ever by accident which quickly leads to panic. Charles was a natural in the water.

So, with our differing views of the day ahead we left the beach in a small, local sailboat made from a mango tree. We were poled out along the coast and then the rough sail was set and we sailed quietly and gently towards the reef to drop anchor. Our fisherman quickly kitted Charles out with a mask and snorkel and after a rather undignified dive into the warm, turquoise water he was happily gazing downwards to the sea bed below. I ventured more gingerly into the water and made a short test swim away from the boat. I felt surprisingly buoyant and was encouraged by that enough to accept the offered mask and snorkel. I found the mask quite claustrophobic and putting my head under water gave rise to familiar feelings of panic but with a firm grip on the side of the boat and a bit of determination that this was not an experience to be missed I was able to look down and saw, beneath me, the most amazing scene.

The reef was rugged and still while all about it darted beautiful, vibrantly coloured fish. They were bright blue, mauve, yellow and some even black and white striped. It was unbelievable to me that I could be seeing such a spectacle. Charles swam around and floated lazily with his head down and was clearly transfixed and with a little persistence I even managed to leave the security of the boat briefly. I wished I had the confidence to make more of the experience and fought to persuade myself that whilst I wasn't truly swimming I wasn't really drowning either.

Back on shore new guests had arrived: a Frenchman and two Spanish girls. We joined them for a late lunch and sat reading and relaxing on the veranda for most of the afternoon until the daily catch came in and we were pleasantly distracted by the Frenchman who vigorously negotiated the purchase of four crabs for dinner. The largest crab was dead and the subject of much debate. A small crowd of women and children gathered as the Frenchman poked and prodded and bargained. This was great entertainment and by the time the deal was done to the satisfaction of buyer and seller it was nearly dusk. There was just time before dark to commission a local to climb up and pick a coconut for us which was added to our evening meal. We spent a very pleasant evening comparing various aspects of life in Tanzania, England and France and the rather interesting views of Mbarak who found the concept of free speech and democratic voting a little far-fetched.

All too soon it was time to pack up and catch a ride back to the west coast. The only vehicle which arrived to take us was open-backed and promised a very dusty ride. From the beach we were the only passengers but soon began to stop and pick up locals with toddlers, children and bags of all sizes and shapes. We bounced along happily – at least they were all happy and when we dropped them off in town they waved cheerily. We were not quite so cheery about the whole thing having found out we'd paid five times the fare they had paid. Oh well!

We checked back into the Warere Guest House and asked about the spice tours which took place every day. We were told to go to a meeting point in the morning and when there were sufficient people for a tour it would set off.

We turned up at the meeting point to find a few other people waiting and it didn't take long for enough of us to be gathered and we all piled into a motley motorcade of VW vans and a variety of old Ford cars – MK 1 Cortinas, Zephyrs being the only ones I could confidently recognise from the late 1960s and early 1970s. Our van was full of Australians and New Zealanders who formed the bulk of the tour.

The first stop was the Anglican Cathedral built on the site of the old slave market. Apparently, when David Livingstone's campaigning was successful in bringing an end to slavery the slave market was destroyed and the land bought by two local men who then donated it for the building of a cathedral. The altar itself was on the site of the old whipping post. In the yard dozens of happy, lively local children played, sang and danced. All this was in stark contrast to the preserved slave chambers which were dark, deep stone rooms where upwards of 200 people had been kept. We didn't linger too long there and were much happier in the bright, warm sunlight watching the children play. They seemed as happy to see us as we were to watch them before we moved on to our next stop – a ruined palace.

The palace itself had belonged to Sultan Burghash who ruled Zanzibar in the early 1800s and built the palace for his one true wife and 99 slave wives. The story was that the first wife only married the Sultan on the condition that any subsequent wives were slave wives and their children, therefore, would be slave children and unable to challenge the position of the first wife's children. We saw the baths and changing rooms where all the wives bathed and played whilst the Sultan taunted his first wife by parading the slave wives and favouring them. Apparently, the first wife was a clever woman and never rose to the bait knowing that her position and that of her children was unassailable. I wondered if she was a happy woman.

The tour continued and we were told that each wife had a separate bedroom and that when the Sultan died the wives were given their freedom and allowed to return home although many stayed on the island as they considered Zanzibar to be their home. The tour guide said that when he was a boy in school an old Malawian lady had visited and told them she had been one of the Sultan's wives. During her talk to the school about her life in the palace she emphasised that she had been happy then and could only make a living now by giving talks about her former lifestyle.

We spent the rest of the morning at various roadside gardens looking at a variety of fruits and more exotic produce which included quinine, aloe vera, cardamon, cotton, ginger, turmeric and a substance which was used as lipstick by the local women. We all had great fun smearing the tiny seed with bright liquid on our lips, eyelids, faces and arms – it got over everything. Around midday the drivers parked the vehicles close together and laid out some snacks of falafel, coconut, poppadums, deep-fried potato slices and a spicy dip.

Delicious!

Our next stop was a private farm where the young son shinned up a coconut tree and began to fling down coconuts which the drivers collected and prepared for us. The quantity of sweet liquid in each coconut was too much for any of us to finish.

Cloves were the main crop of the island and the trees had been introduced by the English and became such an important crop that it was illegal for cloves to be sold privately to individuals and the whole crop was managed by the Government for export purposes. The trees were not very big but gave two crops a year totalling 1500 pounds in weight. The farmer would be paid 100 Tanzanian Shillings per pound. Other important crops were cinnamon, breadfruit, star fruit, cacao, coffee and an antiseptic plant known as natural iodine. We were shown vanilla growing wild, tamarind and pineapples as well as jujuba which was used as soap.

Although fascinated we were all now quite hungry so very glad to see a late lunch being laid out on the bonnets of the cars. Rice, salad, fruit and curried fish and there were rush mats laid out on the ground for us to sit on. Lemon grass tea appeared from nowhere and was served by the drivers. Refreshed and rested we climbed back aboard the vans and cars and made our way back to Zanzibar town. We ate dinner from the local stalls again and thoughts turned to our return to the mainland – and Flossie who might be thinking we'd deserted her.

The Salvation Army was full when we got back there so we decided to load Flossie and try our luck at the YWCA. Unfortunately, Flossie had other ideas and refused to start. Her battery was flat. We attempted to jump start her but even with both of us pushing we couldn't get enough speed to start her – nothing. We took the luggage and panniers off and Charles tried running with her – still nothing. Not a peep. By this time we were both hot and sticky so asked around if anyone had jump leads we could use. The askari went off and returned with two cables and asked Charles to go with him to find a suitable vehicle. Charles returned in a car with an Englishman - Major Idwel Evans from Sunbury-on-Thames in Berkshire. The Major formally introduced himself to me and seemed delighted to be of help.

The jump leads and car battery did the trick and Flossie sprang into life. The Major asked what our plans were now and rather than let us go off to town said he would be pleased to give us the spare room in his house. We followed him to a medium-sized, stone house with a kitchen, bathroom, living/dining room and two bedrooms. It was neat and homely with electricity and running water – all the comforts of home and it was quite a novelty to be in a home after so long away from our own.

The Major was very welcoming but excused himself as he had to take some disabled children from the local boarding school to the swimming pool. He told us to make ourselves at home and relax. When the Major returned we found out a bit more about him.

The Major had been in East Africa since 1956 and most of the children (165 of them) he worked with were polio victims or amputees. He gave us some onward names and addresses we could use if needed and told us what he knew of road conditions further south. As he had arranged to meet friends for dinner he left us again and we headed over to the canteen to eat. We got back to the house before the Major and finished our evening relaxing, talking and listening to music into the small hours.

The Major was a kind and generous man we remember fondly. Many years after we returned home he appeared in a television documentary talking about his work for The Salvation Army and life in Africa. A fascinating story.

NOVEMBER 1991

TANZANIA TO MALAWI

DEFLATED AND TYRED

Once we'd packed up and after a spartan, dismal breakfast in the canteen, we discovered Flossie would not start again. She wouldn't respond to pushing either so we prevailed on the Major for his jump leads and battery again. With the engine running we said our thank-yous and goodbyes to him and drove back to town and the YWCA. Charles took a look at Flossie's battery terminals and gave them a clean. We had lunch in the canteen, vowing to eat out in the evening as we were tired of canteen food which always seemed to be chicken and mounds of rice. Tomorrow we planned to travel - both ready to move on. We'd seen enough of Dar Es Salaam and looked forward to pastures new.

Before we could set off, however, we had to break a $100

bill into smaller change and find a money changer. The big hotels all refused to change our bill for smaller denominations but we found a small hotel that obliged us. Once we were packed and checked out we found a bookstall, traded some books and changed our smaller dollar bills into local currency with them. We agreed a rate of exchange and counted the money seated on the shop step. No-one seemed to take undue notice of us and when we'd finished we got on Flossie and set off for Morogoro and beyond.

We made good progress to Chalinze for lunch of peanuts, hard boiled eggs and bananas and quickly went through Morogoro to Mikumi National Park. The road went straight through the park for about 30 miles and although we saw no game at first we did surprise a zebra crossing the road. A very literal zebra crossing! As we approached it paused and then broke into a run. Not long after that we had to slow and pull up to let two large elephants and a baby elephant cross just 30 yards in front of us. Magnificent!

Unfortunately, we weren't allowed to camp at the park camps so went on to the town of Mikumi at the centre of roadworks. The first hotel we pulled up at said it did not take guests. The receptionist very carefully explained: "We're only a hotel, we don't have guests". Puzzled we followed his pointing finger and tried the New Kilimanjaro Guest House. Here we booked in and showered. The parking wasn't good but we were told to give the askari 200 Tanzanian shillings and all would be well.

The guest house didn't offer food so we went to a bar for a beer and then back to the hotel (which didn't take guests) for what was a very dismal meal because we were the only diners and the menu of a dozen or so dishes (combinations of rice, chips, chicken, beef and goat) came down to just chicken and rice - the only thing left. We couldn't face more rice so just had the chicken which was small and overcooked. We spent a miserable evening whinging about lack of variety and remembered our camp stove staples of corned beef hash and sausage casserole with the affection of hindsight. We peered in the shop —a shop no-one was allowed into but only saw the usual, boringly familiar array of Omo, Blue Band margarine etc.

We filled Flossie up with petrol the next morning and left Mikumi for Iringa. There was no apparent camping so we asked at the Lutheran Centre which Major Evans had recommended. Whilst they agreed we could camp "and welcome" we didn't fancy a dreary afternoon and evening in what was, effectively, their car park so headed off a little way out of town. Nothing better presented itself so we pulled into a little roadside restaurant for what was supposed to be egg and chips but turned out to be a chip omelette.

We were sick of chicken, eggs, rice and chips in every possible (and some impossible) combination. The table was filthy and the air was crowded with flies so we found a market, bought some vegetable and determined we would camp – roadside if necessary.

We headed out into a warm afternoon on a good, quiet road which was straight for mile after mile through a cool forest plantation. Mid-afternoon we started to look for a suitable place to camp and after a couple of unsuccessful stops we found a small clearing screened from the road by piles of newly-felled trees. We made tea, pitched the tent and cooked tomato and carrot stew. As it began to get dark we cleared everything away, secured what we could and settled down for the night. We'd seen no-one and only heard the trucks rumbling past on the road. We were a bit nervous of showing any light though and lay in the dark tent for quite a while listening to the night sounds of Africa until we fell asleep. We slept on and off through the night and whenever we woke up we could hear the sound of not too distant, quiet chatter and the squeak of bicycle wheels as locals passed on the road. We wondered if they knew we were there listening in the dark.

We woke early and in time to see the sun rise and climb above a spiky horizon of plantation treetops. It was a chilly start to the morning but we were soon on our way and making good progress until we saw a tour truck parked at the roadside. We stopped to talk to the driver and see what, if any, information he had about the road ahead, towns and the likelihood of a camp site. He said he was pushing on for Malawi and a good camp site just across the border. He told us about the border crossing, where to find the local black market and that the road was "not too bad" so we decided we'd head for the border and Malawi.

Almost immediately the road deteriorated and we rode on mile after mile of the most variable tarmac and had to weave around the worst potholes we had yet seen. We couldn't find anywhere for lunch and only managed to find a drink after much asking around. We were glad to be leaving Tanzania and had high hopes of Malawi. The Tanzanian road continued to the border in an appalling state of disrepair and neglect until, suddenly, smooth, new tarmac stretched ahead to a neat roundabout with a large green sign directing us to the border three miles distant.

This was our cue to stop and make our preparations for the

border crossing. We had to check our money was correct for the border. We'd come into Tanzania with US dollars hidden in the tail light and the tubular frame of Flossie and had used this for our black market transactions. We now needed to make sure we only presented the correct balance shown on our currency declaration form. We hid our copy of the travellers' bible ('Africa on a Shoestring') under Flossie's seat in the tool tray as we had heard that Malawi 'disapproved' of it and would confiscate any copies found. I also put on my skirt ready to enter Malawi as women in Malawi were not allowed to wear shorts or trousers or show their knees – it was against the law. I kept my trousers on but rolled them up to my knees and hoped this would go unnoticed.

We got through the first part of the border and left Tanzania without any problem and drove 200 yards to check in with the Malawi police. There was then 8 miles on good, fast tarmac to the Malawi Customs which represented the actual border point – Malawi.

Passport control and Customs checks were soon done but then we had to wait for 'checking'. Eventually, someone came to do this and asked about any books we had. Charles was just about to show him our books (not 'Shoestring, of course) when another officer waved us through. At that exact moment yet another officer appeared and said I could not proceed as I was wearing trousers under my skirt.

We explained about the impracticality, when riding, of a skirt but the officer insisted that the local Malawian women rode bikes in a skirt and, therefore, so could I. The officer addressed himself to Charles most of the time, referred to me as "this woman" and never made eye contact which annoyed me more than the trouser versus skirt debate. However, there was no arguing that locals only rode small bikes and nothing as big or fast as Flossie and we eventually conceded defeat. I was shown to an office and removed my offending trousers.

Suitably dressed, at least for the moment, we were ready for Malawi. Swinging my leg over Flossie and the luggage and sitting astride her in my skirt showed a lot more than my illegal knees and anyone who cared to be looking would have seen a fair bit of thigh but the law was the law. We had, in any case, decided that when riding I would risk trousers under my skirt and would roll them up and down as required.

The road from the border was good and we were soon in Karonga and the lakeside Marina Club which the tour truck driver had suggested. We changed money at the bar and were told it was safe, and free, to camp on the beach so we pitched under a large and shady tree with a small audience of locals to watch our every move. A policeman shooed them away and warned us not to camp. It seemed camping wasn't safe for a lone tent which gave us a problem. We didn't want to move to the guest house and although we wanted to eat there we couldn't risk leaving the tent. So, as it got dark we cooked baked beans and ate beside the tent and Flossie surrounded by gnats and mosquitoes and then went dismally to bed. We were very depressed with our first impressions of Malawi after such high hopes.

The next morning we found breakfast of scrambled egg, tomato and thick slices of fried bread and coffee in the town. We filled Flossie up and left for Livingstonia - a settlement named after David Livingstone. Mr. Livingstone had originally settled his mission on the shores of Lake Malawi but the malarial mosquitoes were a constant problem so moved to higher ground.

Livingstonia was six miles up a steep, winding dirt road and we steadily climbed to about 3,000 feet in those miles to arrive, hot and sticky, at the village. The museum house was interesting and told us a lot we didn't know about David Livingstone but the nicest part of it all was being able to touch and handle the books, his camera, hat and morse code tapper. Nothing was in cabinets or under glass.

The road out of Livingstonia towards Rumphi was flatter and better and we hoped we could make good time to Nkhata Bay on Lake Malawi. Flossie ground on and we reached the tarmac around late afternoon and headed to Mzuzu.

As we travelled I had time to re-think our initial impression of Malawi. I noticed that the local people were slightly better dressed than their Tanzanian neighbours and the Kenyans and that the rural areas were generally better organised and neater, more 'finished' than we'd seen elsewhere. Buildings were often neat brick with thatched roofs and there was much less corrugated iron. Footpaths and phone boxes gave the country a structured look.

We arrived in Nkhata Bay just as the sun was setting and were pleased to see that Simon and Belinda from Ma Roche's in Nairobi were already there. We were surprised to see they had passengers and that they included the New Zealand/Canadian couple we'd met on Zanzibar, Stephen and Linda, and a blond Swede called Carl. We caught up with each other's news and were told there was going to be a bonfire party on the beach that evening – it was Guy Fawkes' Night!

The good news kept coming as we also found out that the local population came round regularly selling firewood, cake, fish, peanuts and a laundry service. We decided, there and then, we would be spending a few days at this pretty, lakeside camp site.

Formal greetings over, tent pitched and we took our contribution of carrots and onions to the communal salad at the party on the beach. The bonfire was alight and everyone gathered around. Simon lit several flares he'd been carrying which made a decent substitute for fireworks and as the bonfire burned down we cooked rice, potatoes and fish, shared beers and the salad and generally relaxed. It was good to be with people we knew again and we were looking forward to a good night's sleep as we strolled back to the tent. Everyone said the askaris here were very conscientious and security was not a problem.

We started the next day with a swim in the lake which was warm and very pleasant. Breakfast was banana cake bought from a local boy and then we settled down to do absolutely nothing with our morning except eat more banana cake and peanuts and organise another local to do some washing for us. We did take a trip to the local supermarket which was a revelation with bread, eggs, milk, yoghurt, cereal and all sorts of tinned goods including corned beef and baked beans. We returned to camp with as much as we could carry. The road from the camp site to the local town was unmade and quite sandy so not something we wanted to do on a daily basis.

The afternoon provided a bit of excitement as Linda discovered a mark on her toe which someone thought was a worm as he'd had one burrow under the skin of his foot. He offered to cut the worm out and we all gathered around to watch. After some time with a Swiss Army knife the 'worm' turned out to be a blood blister and whilst Linda was undoubtedly relieved I think the rest of us were a bit disappointed with the anti-climax.

We were soon distracted from our disappointment though with the new excitement of Simon who turned up in a dug-out canoe he'd borrowed from a local. All the men wanted a go and Belinda, Linda and I spent an hour or so watching Charles, Simon, Stephen and Carl attempt to all be in the canoe at one time and paddle for more than a few seconds before it turned over and pitched them out into the lake.

There was a lot of giggling and splashing but not much success and they eventually decided to retire, defeated, to the bar for beers. As it got dark we lit our own camp fires and settled down to eat. At this point, Charles and I discovered that we should have altered our watches to Malawi time which was an hour behind Tanzania. This meant it would be light even earlier in the morning and dark by 6.00 p.m.

As we settled to a daily routine the lake, and the locals who lived nearby, provided so much. We washed ourselves in the lake every morning, washed our clothes and our dishes and used it to cool off in the heat of the day. We bought fish from local fishermen and local boys gutted the fish in exchange for the head, tail and other 'waste'.

The weather and our routine was settled and calm until one night there was a deafening clap of thunder and then, just before dawn, lightning flashed and thunder rumbled regularly. The rain this produced was just a light shower but it was slightly unnerving as only the day before Linda had told us the story she'd heard of lots of locals being drowned on this very beach in flash floods. The scars in the earth caused by the floodwater were still visible and since that event the locals had been encouraged to leave the bar area for higher ground.

One of the high points of excitement during our stay in Nkhata Bay was the opening of the new toilet – and I was the first to use it, with very little ceremony. The old toilet was just a hole in the ground and had been rapidly filling up and the flimsy structure around it was in a very sorry state. The low roof had a large hole which had the only advantage that taller users needn't stoop but could stand tall with their head through the hole and admire the scenery or conduct a conversation with passers-by whilst both parties went about their individual business. The straw walls had no door but a screen slightly offset provided an obstructed view of the interior.

The smart, new toilet had no roof but tall walls and a hinged door – all in straw, of course. The ground within this capacious new structure was piled high around the new, very small, hole in the ground. All in all we agreed this was a significant improvement to the sanitary arrangements.

After a week at Nkhata Bay, and a total of four miles ridden in that week, we decided it was time to move on again. We were on our way to the capital of Malawi – Lilongwe. The road was good and fast through very pretty scenery of hills and forestry plantation. Although there was very little traffic on the road there seemed to be endless numbers of trucks on their sides or at unnatural angles in the ditches. One truck had slewed down the road and was lying on its side across two lanes but we managed to squeeze past until we reached Lilongwe – a very neat, new but sprawling city.

The Lilongwe Golf Club had a camp site and we drove in to a sea of old, familiar faces: Simon and Belinda, Stephen and Linda and Ron and Anka from Ma Roche's who still had their chicken. It was still only mid-afternoon so after we'd pitched the tent we went off to find the supermarket which was well-stocked with all sorts of interesting and varied Western goodies we had not seen for quite a while.

Malawi traded with South Africa and was, consequently, better off than neighbouring Tanzania and Uganda and Kenya. A lot of the food (and wine) in the shops was South African or Zimbabwean. There were also a lot of well-stocked, thriving book shops.

As a group we were barbequing that evening so we bought steak and potatoes and a contribution for the communal salad. Cold beer from the clubhouse and steak felt like unbelievable luxury.

Next morning we were not quite so happy as we noticed our box of cooking equipment was gone. We hadn't locked it away in the panniers. Charles set off immediately to find the askaris.

The night askaris had left but the Security Manager came to see us and proudly told us that because of three (THREE) night askaris there had not been a robbery for three months. THREE MONTHS! Well, impressive though he thought his record was there had been a robbery now and word quickly spread round.

Simon and Belinda made us some tea and breakfast and

donated a plate, bowl, knife, fork and spoon to us. The stolen box had been our cooker, pans, cutlery, plates, bowls and cups and a variety of food and spices. The rucksack was also stolen. We sat around miserably and thought about how we would manage with no cooking facilities.

Today was the day our original travel insurance expired and we hoped that Charles' mum had received a recent letter asking her to renew it. But, despite insurance we knew that not having cooking facilities was going to be expensive and inconvenient and that not everything could be replaced locally. Eventually, we stirred ourselves into action and went to the police station to make a statement. This was a formality for an insurance claim with no real hope of any investigation or recovery of our things. Later in the day we decided to find a machine shop as a Dutch biker in camp had suggested a possible repair for Flossie's persistent oil leak.

Flossie had been leaking oil for a long time. Charles thought the cylinder base threads had stripped (I had no idea!) and the Dutch biker was riding an R80GS north from Botswana and suggested that a wire wound around the stripped thread might stop the leak. We tried it. It didn't work. In fact, we never got the problem sorted until we were home and she could be stripped down for a full repair.

That evening we cooked sausages on the barbeque and had baked beans cooked in a pan loaned to us by Simon and Belinda. Before heading off to bed we approached the askaris huddled around their fire and asked them to keep a good watch on our tent. They said our tent was too far away so we stomped off to see the boss. We persuaded him to come to the site and he then explained that our own, and several other tents, were not actually within the bounds of the camp site. A heated discussion then began to the effect that we were paying 20 Kwacha a night and hadn't been told we were outside the boundary – there being no fence. The night askaris had no idea there had been any theft the night before and insisted that everyone move their tents closer together and closer to the askaris so they could keep an eye on everything without straying from their fireside. The askaris' boss seemed satisfied with this suggestion but did comment they'd be fired if there was a theft that night. We were not entirely convinced with the new arrangements so locked everything in the panniers, locked the panniers on Flossie and set her alarm.

The evening's entertainment in the bar was a slow-worm, or snake (no-one knew which) which slithered towards our group. Anka saw it first and we all lifted our feet up on to the table. Ron called a waiter over to deal with it. The waiter, however, took one look at it and ran off screaming. A small crowd of interested drinkers gathered around as Ron approached the 'snake' although he was not entirely sure what he was actually going to do. Charles suggested Ron grab the snake by the neck and fling it in the bushes. We all thought this was a good idea and Ron was about to do so when he stopped to ask the exact position of a snake's neck. Fortunately, by now the 'snake' was so confused it decided to slither away and we resumed our drinking without another thought for it.

Simon and Belinda left the next morning with Stephen and Linda as passengers and we moved into their vacant site which was very central and very shaded. We went off to the local market to buy some cutlery and cooking pans.

We had also decided to find the local hospital. I hadn't been feeling well for some days. I was constantly tired and we decided I should have a test for malaria. After a lot of walking around endless corridors and nameless departments all congested with sitting or standing, glum-looking locals I found someone in a white coat and was sent off to wait in a queue where I filled in a form and paid 8 Kwachas. In the treatment room the test was a quick pinprick for a smear of blood on a slide which then went off to the laboratory. I had to wait for the results.

Whilst I was form-filling and waiting Charles had gone to cash a eurocheque. When he found me, still waiting, he said he'd been in conversation with one of the girls from the tour truck in the camp site. Things were not going well for them all: she was trying to get a vaccination for Yellow Fever but it wasn't 'Yellow Fever Day' and they wouldn't open a whole batch for one person. Neither could they be persuaded to let her buy the whole batch and take it back to the truck for a nurse they had with them to do the actual vaccination. Another of the girls from the truck was in the X-ray department as she'd fallen down a hole in the dark in the camp site. We'd all seen these holes being dug (for a perimeter fence) and had all remarked that these deep holes would be a danger in a dark, African night.

My malaria test eventually came back and was negative. If I wanted to see a doctor I'd have to go back the next day and wait my turn. Satisfied I didn't have malaria we decided against that idea and headed back to the camp site just as the sky darkened, thunder rumbled and lightning flashed. The weather didn't improve much and the next day we headed south to Blantyre under a cloudy sky.

Riding on a bike is a very sensual experience – you can

hear and smell so much more than when in a car. We could smell the rain coming and put our waterproofs on just before the rain really fell down. We'd seen the darker, threatening skies in the distance over Mozambique and could see brighter skies behind so kept going to Blantyre and the Sports Club which was the local camp site.

Blantyre Sports Club camp site was actually a small patch of grass overlooking the cricket pitch with a narrow gate Flossie just squeezed through. Two Canadians were already insitu and once we'd pitched they suggested tea in the Clubhouse. Tea turned into beers and dinner of a good chomba (fish) and prawn pie. The ex-pats in the bar and restaurant were a mixed bunch with some being casually dressed whilst others were in shirts and ties with the ladies wearing dresses and high heels. The ex-pat life looked rather easy and comfortable – very pleasant.

Blantyre was a very neat, compact town and reminded me of a medium-sized, provincial English town. There were large supermarkets with white locals pushing trolleys of food and streets with traffic lights, white lines and pavements – real pavements. It was all very urban and suburban. We spent most of our first day in town enjoying the feel of it all and noticed that signs of Christmas were appearing in the shape of gold and silver decorations, cards and wrapping paper in the shops. It was mid-November.

Our next destination was Mulanje and although the road was narrow and quite worn out in places we arrived there and at the foot of the mountain by lunchtime. We asked about camping attached to a hotel but it didn't look very secure so we decided to head up to the Forest Gate. The road to the Gate was a dirt road through acres of tea plantation until we got to the office and a Rest House.

The Rest House was very expensive and although they suggested we use a corner of the car park for the tent this was no good for us. We wouldn't be able to leave the tent and go walking and were already being pestered by souvenir sellers, begging children and locals offering to act as porters or guides on the mountain. We had little choice but to return to a nearby village we'd passed and find accommodation where we could leave Flossie and the luggage. The Mulanje Motel was clean but depressing with the same basic furniture and heavy, brown coloured walls so typical of Africa. The weather was unbearably hot and humid and after some bread and marmite for lunch we flopped out, exhausted, until mid-afternoon.

In what we hoped would be the cool of the evening we headed out to see the village. We found a park and watched a very energetic game of Sunday football. Thunder rumbled in the distance and rain fell on the players as they trooped off the field but the weather was still hot and humid. We cheered ourselves up with dinner of only slightly chewy steak with fried egg and chips and watched a silent group of 10 or so African women amble in, sit down and voraciously eat a very plain looking meal before leaving. The whole process took about 20 minutes and not a word was uttered during the whole time.

The night was oppressively hot and our room was hot, airless and ridden with mosquitoes. There was no netting, no screens and no fan – memories of Egypt. We could also hear mice scurrying around above the ceiling and the steady, heavier thuds of what might have been a cat in pursuit followed by a sharper, heavier thud of a paw and the squeak of a mouse. Visions of Tom and Jerry came to mind!

We woke unrefreshed and still hot. I had a headache. We decided not to do any walking. It was too hot, we didn't have a rucksack and there was nowhere locally to buy or hire anything to make more than one day's walk possible and it just seemed too much hassle so we left for Cape McLear to, hopefully, find some other travellers, get cleaned up and rest. We were both pretty tired of feeling grubby and were looking forward to using the lake to clean up and cool off.

Before we left we had to go to the bank and while Charles was inside I saw Stephen, Linda and Carl. They said Simon and Belinda were at the Mission because Simon had a very bad case of malaria. Stephen, Linda and Carl had spent two nights on the mountain walking and were now trying to hitch a ride back to Blantyre. It was by now late morning and Charles and I agreed to backtrack to Blantyre and meet them at the Sports Club.

Back in Blantyre we pitched and spent the afternoon in The British Council reading newspapers to catch up on world events. We were surprised to be the only Europeans in the reading room and everyone, but us, seemed to be reading The Times or The Independent. Occasionally, I glanced up to find someone looking intently at us rather than their newspaper. This habit of locals has begun to get to me recently and I have become tired of being watched and stared at and questioned. It seemed particularly odd here because Blantyre had a large, white European population and we shouldn't have been a novelty.

Next morning we met some Dutch people on the camp site. They were travelling north and added to the growing list of travellers singing the praises of Zimbabwe: good food, good wine, good camping and cheap, very cheap. We were able to give them some information about Zanzibar and Kenya before we set off to Cape McLear and Golden Sands camping.

We pulled off the tarmac road onto a dirt road and bounced along on the bone shaking, corrugated surface. The lake was nowhere in sight but, hot and sweaty, we got to the National Park gate and paid our 3 Kwacha entry. The camp site itself offered more than Nkhata Bay but was not as pretty or tranquil and the only food to be bought was in Monkey Bay – 12 miles back along the dirt road and another three miles on the tarmac. We were, however, very pleased to see Ron and Anka and went straight to the bar with them for a cold beer.

We were woken by monkeys swinging through the trees at dawn and 'borrowed' some hot water to make coffee. A local chap took a large pile of our dirty clothes off to be washed while Charles and I walked over the headland to a very pretty outcrop of rocks and little pools known as Otter Point. We sat there all afternoon on the rocks and looked into the pools full of brightly coloured fish.

We got back to the camp site in time to wave Ron and Anka off as they are moving to another camp site, Stevens, just along the beach which was a lot cheaper. This camp site was 6 Kwacha a day plus 3 Kwacha for being in the National Park and 7.50 Kwacha a day for a vehicle – their Land Rover. We didn't have to pay for Flossie which made it more affordable. Stevens' camp site was outside the Park and had a good restaurant so we'd arranged to eat there that evening. Ron and Anka would drive over, order our food and we would walk to it along the beach.

Stevens' camp site was actually much less attractive with no shade and a featureless beach but most of the guests were backpackers staying in block built rooms on the beach. There was some worrying news circulating when we arrived because someone had gone off for a swim to the offshore island in the early afternoon and had still not returned. There was concern that something had happened to him but whilst we were all discussing what we should do about it he appeared from the lake impervious to any worry or concern he had caused anyone. We got back to our tent quite late after a moonlit walk back along the beach and found Simon and Belinda had arrived. Simon was asleep but said to be feeling a lot better.

We only saw Simon briefly the next morning because we planned to bounce and bang back down the dirt road to the tarmac and have breakfast in the town. We filled Flossie and set off for Lilongwe. We needed to change some money and do some shopping as preparation to leave for Zambia. We were not looking forward to Zambia and wanted to get it behind us.

The road to Lilongwe was very variable with worn tarmac and some strips of dirt road. A new road was being built and there were quite a few diversions to negotiate. Even so, we made good progress and got to the Golf Club by mid-afternoon. Two very battered BMW bikes and a Tenere, equally battered, had turned up and we met their riders: two German brothers and a Swiss man respectively. We had a chat and checked out each other's bikes and luggage. Charles spotted two other new arrivals cooking with what looked like our stolen stove but when he asked them about it they said they'd flown into Lilongwe that morning.

As we had no cooker we opted, without much choice, to eat in the bar and fell into conversation with two Americans. Colin was ex-Peace Corps who had been in Cameroon teaching chemistry and the other was Ramses who was an Ethiopian by birth but left when he was 12 years old. Ramses' father had been a civil servant in Ethiopia in 1974 when the first signs of unrest began. He was sure things would get worse and applied to leave for the USA on the grounds of studying there. He fought hard to take his family and eventually succeeded, just in time. Ramses had many fond memories of Ethiopia and hoped to go back. We spent a pleasant and interesting evening talking about Africa and comparing travel notes.

The next morning we cashed a eurocheque each in the bank to get cash dollars and some dollar traveller cheques. It all took hours and when we emerged the whole town seemed to have closed. President Banda was arriving back from England after an operation and the whole city had gone to the airport to welcome him home. We'd seen truck and busloads of happy and singing locals going out of town and just as many on foot. A lot of the women wore skirts and tops in a patriotic print of the Malawi flag and the President's face – usually emblazoned across an ample bosom or bottom.

Back at the camp site a huge, very smart coach had pulled in. The front half of the coach had luxury, airline-type seats whilst the rear had individual sleeping compartments. The passengers were all German. The driver and an assistant leapt off and the luggage boxes revealed tables, chairs and a huge cooking set up with all sorts of food and utensils neatly fitted in it. Within half an hour they were all eating. A second vehicle then pulled in which was the twin of the first. The passengers all leapt off and ran about calling "Willy, Willy" and "Hans, Hans" whilst waving their arms around and kissing each other. After some while a rather robust woman clapped her hands and called loudly "Rotel, Rotel" and they all quickly gathered around her. The whole thing was rather odd – but, amazing!

The weather recently had been cool but I was feeling very 'at one' with Africa and quite content. Simon and Belinda had arrived in camp with Stephen and Linda and Carl and as we were all desperately short of cash we decided to pool our resources and go shopping for food. We split up and toured the local Rest Houses looking for a good, or even decent, rate of exchange. None of the usual locals would change as little as $10. We managed to scrape together enough local money to get bread, milk and some meat and vegetables so that was dinner. As the evening wore on it got quite cool and we huddled closer to the barbeque despite long trousers, jumpers and coats.

The next morning we all still had the problem of lack of cash so pooled our combined food stock for breakfast and then Charles and Carl went off with $100 we had scraped together which included a newcomer (Colin) adding $30. Fortunately, this amount did the trick and we got the best rate of 5 Kwacha to $1 which cheered everyone up as we set to our chores. That evening our good humour was spoilt, however, when Colin came back from his tent to report that his sleeping bag had gone – stolen. Another robbery! We all checked our vehicles and tents while Charles went off with Colin to complain to the manager. We could all see the askaris gathered around their fire but they had a clear view of Colin's tent which was also practically floodlit.

The Security Manager arrived and shouted at the askaris before going off with Colin to the police. The askaris did some pacing around for awhile but detected our disapproval. Two robberies in two weeks despite the price we paid to camp and the 'security' of the askaris on site. But, there was little sympathy for us from the police, management and, consequently, the askaris as we appeared, to them, to be rich and spoilt and well able to afford to lose belongings.

Charles and I were now planning our journey to and through Zambia but needed to cash a travellers' cheque. We'd been trying for days but finally managed it despite everything closing early because President Banda was off to Blantyre and, again, truckloads of patriotically dressed, singing Malawians were going to the airport to see him off.

The next morning we'd got cash and a second-hand petrol can for spare fuel and were packed and ready for the road just after 7.00 a.m. Lilongwe to Mchinji and the border was 75 miles. After 15 miles Charles pulled off the road – Flossie had a puncture. We unloaded Flossie and Charles set about changing the rear tyre but the tyre levers we had were too small. I stayed guard over everything while Charles walked to the nearby village in search of better tools but there was nothing suitable. I settled down beside Flossie for what might be a long wait while Charles took the wheel and stood by the roadside in the hope of hitching a ride to a bigger town which might be as far as Lilongwe.

The first vehicle to come along the very quiet road was an Irish Nun from a school near the border. The Nun pulled over and she and Charles disappeared. By now, my small crowd of onlookers were bored with a lack of activity and drifted off which left Flossie and I quietly waiting.

As I sat in the shade a local man came along and stopped for conversation. "Hello Madam," he said. I replied. "How are you?" he asked. "Fine", I replied. "What is the problem?" he asked. "We have a bad tyre and my husband has gone to fix it," I told him. "I'm going to that building there. It is the tailor. I'm collecting my trousers which I left there some days ago," he said. "OK," I replied. This sort of exchange was what counted as conversation in these parts. Just as he was about to set off a truck went past and he felt the need to tell me it was from Tanzania and going to Zambia. I hoped we might be doing the same soon.

The same man came back sometime later with his trousers and remarked "I have been to the tailor and I'm going along home now." "Fine", I replied. It passed the time.

Charles, meantime, had arrived at the Mission garage just a short way down the tarmac road and six miles or so of dirt road. The garage was superbly equipped and they patched the tyre and put a tube in. Charles hitched a ride back to Flossie and I, fitted the wheel and loaded the luggage. Charles decided we would go back to Lilongwe as he'd seen an old tyre lying around which would be a suitable replacement. The tyre was no longer there so we started searching Lilongwe for a spare inner tube, puncture repair patches and glue. As we hadn't planned to still be in Malawi we'd run our cash down to the last Kwacha so also had to change money to pay for the things we needed. Re- equipped we headed off again and sped past the site of our earlier puncture en route to Mchinji.

A brief stop at the Mission garage to settle up for their earlier help and we were making progress to the boarder and Zambia.

Thirty-five miles later the tyre went down again. This time Charles could repair it himself and as we unloaded Flossie and Charles set to work we gathered a small crowd of onlookers. Under their steady, fascinated gaze Charles repaired the tube and tried re-inflating it. But, our bicycle pump couldn't give us sufficient pressure to 'seat' the tyre and seal it to the rim.

By now it was late afternoon and although we'd given up on Zambia we did hope to, at least, get back to Lilongwe for the night. A Land Rover slowed and gave a questioning 'thumbs up' sign. I shook my head and it pulled over. The driver was a white Malawian who had a hand pump. After several attempts and some washing up liquid to ease things the tyre popped into place. We were off again – back to Lilongwe. Again.

The rear tyre was now so chewed and split from the bad roads that the actual tread blocks were separating from the tyre so we'd have to get a replacement before attempting to go any further south. Seven miles later the tyre went down again and even getting back to Lilongwe was looking doubtful. We considered camping at the roadside but that didn't solve anything. We wondered about the likelihood of getting a ride back to Lilongwe – for us and Flossie. The first vehicle to stop was a container lorry which couldn't help and although the second to stop was a pick-up which might have been OK they weren't sure they could take the weight of Flossie. They suggested we hide her in a bush and go with them to town but we weren't happy to leave her.

Charles had another go at fixing the tyre. By now the sky had turned a vivid red as the sun set and we only had one onlooker who did his best with mime and gestures and two words of English ('yes' and 'sorry') to help. He and Charles took turns with the pump but it was no use. One side would seat but the second would not – despite our entire stock of washing up liquid and water and much swearing. I flagged down another vehicle and the driver lent us his foot pump. He knew our local helper and it was arranged he would return the pump the next day. The foot pump eventually did the trick and the tyre seated. We paid our helper some Kwacha and waved as we drove off to, hopefully, Lilongwe.

On the back of Flossie I was offering up desperate, silent prayers that we'd make it to Lilongwe. We'd never driven in Africa after dark before and all the good advice said it was to be avoided but we had no real choice. It wasn't long before the inevitable happened and the tyre started to go down again. We stopped by some buildings with lights showing and I went to ask if they could help although, to be honest, I wasn't sure what I was asking them to do. As it turned out there was no point worrying about what to ask for because the building was a Tobacco Research Institute – empty and guarded by watchmen who didn't speak English.

Charles had now used one of our precious 'gas' bombs for the tyre and with just enough pressure we set off again with just four miles to go to the outskirts of Lilongwe. But, the tyre was probably not going to make it that far and as it started to go soft again we stopped and I got off to walk while Charles nursed Flossie along slowly. I jogged and walked behind her red tail light and we reunited at the junction for the main road. Charles felt Flossie would make the distance if we could lighten the load further so we unloaded the luggage and flagged down a car. We asked the driver if he would take me and the luggage to the Golf Club and Charles would follow on Flossie. We piled the panniers, tent etc. into the car and I leapt in as the driver instructed Charles to stay close behind.

Our saviour turned out to have spent six years in Glasgow studying mechanical engineering and he drove me straight to the camp site where a cyclist we'd met briefly helped me unload the luggage from the boot of the car. The panniers were too heavy for me to lift on my own but I thanked our driver and sat down on one to tell my story and wait for Charles and Flossie. I didn't think they could be far behind but they hadn't managed to stay close to the car.

It wasn't long before I heard Flossie's distinctive engine getting closer. Charles had stopped to put the second (and last) 'gas bomb' in the tyre and driven fast to get back before the tyre deflated again. Exhausted, hot and dirty we went to the bar where everyone, by now, knew the story. They helped us pitch the tent and we laid down to sleep unable to quite believe we'd spent over 14 hours driving up and down a 20 mile stretch of road to end up exactly where we'd started – dirtier and poorer.

Our first stop the next day was a large garage but they had no suitable tyres for Flossie. We asked around several tyre dealers and anywhere that looked vaguely likely to have something and even took the old tyre to a re-tread company just to hear it was, as we thought, beyond repair.

Whilst I was waiting around I got into conversation with a Zambian man who wanted to ask me why Europeans thought the African was like a monkey and ate the flesh of other humans. I said I didn't think this was so but he insisted he had heard this about us. I explained that, maybe, many years ago when the early missionaries first came to Africa they believed this and took stories back to Europe but nowadays we knew better and many African and Asian people lived in England and Europe. The Zambian said that when he'd been in England the family he stayed with had commented, with surprise, about his ability to use a knife and fork and hold an intelligent conversation. I was rather embarrassed about this and had no real answer for the ignorance he experienced and the Zambian concluded that life in Africa was much simpler and we Europeans should learn to be the same. Fair comment, I suppose.

Back at the camp we were approached by a South African who seemed to know a lot about BMW bikes and made a few suggestions about where we might find a tyre. Most of the suggestions revolved around ex-pats who might know someone, somewhere but one possible lead was that the local Police had similar tyres so we will follow that up – somehow.

We spent all the next day fruitlessly chasing down possible sources of tyres. We managed to find out that old police tyres went to auction. We found the auction house and although the chap in charge said we were in the wrong place he would take us in his car. We had to help him bump start his Morris 1100 and chugged slowly around to another large Government depot. On the way we had to go over quite a few speed bumps and at each one our driver stopped and said we'd have to get out as his suspension was so low there wasn't enough ground clearance with us in the car. In the end it was all a waste of time and our last resort was to phone a company in Johannesburg who took our credit card payment and promised to air freight the tyre immediately.

That evening we met the two brothers, Philip and Michael,

we'd met here before. They'd just got in from Nkhata Bay. We asked them if they'd seen an Englishman (Peter) on a blue Tenere and they said they had and he had said he was on his way to Lilongwe. Peter won't be expecting to see us still here but it will be good if we can catch up with him for a few days. Chatting to the brothers it seemed they had crossed paths with quite a few of the crowd we'd been meeting here and there – small world!

While we waited for our tyre to arrive we decided to do a little clothes shopping. At least, we took one of Charles' tattered t-shirts and some material and gave the whole lot to a tailor. Two new t-shirts will be ready to collect in 24 hours.

A chap in a bar engaged us in conversation and it seemed he'd heard of our hunt for a tyre. We told him the hunt was over and we were waiting for one to be air freighted in. He explained that, in normal circumstances, we'd be expected to pay nearly 100% tax importing a tyre and we should insist on a reduced rate as we will be re-exporting it again when we travel on. He suggested we offer to pay 5% tax and 2% surcharge (against the usual 45% and 35%) and slip the Customs man 10 Kwacha. Useful advice – we'll give it a try.

As we still had a few more days to wait for the tyre and the tailor-made t-shirts had worked out well we bought some more material and commissioned a skirt for me.

The evening passed in good company in the bar. The man who tried to help us with the Police tyre was there with his family and his wife borrowed a guitar and was encouraged to sing for everyone. She had a sweet, gentle voice and sang some favourite classics by John Denver and Simon & Garfunkel. Two Frenchmen with guitars and a local joined her although they knew few of the same songs so it was all rather haphazard. Outside it was raining heavily.

DECEMBER 1991
MALAWI TO ZIMBABWE
A WET, WET, WET CHRISTMAS

Charles woke up during the night to the sound of more rain falling. He then woke me up with the news that all our shoes (riding/walking and casual) had been taken from under the fly sheet of the tent. Only our flip-flops were left – how kind!

Charles got up and called the watchmen over but, as usual, they were apathetic and said they'd seen nothing. We laid awake awhile in a quiet depression and unable to quite believe this had happened again.

We woke with daylight and went in search of the manager to complain. He was concerned. Concerned, no doubt, because camping fees and our spending in the restaurant and bar was valuable income for the Club which might disappear if the camp site was not considered 'safe'. We carefully explained the spate of recent thefts and said we weren't sure the night watchmen were entirely honest. He said he wasn't too sure about them either which rather took the wind out of our argument. We pointed out that the main problem was that if the night was cool or wet the watchmen took refuge in the toilet block and then couldn't see what was going on – even assuming they stayed awake, which we doubted.

Charles and I went off to the police station to make a statement and we asked the CID officer to come with us to the camp site and at least make an attempt to investigate something. We met the security manager, walked around our tent, explained what happened and left him to ask a few questions of the day watchmen. They assured us everything was 'in hand' but goodness only knows what that meant – probably not much.

We now had to replace our shoes and walked around the shops to see what was available. Not much. The main problem would be finding anything large enough for Charles who has quite large feet. The second problem was finding something of suitable quality for riding a large bike off-road. Our stolen boots had been fairly sturdy and although not specifically for motorbike riding they were strong enough and could double as walking boots.

The next day we took a bus to the New City and a large shop which looked promising for shoes. I found some canvas shoes and an assistant drifted over to help. I asked if they had the same in my size. "I don't know," she replied. "Shall I look?" Once she found some and I said I'd buy them she was galvanised into action and I left wearing them.

Charles was more difficult to satisfy and nothing but expensive leather 'town' shoes were available and not in his size. It was suggested we try in the Old City but first we had to sort out our cash situation. We'd recently been told of a 'scam' of telling the bank that we were leaving the country the next day and had too many Kwacha so could we change them for $25 each. We tried this and it worked like a dream so we were soon on our way to the Old City.

We found a European shoe shop (Bata) but they told us the largest shoe size they make is a 10 – Charles is size 12. We trawled around every shoe shop we could find but no-one had anything larger than a size 10. We eventually found a size 11 which did fit but it was in thin suede so hardly suitable for riding. Just as we were thinking we'd have to give up we found a shop selling trendy LA Gear baseball boots in size 12. The shop owner was so thrilled to finally be rid of these unwanted, large boots he discounted them for us.

Resplendently, newly-shod we made our way back to the camp site to find Peter's blue Tenere and his tent right beside Flossie and our tent. Peter had already heard some of our tales of woe from fellow campers and we exchanged more news on the way to the bar.

Shoe problem solved for us and the next day we took a bus out to the airport to collect Flossie's tyre. The bus only went close to the airport but a helpful passenger told us when to get off and that it was only a short walk. It actually looked quite a distance but someone stopped to give us a lift. Inside the terminal they told us to go to the freight terminal and we were offered another lift and, finally, got to the right place – cargo enquiries.

We were told there was nothing for us and when we asked if we could check in the warehouse for ourselves they happily obliged. But, there was no tyre. It was suggested the tyre might arrive on the afternoon flight and we could phone Johannesburg from the passenger terminal to check. We walked to the passenger terminal to find all the phones out of order so sat down to wait. For want of nothing better to do we tried the bank 'scam' again and, again, it worked like a dream which meant we could splash out on lunch in the 'Spectators Restaurant' although, sadly, there was little to spectate – one landing and one departure.

The phones were still out of order after quite a lengthy lunch so we went back to the freight terminal to be told our tyre was manifested and before too long we saw a warehouseman bowling it along towards us. We had to go through Customs and they wanted to charge us import duty on it. Charles explained that we were only temporarily importing the tyre and would be leaving the country tomorrow when our visa expired. Our passports and Flossie's carnet backed this up and it was agreed no tax would be due so we rushed back to the warehouse, paid the handling fee and a tip for quick service and left clutching the precious tyre.

We'd missed the bus back to town so we approached a couple of backpackers to see where they were headed and maybe we could share a taxi. They explained they were flying out but the third member of their party had gone back to their hotel to fetch a forgotten passport. They were quite anxious about her arriving in time for the flight as she had all the tickets. We waited with them on the basis that her taxi could take us back to Lilongwe and when it drew up and she rushed into the terminal with her friends we spoke to the driver. We asked him to wait for a while in case the backpackers also needed a ride back to town but once we saw them being rushed through the terminal we were on our way back to Lilongwe.

In town again we called in at the police station about our insurance claim form but were told we'd have to come back tomorrow as CID had gone home and they had the only rubber stamp for our form. Tomorrow Charles will fit the tyre, we'll pack up and head for Zambia – again.

Charles fitted the tyre while I did some chores and when Charles and Peter took the tyre off to find an airline to pump it up the watchman who collected 'rent' came up to me. He'd been avoiding us for days because he was frightened of Charles. I told the watchman that we hadn't paid because we'd lost 1,000 Kwacha of our belongings and our shoes and that Charles was very angry. The watchman wandered off not quite knowing what to do and before too long Charles and Peter came back and fitted the tyre on Flossie. So, now we all had new footwear and were ready to go.

Our happy mood was soon cut short though when the watchman with his rent book returned and asked Charles to go with him to the manager. I gather there was a heated argument between them all and Charles agreed to pay 80 Kwacha of the 154 Kwacha bill. But, the camp site hadn't finished with us yet and once we were packed and ready to go Charles discovered his sunglasses were missing. The watchmen, as usual, denied all knowledge of anything and I questioned the woman who cleans the toilets. At least, she took an hour to clean them and then washed her clothes, used the showers herself and lounged around until midday. The sunglasses were the final straw so we just left – very happy to be leaving and keen to get out of Malawi.

We pushed on through a short shower of rain and whizzed past the previous puncture sites to reach the Malawi border mid-afternoon. We were quickly through the formalities, changed our Malawi Kwacha to Zambian Kwacha and drove the six miles to the Zambian border post. There was no delay and in Chipata we spoke to the Zambian National Tourist Board office who sent us to a neat, clean hotel with a friendly receptionist who tried very hard to speak perfect English.

Our room was one of the smartest so far in Africa and a wonderful notice on the back of the door told us that the toilet paper, tissues and soap were only for our use whilst we were in the hotel and that we should "not take them away or home as other guests have been found to do. By Order of Management"!

We found the bar and were asked to order dinner (chicken and chips) for later. The large, bright room boasted sofas and comfy chairs and a large television with a larger notice telling us not to touch it – "Let alone the receptionist to operate." Again, "By Order of Management".

Zambian television was interesting. The adverts were quite dated in their style of asking housewives in the street which washing powder they preferred and there were quite a few country-building type slots for the national electricity company which encouraged everyone to pay their bills promptly. The big news was AIDS though and a rather cute advert featured a woman who refused to marry the man she loved because he had been married before and she was concerned he may be carrying AIDS. The man protested he had not been with his wife for several years and, displaying his portly physique, that he was bursting with health. The scene faded and a serious looking woman came on screen to explode various myths about AIDS – all very educational.

When we got back to our room the receptionist delivered the tissues and soap which we must not take away with us. Then, a fan and insect killer spray arrived. Next to arrive was dinner but we sent that to the dining room and by the time we followed the television was broadcasting news and criticism of the previous Government and the level of corruption.

Before we'd come to Zambia we had been nervous about the political situation. Official news and travellers we met who'd been here were very negative about it all but so far we were impressed with the roads, the people and felt quite relaxed.

Next morning we were on the road early with just a quick stop to fill Flossie's tank and petrol can. The road was variable but it was certainly not as bad as we'd expected and better than Tanzania had offered. We soon reached Kacholola where we had thought we'd spend the night but it was only midday and as the road seemed good and the town was very quiet we decided to push on to Lusaka.

Although the roads were good the scenery was very tedious with no houses, schools, villages or people to break up the green countryside. The only event to break up the monotony was a police road block but the policeman merely wanted to admire our 'Honda'. Yes, that's Honda spelt B. M. W!

Lusaka itself appeared to be modern and organised but it was, on closer inspection, run-down, ill-stocked and rather sad. We found The Salvation Army who offered camping in their secure compound already occupied by an English couple, a South African called Jeremy and an English cyclist we'd met before - Chris. We chatted together but then Jeremy pointed out that if we wanted to eat in town we should do it early and before everything closed down for the night. We found a local place which offered burger, chips and a glass of milk and then found a lively, local bar with live music. The noise was throbbing and deafening and the room was full of gyrating, shouting, smiling locals.

Back at The Salvation Army we settled down for the night. We were exhausted after our longest driving day of 357 miles and a night on the town. We knew we'd sleep well as the compound was surrounded by an eight foot high wall topped with broken glass and barbed wire.

Lusaka to the border next day was fairly straightforward with scenery being very much "more of the same" until we passed through the gently winding and rolling Katue Gorge. At the turn off for Kariba we planned to cross into Zimbabwe but were short of petrol so detoured to Chirundi and used the last of our Zambian money. We tried to change $5 to get enough petrol for the border and Kariba town but no-one was interested. Fortunately, we had 17 Zimbabwe Dollars we'd bought from a traveller way back in Lilongwe and although it had just seemed a good idea at the time it was now our saviour.

With as much petrol as we could afford we took the winding road along the gorge and saw Lake Kariba glinting in the distance. At the border post we passed through almost exactly 48 hours after we'd arrived. So, that was Zambia!

We drove across the dam wall between the two border posts and stopped to admire the impressive, well-landscaped structure which makes Lake Kariba Zimbabwe's beach resort.

Getting into Zimbabwe was easy enough. The form filling formalities were very organised and efficient and we showed our credit cards as proof of 'sufficient funds'. It was a good job they didn't ask to see the latest statement!

Zimbabwe seemed, oddly, less 'African' and quite strange. We found the Lions Camp we'd been told about and had a quick look but decided to check out the MOTH Camp as well. This was run by a white Zimbabwean and seemed very well organised so we chose a site and pitched the tent before using firewood lying around to make a fire and some tea.

We took a discreet look at our fellow campers who were exclusively white and seemed mostly to be Zimbabwean or South African. There was a group in a chalet who had even bought their black 'houseboy' with them.

Having settled in we faced the problem of no cash and the bank being closed until tomorrow. We asked at reception if local hotels had a change facility and were told the owner's husband would change some money but at the bank rate and not on the black market. When Charles met him he took $20 at the black market rate and we were solvent again.

The hot showers in the camp site were some of the best I'd ever been in and it was a joy to put my trousers back on after a month in Malawi wearing a sarong skirt getting tattier and dirtier. We took Flossie out and headed for the Lake View Inn looking forward to the good, cheap food we'd heard everyone talking about. As we pulled into the car park we saw Ralph and Anna's Land Rover. We'd expected to meet up with them here and joined their group.

Two cold beers quickly arrived and we chatted about recent events, impressions and experiences. We decided to eat at The Country Club a few miles along the road where we found tables were properly laid with linen tablecloths, quiet music played, the waiters were attentive and efficient and the food was good. It all felt rather like a dream.

The Country Club was exclusively for white clientele and I was so amazed to see a whole double page of food on offer I never thought to turn a page and find even more. How could a few miles across an imaginary line on the ground make such a huge difference? Surrounded by well-heeled white Zimbabweans we felt rather odd not to be the odd ones out although we were, of course, odd because we were considerably scruffier than the local white population.

We went back to The Country Club the next day and although we weren't members there was no problem getting in. It was the 7th December and they were hosting a Christmas party for the local children and Father Christmas was rumoured to be arriving. It was fascinating to see the children dressed in their party frocks with lace and ribbons and reminded me of similar events I went to – back in the 1960's. As the party got into full swing we headed off to the supermarket and returned in time to see the children getting their presents from Father Christmas. We spent the rest of the afternoon at the bar and were only asked to leave because after 6.00 p.m. 'gentlemen' were required to wear a tie and jacket in the bar. We were, by no means, being thrown out and just asked to move to the lounge or dining room. It was all getting very surreal!

But, the Christmas party reminded us that the clock was ticking and we had places to see and miles to cover before re-grouping at Victoria Falls with Peter, Simon and Belinda for Christmas. So, we headed off next day on a good, tarmac road which wound steeply through green countryside with a few villages. We stopped at Karoi and reached the Chinhoyi Caves and its camp site by early evening. The caves were interesting if not spectacular: the Sleeping Pool was rather smelly although very tranquil and blue in its magnificent sunken setting. The viewpoint from above was less than breath-taking although the smell from it was and the Dark Cave was not exactly 'dark' with the addition of modern lighting.

Back at the camp site a tour truck had pulled in and I met a South African girl from it in the shower block. She was desperately scrubbing at her toilet bag as her shampoo had leaked and although she was only three days out from the start of her trip in South Africa I doubted she was cut out for more of Africa. She didn't seem to know where she started the tour or where she'd been and described the shower as a "den of horrors" as it had spiders and a blocked drain. "I'm from South Africa and I'm not used to this sort of thing," she announced. When she found out I was from England she asked if it was nice "down there". I left her to her toilet bag, the spiders and the blocked drain but wondered what she would make of Africa if she travelled any further north.

After breakfast the next morning we headed to Harare. The road was, again, good and fast and quiet and despite sheltering from rain for 15 minutes we made good time to arrive in the capital by lunchtime. The city was smart, modern and Western European in its style and the first person we bumped into was a New Zealander we'd met in Lilongwe who was able to tell us where to find the black market. Our next stop, cash-rich, was a camping shop to buy a stove, some gas canisters, mess tins and a torch to replace stolen items. Our next stop was camping at Sable Lodge where we expected to meet a few other travellers.

Sable Lodge was a guest house offering dormitory accommodation and cooking facilities for backpackers with a small area at the rear for vehicles and tents. The place was full to bursting and quite a few of those gathered looked a bit down at heel - shabbier than the normal traveller. The only other vehicle was a Swiss bike and rider who wanted to know all about Flossie and how she handled. As luck would have it we then saw someone we knew and asked if they knew of any other camping. Most of the alternatives were some way out of town and as we'd got quite a few errands we wanted to stay in town but were not keen on Sable Lodge. The camp site area had recently flooded and the sight of the crowded wet tents, wet cats, dripping washing and bedraggled occupants was depressing.

We were persuaded to stay the night so pitched on the only dry patch of grass and determined to get everything done in town tomorrow so that we could move out. When we ventured out the next day we saw Simon and Belinda's Land Rover parked and looked around for them. They said they were staying with friends but that the camp site a few miles out of town was OK and that Ralph and Anna were there as well as Susie and Alfie in a Land Rover and we hadn't seen them since Nairobi.

We decided to drive out and have a look for ourselves but forgot that we had driven into town on reserve, gone onto the second reserve and hadn't filled up since. So, we ran out of petrol.

A motorcycle petrol tank is shaped over and around the main frame. Motorcycles of Flossie's vintage did not have fuel gauges or petrol pumps and the engine was fed with fuel by simple gravity. A tap at the bottom and on either side of the tank would be turned on to start the engine and turned off when parked. The tap would open a pipe to the petrol supply but once the petrol level fell below the top of this pipe the tap would be turned again to open a hole in the bottom of the tank to allow the remaining fuel to drain out. The change in engine tone as it was starved of fuel would be the only indication of the level of petrol in the tank. So, there was the main supply of petrol in the tank and then a first and second 'reserve' at the lowest point of the tank on either side of the frame.

We ran out of petrol at traffic lights at a major road junction. We emptied out one of the water containers and

Charles set off with it to hitch a ride to a petrol station. As usual, I stayed with Flossie. Charles was lucky and got a lift immediately and they even bought him back so we were quickly on our way again but abandoned our plans for the camp site and went back to Sable Lodge.

We woke early next morning with the sun on the tent and a determination to get out of Sable Lodge. We packed everything up and headed into town for bacon and eggs, coffee and hot, buttered toast for breakfast. We made another stop for fuel and were in Coronation Camp by 9.00 a.m. and chose a spot for the tent just as everyone else was waking up.

The first people we met were an English couple we had heard much about – Bill and Gina. We'd heard of this couple travelling in a new, beautifully fitted Land Rover. We went over to introduce ourselves and found they had heard of us too. We were 'different' from the crowd as a couple travelling on one bike.

Bill and Gina's Land Rover was truly beautiful: well-fitted, neat and clean. They even boasted they still had some Marks & Spencer frozen food in their on-board freezer! However, the Land Rover had been sold locally and tonight would be their last night before they headed for Victoria Falls as backpackers and for a flight home just before Christmas. In the meantime, they had nearly 8,000 Zimbabwean Dollars to turn, somehow, into US Dollars. We gave them an English cheque for some of their local currency which helped us both out.

We gave our dirty laundry to a local woman and I languished in a hot bath. I then felt sufficiently restored to re-write the letter to our insurance company to include the second theft of shoes before we headed into town to eat.

The town was busy with local shoppers fully engaged with their Christmas shopping and the shops were decorated with all the usual, traditional paraphernalia of Christmas. We found a clothes shop and I tried on a couple of blouses. I didn't think my scruffy t-shirts would be good enough for Christmas Day in Victoria Falls and after eight months on the road I wanted to dress up a bit. A blouse with my clean skirt from Malawi would feel like dressing up!

And, that completed our chores so next day after breakfast we headed out of Harare. With a stop at a map shop and supermarket it was nearing midday before we really left the city behind but we rode for an hour before a quick lunch stop and as the afternoon warmed up the distant Eastern Highlands came into view. As we got nearer the magnificent mountains of green rose up as far as we could see – so many peaks.

A lot of the scenery of Zimbabwe had been green and vegetated with strange rocks poking through the earth. Some of the rocks were garden rockery size while some were the height of a tree. Others were low and flat, some larger outcrops balanced precariously and others were almost decorated with bushes and trees. This strange landscape had now given way to a mountain range of familiar beauty – rolling green hills and remote majestic highlands.

We found the Vumba Botanical Reserve, signed ourselves in and drove to the camp site which was lightly perfumed with the scent of magnolia and lightened by the sight of many pale blue hydrangeas in bloom. In this pleasant, fragrant garden environment we quietly celebrated eight months of travelling. Eight months from home.

Our celebration included coffee and chocolate cake at the very English tea room set beside an ornamental lake. The very English garden which surrounded us with a myriad of paths, neat hedges and pretty flower beds had been laid out by an English mayor and showed off very English flowers beside more exotic varieties. A roaming peacock, peahen and some chicks completed the picture postcard.

But, we had a deadline and couldn't afford the time to linger too long and the next day we were off again on a fairly boring road which took us to Chimanimani village and the turning off to a dirt road which wound and climbed through beautiful wooded hills to the camp site clinging to the terraces. I was so pleased to arrive and get off Flossie. I really hated dirt roads and had never got used to them. But, in this instance the road was worth the effort and our view was impressive. We had a cold meal and an early night ready for an early start.

Just after daybreak we packed our lunch and some other essentials into the rucksack and headed up the hill through the camp to the path signposted 'Bailey's Folly'. The path steepened and as it wound through the rocks it became almost a climb on hands and knees and a path which was difficult to follow. At least, I found it difficult because I was concentrating so hard on where to place my feet that I forgot to look for the marker cairns. Fortunately, Charles had his eye on the track and the markers as we climbed and climbed until we reached the peak and a more gentle walk across the plateau to our first sighting of a hut.

We sat on the hut's veranda and snacked on peanuts and banana before heading down a steep path behind it which led to Digby's Waterfall. The scenery reminded us both of Mount Kenya until we arrived at the base of a very pretty waterfall. We sat on the rocks to rest and then followed the stream along to Peterhouse Cave. We'd heard that this, and the waterfall, is a popular overnight stop for hikers and although the rock overhung with a grassy patch in its lee would provide some shelter it offered little real protection.

We ate our lunch on the rocks above the waterfall overlooking the green fringed pool below. The climb back up to the hut was wickedly steep but with our heads down we slowly gained height and were grateful for a gentle breeze and light cloud cover which cooled the afternoon.

Once the path became a descent we made fast progress on the rocky path and were back at the tent before dark. I went off for a shower which was one of the coldest ever. A woman coming out described it as "beastly" which rather summed it up. There was a bath in the shower block but I can't imagine anyone would ever use it and as it was I kept ducking in and out of the shower as it was just too cold to bear for more than a few seconds. The water running off me was shockingly dirty – the red mud of Africa. The men's shower block was no better but had a long queue so I persuaded Charles to use the water in our water containers which was no less unpleasant than a shower. The Spartan facilities were pretty much of a one-ness: one loo, one basin, one bath, one shower, one temperature – bloody cold!

Next day we were ready to leave the Highlands and although the scenery for the first part of the day was very pretty it soon became ordinary and mundane. The only excitement to the day was almost running out of petrol – again! Certainly, we did at least six miles on the second reserve and rolled into a petrol station just about under our own steam.

Re-fuelled we arrived at Lake Kyle just beyond the Great Zimbabwe Ruins although the lake was more of a puddle set in pretty gardens with neat chalets and a very shady, spacious camp site. We asked about the price of chalets but after more than two weeks of camping we didn't wait to hear the answer. Three beds in the bedroom with a dressing table, a reasonably well-equipped kitchen with a table and chairs, a bathroom with a large shower cubicle with hot water and, best of all, large, white fluffy towels. This was luxury with a capital 'L'. I couldn't remember the last time I'd seen a white towel – let alone a fluffy one!

The camp site shop provided milk and eggs for breakfast but we were distracted by two bikes which arrived – both Swiss. He (Rene) turned out to be a Swiss motocross rider on a Husqvarna whilst his girlfriend (Olivia) was on a 125 Gilera and had only passed her test two days before the bikes were shipped from Switzerland to Harare.

Next morning we enjoyed a rare lie-in and then breakfast of cornflakes, scrambled egg on toast and coffee finished off with a decision to stay another night. Bugger the camp site!

We drove out to the Zimbabwe ruins and spent the morning climbing up, around and over the ancient monument. No-one seemed quite sure what the purpose of the rocks were and they weren't thought to be religious or defensive although the vast structure built on a hill looked like a pretty defensive position to me. The dry stone walling around the ruins seemed oddly out of place and not at all primitive. Certainly not primitive when compared to the mud huts with thatch the natives inhabited later.

The road and the miles to be covered before Christmas made themselves felt the next day as we packed up and hit the very boring road to Bulawayo. The camp site we found was green, grassy and shady and once settled we went in search of the means to repair a small crack which had appeared in one of the welds of the pannier frame. The panniers were carrying a lot of weight and took the strain of the rough roads so an early repair seemed a good idea.

We found a petrol station with a service centre with gas bottles outside so asked about welding. Charles unloaded the luggage and watched over the repair which took only minutes. A tip to the welder and we were off again to Matopos.

Motorbikes were limited to driving only on the tarred roads. This didn't bother me at all although I think Charles felt the restrictions of where we could go. We were, however, more often limited on visiting tourist sites by a lack of enthusiasm for commercialism and crowds. But, the grave of Cecil Rhodes at Matopos defied both these things as it occupied a lone, high spot chosen by the man himself who left very explicit instructions for his burial place. His body was brought from Cape Town to Bulawayo and to Matopos with great ceremony and laid to rest in a large grave deep in solid rock. The site was aptly named 'World's View' and surrounded by large, precariously balanced rocks with a commanding view of the countryside below. A simple plaque marked the spot – "Herein lie the remains of Cecil John Rhodes".

Having visited the grave and enjoyed the view for a while we went in search of 'White Rhino Cave' which was actually a large overhanging rock and not a cave at all. The 'cave' was famous for its prehistoric paintings. We picked out the small red figures of running warriors and the crude drawings of animals but couldn't make out the outline of a rhino supposed to be there. Despite squinting, standing back, looking closely and peering from all angles it eluded us completely. The subtlety of the artist's work was clearly too much for us so we gave up and returned to camp for a cup of tea.

Next day we were en route for Victoria Falls knowing we would break the journey at Hwange National Park. The road was tedious and we got a soaking from a passing storm which caught us, without warning, on the open road. Something else caught us, without warning, on the open road – an elephant. As we entered the park's boundary we met a huge elephant walking slowly towards us along the white line. We stopped Flossie and turned off her engine. Charles then decided the better course of action was to start the engine, make a U-turn and retreat along the road a little. By this time several other vehicles had arrived and stopped – no doubt they were considering the options. The elephant kept coming and we all looked at each other for support, advice, guidance – anything really. We, of course, felt particularly 'exposed' on Flossie. What would an elephant make of her?

We will never know what the elephant was thinking because a local driver with his family on board made a slow U-turn of his car and reversed, slowly, towards the elephant. Apparently, this is considered the sensible approach. The elephant will, probably, decide not to charge but if he does the driver can slam the vehicle into a forward gear and make a high speed retreat. I don't know how the 0 – 60mph speed of an elephant might have compared with the Zimbabwean's car but, fortunately, there was no need to put them to the test. The elephant looked at the approaching vehicle ambled to the side of the road and meandered back into the bushes and trees. The sigh of relief from us all was audible and we drove slowly, carefully, on to the safety of Main Camp. A very close encounter.

Once we had all got to camp and relaxed an Australian put the thoughts of us all into words "We come to Africa to see animals in their natural environment but when we see them we think 'Hell, shouldn't they be in a cage or something?'". How right he was in summing up the desire to see something close against the realisation that the something which is close is also very dangerous.

The 22nd December dawned and we pressed on under a bleak, grey sky towards Victoria Falls, Christmas and our friends gathering there. In the town of Victoria Falls we drove into the camp site and saw Simon and Belinda's Land Rover parked so we pitched beside it just as it began to rain. We took refuge under the Land Rover's awning until their passengers arrived and, eventually, Simon and Belinda who had been white water rafting on the Zambezi River.

It rained steadily all night and although we were warm and dry in the tent it was a very noisy and depressing night. We cheered up a bit next morning when Peter drove in. Peter had bush camped for the night in Zambia and had got wet riding in but we all had hopes the sun would come out and Christmas would be warm and dry.

The 24th December (Christmas Eve) dawned and it was still raining. And, raining hard. There had been thunder and lightning and no hope of doing any washing or drying any clothing or bedding which was all beginning to feel, and smell, decidedly damp.

In light of the weather it seemed a good idea to visit the Falls themselves. A truly magnificent sight was slightly obscured by the veil of rain and low cloud but their local name of Mosi-a-tunya (the smoke that thunders) was very obviously apt as the water roared and catapulted itself over the great drop to the mighty Zambezi below. We got wetter and wetter as we viewed the various falls from the different viewpoints and were eventually wet enough to have had enough and went back to camp to take advantage of the luxury of the hot baths.

Warm and in dry clothing we headed to the bar and as the rain fell outside in torrents it got louder and louder inside and out. Cooking and eating out of doors was clearly impractical so we made damp tracks to the local Wimpy for hamburgers and then back to the bar. We were all now soaked - again.

Christmas Day dawned and as I opened my eyes I became slowly aware that I was warm and that it wasn't raining. Perhaps, it was brightening up. We all crept slowly from our various tents and tentatively peered at the sky for signs of better weather. We were rewarded with small patches of blue and a weak sun trying its best. I had a hot bath and tidied the tent (now very smelly from damp, unaired clothes and bedding) and then we all gathered for porridge and tea with an eye on the sky and growing patches of blue. We all spent the morning on chores to tidy ourselves and our tents up and despite several short rain showers the weather did seem to be improving.

At 11.00 a.m. we all called a truce on chores and started on the crate of beer and by midday we were smartened up sufficiently for lunch. Belinda had a new dress, I had my Malawi skirt and blouse and sandals. We shared a little mascara and with the boys all spruced up and waiting on us we headed for the Victoria Falls Hotel and the famous 'all you can eat' buffet lunch.

We ordered cocktails and wine and ate our way through

the lavish display of delicious and varied food laid out. We staggered into the lounge for coffee and slumped there for most of the afternoon - just like a real Christmas!

As dusk fell on us in the camp site we realised that none of us could face the steaks we should have cooked last night and although we were concerned about them not being refrigerated we decided they would keep until breakfast. We managed some Christmas cake under a night sky crowded with stars we haven't seen for some time which, hopefully, bodes well for tomorrow. Belinda and I went to our beds and left the boys talking about gearboxes, tyres and other mechanical matters.

We were woken before dawn the next day to the sound of loud music and equally loud swearing from some South Africans who had arrived late the previous night. The morning was soon too hot to lie in bed and as we emerged from our tents we lit the barbeque, put food on to cook and opened the last of the beers.

Peter, Charles and I had decided to hire bicycles and do some local sightseeing on them. At a local crocodile ranch we were shown eggs collected from the river banks and crocodiles through every stage of life until the large, mature crocodiles captured as 'troublemakers' for killing cattle and villagers. Capturing the crocodiles after tranquilising them and moving them to the park allowed them to be studied, bred or exported to zoos. The younger crocodiles bred in captivity would be returned to the wild when big enough to survive alone.

The afternoon was warm and the sun was out so we decided to make a return visit to the Falls and see them in the sunlight. As we descended down to the Devil's Cataract from a high vantage point the sun shone brightly and a rainbow appeared in the spray billowing up below. The Falls were breathtaking and the many rainbows were an added bonus which could be seen clearly as a complete arc resting on grass and arching up and over the spray before bending down gracefully into the water. The power and force of the curtain of water and the spray thrown up fell like rain but, on this occasion, we were happily soaked.

Peter and Charles were now quite keen to buy some engine oil as both Flossie and Peter's Tenere were in need of an oil change. But, engine oil was one of the odd shortages in Zimbabwe and there was none to buy. The next day was warm and sunny and forced an early start as the tents warmed up. Peter went off to look for engine oil while Charles and Simon went in another direction to look for a local welder. Belinda went shopping and I stayed in camp on guard which really meant relaxing with my book and watching the ever-changing scene of camp life.

Later that day Simon and Belinda left for onward travel whilst Peter, Charles and I decided to do a local walking safari. We quickly found a footpath beside the river and walked happily along in the shade of the trees with nothing much to distract us until we saw hoof tracks in the dust and then great holes in the soft mud which were hippo footprints heading for the water. Marks on the bank showed a slippery approach into the cool water and increasing piles of dung marked the spot where the hippo had paused. At that point we spotted an impala through the trees and stood still and quiet to enjoy a less threatening animal of beauty and grace. We did see some warthog and more impala and whilst that might have been disappointing I'm not sure any of us really wanted to confront the hippo and crocodile which are supposed to be found in the shallows along the river bank. The Australian's comment about wildlife, natural habitat and cages was in the back of my mind and I found myself jumping at every crackle or rustle of movement.

Back at the camp site we found Simon and Belinda who had carnet problems and couldn't get their vehicle into Botswana so had returned to re-think their trip. They've decided to stay put for the New Year celebrations, park up their vehicle in Bulawayo with a family friend and continue, temporarily, on foot as backpackers.

The New Year was rapidly approaching and we began to plan our celebrations. We booked a 'Sundowner Booze Cruise' for the five of us for that evening and then hired bicycles. We hired the best bicycles money could hire but they weren't very good: uncomfortable and rattling with stodgy brakes and dubious tyres. Ready for a day out we gathered together all our items for trading which was mainly worn underwear, old t-shirts, suntan lotion and vitamin pills and set off for Zambia just across the bridge which spanned the Zambezi River forming the border between the two countries. We pedalled steadily in the blistering heat and a few miles to a petrol station where we bought enough Zambian engine oil for Flossie and Peter's Tenere.

The view of the Falls from this side of the river was quite different: more majestic and impressive – if that were possible. The part of the Falls known as the Eastern Cataract was only visible from the Zambian side and we were rewarded with a perfect rainbow before crossing a narrow bridge to a spot where we could see the 'Boiling Point' and 'Danger Point' where we'd stood in Zimbabwe. A thorough soaking from the spray was a relief after our hot bicycle ride but we didn't hang around for long as we had trading to do.

The 'souvenir scrum' was noisy and quick as we traded our unwanted belongings for wooden carvings and bracelets. Charles' old underwear seemed particularly desirable as the local traders called out to us. "Over here with the pants, please", and "Big man, bring your pants to me." It was all hilariously odd!

All too soon we had to rush back through the border again and get ready for our cruise. We climbed aboard the speedboat and cast off into the middle of the river. Our guide/driver said we should see hippo and crocodile but not much more and we settled down to relax. We opened the champagne and ate the canapés and actually noticed very little but hardly cared as we ate and drank after a hot day of exercise. Apart from the five of us in the boat there was an English/American couple on an extended honeymoon. They had made a previous trip to Asia on a motorcycle and were good company. We did glimpse a crocodile in the shallows and saw distant hippos yawning but otherwise concentrated on the conversation, booze and food in the boat.

After a while of 'cruising' we stopped and went on shore where our guide told us people usually opened the champagne and ate the canapés. We had already happily finished our allotted three bottles of champagne and most of a bottle of 'spare' wine so our guide went off to beg some off another boat. At the end of our cruise we were all quite happy and arranged to meet our new honeymooning friends later at the barbeque being held on the terrace of the Victoria Falls Hotel where we planned to celebrate the New Year.

The five of us rolled back to camp to tidy ourselves up and were a bit concerned to meet others coming from the hotel saying it was already very busy and we would be lucky to get a table. By the time we got to the hotel it was bustling but our new friends were already there, had saved a table and waved us over. We ordered drinks and the evening unrolled towards midnight.

As we toasted 1992's arrival the main dining room began to empty out and we drifted in from the terrace to the remains of the posher, indoor party. Streamers and balloons hung from the spinning ceiling fans, the music played and a few people were still dancing as we found an empty, cluttered table. Simon and Belinda were on the dance floor within seconds while the rest of us chatted and wondered whether to order more drinks. At that point Peter noticed an ice bucket on the floor and partially hidden by a curtain. The ice bucket had a full, unopened bottle of pink champagne chilling in it. It seemed a shame to waste something someone had so kindly left behind (or forgotten) so we emptied it into seven coffee cups from a nearby table laid for breakfast.

It was nearly 3.00 a.m. before we headed back to the tents and were asleep before our heads touched the pillows.

Happy new year!!

THE BACK OF HIS HEAD

JANUARY 1992

ZIMBABWE TO BOTSWANA

UPS AND DOWNS, ON AND OFF AND THOUGHTS OF HOME

A brand new year and the sun was shining so strongly the tent was too hot and, despite the way we felt, we just couldn't lie in it in comfort. So, we were both up by 7.00 a.m. and slumped in the shade until we felt energetic enough for breakfast. We decided to cycle up the hill to a local hotel but the ride up the hill in hot sunshine with a slight hangover and only four hours' sleep was tortuous and I felt quite wobbly by the time we got there. We were subdued over breakfast and free-wheeled back down the hill to the Victoria Falls Hotel to return the bicycles and then back to the camp site for cold drinks and to laze away the rest of the morning and, in the event, lazed away the whole day.

After a good night's sleep we greeted the 2nd January with

a little more enthusiasm and Charles and Peter set to work on Peter's bike which had a stripped thread as a result of an earlier oil change. Charles changed Flossie's oil and we all made plans for where and what next. We and Peter had planned to leave the next day for Sinamatella Camp in Hwange but hearing that Simon and Belinda were also heading that way we decided to delay and all travel together.

Posting parcels home proved to be quite a challenge. We couldn't buy any brown paper but found some lying around outside a supermarket. I made up several small parcels to be weighed before sealing them as a parcel of less than 2kgs would cost Z$5 whilst anything heavier would be much more expensive.

Whilst I was busy with parcels Charles tried, and failed, to buy travellers' cheques with Zimbabwean Dollars we had bought earlier with a eurocheque. Fortunately though, we were solvent, had paid our debts to fellow travellers and planned a final fling over dinner that night.

The day was made even better by seeing a local African fall off his bicycle. Generally, we attracted attention on Flossie and, quite often, passers-by and passing cyclists stared long and openly and turned their heads at the expense of looking where they were going. How often I had hoped someone, one day, would trip over or walk into something whilst gawping at us. Finally, it happened and as a passing cyclist was busy watching us he cycled off the road and into the roadside ditch. He wasn't hurt and jumped up fairly quickly but it amused us – in a mean sort of way.

The day got even better late afternoon as we went to the station to see the famous steam train arrive. The great steaming monster sat just along the track for a while but then, with a belch of smoke and a hissing of steam it chugged slowly into the station. I hadn't seen anything so exciting in a long time and waited until it steamed out of the station in readiness for its return journey to Bulawayo. We had to wait an hour before the train reappeared and after a short pause in the station black smoke again belched from its funnel and steam hissed from every orifice. The whistle blew and the noise of steam rose to a deafening pitch and the connecting rods began to move slowly, very slowly. The rods moved faster and faster and the wheels began to turn and as the noise rose again the train began to move slowly forward. As the train gathered speed it passed us with a hiss and roar and disappeared around the bend in the track with the carriages following in graceful quietness. The station suddenly seemed very empty and ordinary and as we rode back to the camp site on Flossie I couldn't resist making steam train noises of hissing and puffing. Charles was not amused!

The next morning we all busied packing up and getting ready to leave. Two bikes and a Land Rover (Flossie, Dobbin and Sidney) left the camp site in convoy. Peter and Charles went straight off to get petrol while Simon, Belinda and I went to the supermarket to buy food and stock up on beer and wine.

When we came out laden with our goodies Charles and Peter were waiting but as we distributed the shopping across the three vehicles Peter's bike slipped off its side stand and crashed to the ground to land, almost, under the Land Rover. Amazingly, there was no damage to either vehicle and we all set off. Simon and Belinda left before us to sell some spare parts but we passed them on the road before turning off the main road to Sinamatella Camp. We rode a little way on tarmac which then became a good gravel road which then became quite corrugated and made for a noisy, bumpy ride.

We soon got to the camp site which sat on the edge of an escarpment overlooking a scrub plain with an almost dry river snaking through it. The view was spectacular and we were told that lots of game could be seen in the dry season. We had already seen several waterbuck grazing quietly. As we pitched the tents Peter discovered his tub of margarine had lost its lid when the bike fell over and spent the rest of the afternoon degreasing and cleaning the pannier and most of its contents. Charles and I brewed some tea for us all and admired the view while we waited for Simon and Belinda to arrive with most of the food.

Before too long we heard the rumble of the Land Rover's engine which arrived with a very cross Simon behind the wheel. They had been given a lot of wrong information on directions and road closures and made a 60 mile detour as a result. We cheered him up by cooking then all retired early with plans for a game drive in the Land Rover before breakfast.

Charles woke me at 5.30 a.m. and I stumbled sleepily out of the tent and by 6.00 a.m. we were all up and ready to go. Belinda was driving, Charles had the map and Peter, Simon and I were in the back. It wasn't a squash but wasn't very comfortable as the rear seat was designed for only two passengers so it was all the wrong shape for three people and a roll of material hanging on one side restricted the headroom there. Still, it wasn't too bad and it was free. We were looking forward to the morning.

It wasn't long before we saw impala and a boar but little else until we got to the lakeshore where we saw hyrax and hippos splashing and playing around in the shallows of the far shore. A crocodile cruised lazily past. We drove back to the restaurant for breakfast and saw a mother giraffe with her young and a long line of zebras. The restaurant cat chased a squirrel across the veranda and up a tree. The squirrel was much quicker and more nimble and got away across the roof of woven branches which left the cat wondering how to get back to the ground.

Back in the camp site we set about various chores: I did some washing, Peter was writing postcards, Simon cleaned out the Land Rover fridge in preparation for selling it, Belinda wrote her journal and Charles checked Flossie's valve clearances (tappets). The weather was bright and pleasantly cool with a light breeze and fluffy white clouds in the very blue sky. My thoughts turned to home and I realised we probably only had a couple of more weeks before we needed to start planning the journey home. We also had to think about where we would go and what we would do when we got there.

Our last UK home had been in Berkshire and one of the reasons for our trip was to escape the pressures of life in the south east of England. Charles had parents in the West Country whilst my family were in Sussex.

But, thoughts of home did not make me sad as I knew I'd

be ready to go home when the time came. I was getting a little tired of travelling and looked forward to sitting and sleeping comfortably and cooking proper meals. I was also, and more importantly, looking forward to having Botswana behind us. I really did not want to do the route to Windhoek in Namibia that I knew Charles was planning for us. I'd had enough of rough roads and the route he planned was said, by most, to be very poor. By mid-afternoon all thoughts of home and rough roads to Namibia were put aside as we headed out for another game drive together. We saw the usual groups of impala known locally as Hwange goats because of their numbers and also caught sight of a group of warthogs with their young.

The recent heavy rains restricted our progress a bit though as many of the bridges had been washed out. At one point we found a bridge damaged with a 10 foot gap in the middle section. Much of the bank and surrounding mud had been destroyed by the force of water and there was a lot of root debris cluttering the river which was now more or less dry. Charles, Peter and Simon got out, paddled across and inspected the broken lip of the bridge. They crossed to the far bank and examined the damaged banks. Most of the far bank had been washed away to leave the river too wide for the bridge and the riverbed was damp, muddy and flat. The three men agreed they could use debris to make a suitable ramp for the Land Rover to make the crossing. They moved a series of large boulders and put them at the side of the fallen concrete, inspected their temporary and makeshift repair and came back to Belinda and I. Peter and Charles grabbed their cameras while Simon told Belinda to follow his directions exactly and he would guide her to the far bank. I climbed into the front seat.

Belinda drove the Land Rover through the puddle at the lowest point of the bridge and edged towards the bank on the right. Simon beckoned us forward with a concentrated look and made movements with his hands to indicate fine adjustments left and right to find the best route for the wheels. Belinda followed his movements with adjustments on the steering wheel and inched forward until the front wheels dropped slowly down off the edge. Belinda swung hard left and the back of the vehicle dropped down onto the mud and level ground. Hauling on the steering wheel with all her strength Belinda put the vehicle through a tight turn to face up river and after backing up a little and swinging round hard again the turn was complete and Simon took up another position to guide her down the next slope. Again, minor corrections were made to position the wheels exactly and Belinda inched us forward again and eased the car along until we were positioned to drive up the rocky slope and out on the far bank. The first attempt failed so Belinda reversed hard up against the slope behind us, drove the rear wheels up as far as possible and drove forward with as much power as the Land Rover could provide. The vehicle climbed up, turned hard and gained the grassy bank where we bumped over ruts and holes to the road beyond. There were shouts of delight and whoops of excitement as the three men climbed back in.

Now, however we had a very long ride and as we were short of time to be back at camp before dark we had to make good time. Belinda pushed the Land Rover along at a good speed and only slowed for bridges or rougher parts. At one slow point we caught sight of an elephant and her young calf crossing the road but they were quickly gone and apart from a grazing giraffe we saw little else as dusk was fast falling. Our speed and noisy progress made for game viewing of a different kind though as most of the impala, zebra and small groups of giraffe were now running and what a wonderful sight they made – beautiful, graceful and fluid in movement.

The next day we would all be moving on but not before Simon and Belinda sold their fridge and sand ladders to a Danish couple in a Land Rover which had arrived from

Mozambique. They went off to the village to try and sell more of their spare parts to the Land Rover garage whilst the rest of us drifted around lazily in camp. We did need to pack up but there was no hurry as we were only going as far as Main Camp. Charles decided to adjust Flossie's suspension setting and tyre pressures and made a short test ride. Fully loaded she was certainly a more comfortable ride and when we were ready to leave we sped along the dirt road.

It wasn't long before Peter, Charles and I passed Simon and Belinda picnicking at the roadside and we kept going until a dark sky and spots of rain stopped us to put our waterproofs on. The heavens opened and the rain fell and was driven by a strong wind. We found a lay-by and the shelter of a few trees and as we stood there dripping and watching the sky for signs of blue sky we heard the rumble of the Land Rover and Simon and Belinda came long. They stopped to see if they could give us some shelter but we were, by now, so wet we sent them on their way to Main Camp. It wasn't long before the rain eased, the sky brightened and by the time we got to Main Camp ourselves we had dried off.

In Main Camp we parked Flossie beside the Land Rover, pitched the tents and went off on a game drive. We didn't see very much except the usual impala and zebra but there were some very pretty, brightly-coloured birds. We found a viewing platform with a thatched roof and veranda on stilts and sat there to look out over a small pan of water with more birds, small game, a group of ostriches and a lone buffalo amongst a small group of wildebeest. Even without the game to look at this was a very pleasant spot and we opened the beers and sat happily for more than an hour.

On the way back to camp we saw a clutch of vehicles parked at the roadside. This could mean only one thing – large game. A lion, elephant or rhino must be close by. It was an elephant standing just beside the road ripping and chewing on the trees with no concern for the audience clicking away with cameras. The elephant was an impressive sight and appeared untroubled by the vehicles. The vehicle owners were, however, slightly more troubled by the elephant being so close to the road and no-one wanted to drive past. Eventually, a van did start its engine and inch forward but the elephant merely paused, raised his head, flapped his ears and turned his head to the noise. We all watched. The van paused and the elephant took a few paces towards it. The van moved forward again towards the elephant and sped past. The elephant began to move in our direction and to 'charge'. Simon started the engine, slammed the gear lever into reverse and retreated at speed with the oncoming elephant only inches from the front of the Land Rover. The elephant seemed to fill the windscreen. Fortunately, the charge was one of the 90% of mock charges and as soon as it realised we had been warned off (as we certainly were) it stopped and returned to feeding. We were all a little shaken – especially when Simon said the Land Rover had recently not always started at the first turn of the key!

Other vehicles arrived and jostled for position to get a good view. We decided to let them jostle and made sure we kept a clear path out of trouble – should it be necessary. The elephant began to look less relaxed at the commotion and edged into the trees but didn't quite leave and no-one was going to drive past. But, we'd seen enough so turned around and left him in peace. We would all write up the elephant's charge in our diaries and journals with, no doubt, wild exaggerations although my account here is, of course, entirely accurate and detached!

We were up early again the next day for a game drive and took our breakfast to the viewing platform. On the way we saw a group of jackals on the road struggling to drag their recent kill, an impala, into the long grass. We watched for a while and noticed a tail standing up in the grass and slowing flicking from side to side. A leopard! The leopard rose up and slowly, elegantly, walked towards the jackals. They began 'worrying' the leopard to keep it away from their kill. The leopard roamed around in circles while the jackals barked and tried to draw it away from the food but never dared to get too close. We watched and moved a few yards back and forth for a better view until, inevitably, the leopard trotted off triumphantly with the jackals' impala breakfast in its mouth. The leopard disappeared into the bush to eat in peace.

Back at camp the 'For Sale' sign on Simon and Belinda's Land Rover had attracted attention and an English vicar and his wife showed a keen interest. They had been in Zimbabwe for seven years but planned to drive back to the UK next year and were looking for a Land Rover to make the journey. We all chatted and they were very interested in our adventures and any useful information we could share. It was soon agreed that Simon and Belinda would take the Land Rover to the couple's house in Bulawayo at the weekend and as it was very close to the camp site we were all invited to dinner.

Selling the Land Rover to this English couple would suit everyone. The vehicle wouldn't need to be imported to Zimbabwe and then exported and wouldn't need to be imported to the UK at the end of their trip.

As the day wore on it got hotter and we all decided to head

to The Safari Lodge a few miles along the main road where we could enjoy some cold drinks and make use of their swimming pool. Charles and I went in the Land Rover and Peter followed on his bike. Halfway there we were stopped by the sight of several elephants at the roadside. We then noticed large, flapping ears behind almost every tree in a small clearing – 13 of them in all. The group of three smaller elephants at the roadside then decided to cross the road and we were a little wary bearing in mind our previous, recent encounter. We waited patiently even though the last one was a little stubborn to follow the others. We inched slowly forward and as we drew level with the last elephant we were only half the width of the road from the tip of a long white tusk and an enormous head which turned slowly to watch us go.

At the Safari Lodge we sat in the shade, ordered beers and intended to relax. Almost immediately a small group of elephants gathered at the boundary to the hotel grounds. There was just a low wooden rail and a small ditch between them and us and they stood for some time watching us watch them before they drifted off to a nearby waterhole for a wash and to splash around happily with no concern for us. A group of baboons arrived, invaded the hotel grounds and raided the litter bins for food.

Back at camp we were all ready for bed and as we settled down for the night we could hear the low roar of a lone lion not very far away. We'd been told there was an old lion prowling in the area. He was too old to hunt effectively so had taken to scavenging for food. He didn't keep us awake though as we'd had an early start and another planned for tomorrow.

The low roar of the lion woke me in the night and we were up at dawn for a walking safari. We joined a group of about a dozen with two guides – both armed. They told us there was a small pride of lions close to camp and that the female was in heat and during the mating season lions do not hunt but stay close to the female so that she can choose her mate. As we set off the guides said they would try and pick up the trail of the lions and did show us several sets of tracks and clear paw marks but although we walked for two hours we didn't see any sign of the lions. We got quite close to all the usual small game and saw distant buffalo and lots of birds. The guides pointed out a zebra with a large, open wound on his rump and leg. This was said to be the result of a lion attack which it survived but would make it easy prey next time.

We lazed around for most of the rest of the day. Simon and Belinda were heading off the next day to Bulawayo to clean and sort out the Land Rover for the weekend visit to the vicar and his wife. We planned to stay another day with Peter and then head back. One last game drive together didn't result in anything exciting except for a good view of a lazy elephant drinking at a waterhole before ambling away and when we got back to camp there was no hot or cold water. We headed to the restaurant to eat but the power went off quite early so we finished eating by candlelight and headed off to bed.

The grumbling growl of the lion could be heard quite close to camp in the night and we woke to light rain in the early dawn. When we did get up there was still no water except a slow trickle from the cold taps and I spent the morning watching Peter and Charles tinker with Peter's bike while Simon and Belinda packed up and left. We were on the road by mid-morning and the road back to Bulawayo was straight and boring. As we drove into the camp site we saw Simon and Belinda with the contents of the Land Rover spread all around. Belinda was busy cleaning the inside of the vehicle whilst Simon was covered in oil and grease and fully occupied under the bonnet. Everything was getting a real clean for its big day tomorrow.

The camp site was green and grassy with tall trees for shade and an abundance of flowering hedges and bushes. The toilet and shower facilities were really good and clean and

Charles and I were both looking forward to a good weekend in good company getting ready for Botswana and, most importantly, onward travel.

Saturday dawned after a windy night which probably sounded worse than it was because of so many surrounding trees and hedges to rustle. In the evening we all headed out to the vicar's house for dinner. They lived in a pleasant, sizeable bungalow and the Reverend greeted us warmly, invited us in and then immediately went out with Simon and Belinda to look over the Land Rover. The Reverend and his wife (Irene) had three young boys who were all very quiet and polite. The house was homely and modestly furnished although the atmosphere was, naturally, a little strained and I daresay the boys thought we were a rather odd group.

We had bought white and red wine and took our drinks out into the garden. The garden was very English with a lawn and flower beds but the give-away to where we were was the high brick wall topped with broken glass and the garden furniture being chained together and attached to a large ring secured into a concrete post set in the ground. We asked, very politely, if security was a problem in the area. "Not at all," said the Reverend "Why?" We pointed out that it would not be 'usual' in England to have the garden wall topped with broken glass or to chain up the garden furniture. They both looked at the wall and then the chain, ring and concrete post and agreed that they had come to think of this as 'normal'. Irene told us that they didn't really have any problems with theft because their maid mixed socially with the other maids and made it clear to everyone that the Reverend and his family were "poor", that they were guests in the country and working hard for the local people. They relied heavily on the natural grapevine preventing any attempt at theft. The grapevine and the wall topped with glass!

During dinner we talked about our travels and the Reverend and his wife were very interested in everything and looking forward to their own journey home. As the meal finished and was cleared away I managed to ask Belinda, quietly, if the Land Rover had sold. Belinda whispered hastily that it looked very positive but no money had changed hands. As we took our leave it was agreed that Simon and Belinda would come back tomorrow to agree a price and make arrangements for the money transfer etc.

Next day, it all went well – Simon and Belinda had sold the Land Rover and most of its contents for the full asking price. Peter, Charles and I left them celebrating and planning and headed off to the Natural History Museum which had a good reputation but at only one Zimbabwean Dollar entry it didn't have to be too good to be good value. The first exhibit hall had a very impressive collection of stuffed animals including a magnificent elephant with its trunk held aloft. This was marked as being the second largest stuffed animal in existence. There was also a very life-like frieze of lions with their kill and as we moved along we were faced with glass cases displaying all manner of stuffed animals in what was described as their "natural habitat". All quite odd!

The next section was less grim with displays of rocks, precious metals and minerals and information about how they were mined and what they were used for. It was all very imaginative and educational and all too soon the museum was closing for lunch. We still had loads to see and decided a return visit would be made.

Back at the camp site we found the Reverend wandering around looking for Simon or Belinda. He wanted to ask if they would drive his car to Harare as it had to go back there and they were going that way. We knew this would solve a problem for Simon and Belinda by giving them transport for things they wanted to air-freight home and promised to pass the message on. When Simon and Belinda returned we all decided to go out to the Khami Ruins. We had to push the Land Rover to get it going as the starter motor was playing up and Simon was thankful the Reverend was not around.

The Khami Ruins were very much like the Great Zimbabwe Ruins although not as impressive. The afternoon was hot and still and although we did the two recommended tours around the main points of interest we spent most of the time perched on a high rock overlooking the river and watched it flow lazily along. The dam was unimpressive as the water level was so low. Charles and I sat discussing our onward travel options. He wondered if we should go directly from here to Johannesburg although I knew this was not what he really wanted to do. Charles was very keen to go to the Okavango Delta in Botswana and go to South Africa via Namibia. He knew I wasn't bothered either way about Namibia but really did not want to go off road through the Kalahari Desert.

At this stage in our trip everyone we met was nearing the end of their journeys as most planned to finish in South Africa. Everyone talked of final plans and how to get home. We were no exception and our thoughts were of the practicalities and details of going home and organising our lives again. We had originally planned to sell Flossie in South Africa and fly home but she was now so integral to the trip and we were so fond of her we couldn't leave her behind and go home without her. So, we could fly with her to somewhere in Europe and drive her home or ship her home and fly ourselves or arrange for Flossie and ourselves to return home by sea. The final leg of any route would be to ride the last part together to Sussex (and my family) or to the West Country and Charles' parents. Of course, there was a fourth option which would be none of the above!

We agreed not to make any firm plan and, for the moment, concern ourselves with the next few weeks which would include releasing some capital as a 'get home' fund. We also agreed we would not renew our travel insurance again which gave us an end date of 14th March – two months ahead. Ample!

Next day we went back to the Natural History Museum and spent happy hours in the Hall of Man, the Hall of Chiefs covering Zimbabwe's culture and history and then a section of memorabilia detailing the life of Cecil Rhodes. We admired the National Tapestry which was a project born in 1946 when it was suggested that the Federation of Women's Institutes of Southern Rhodesia should create a tapestry charting the country's history and landmarks - a sort of African Bayeux Tapestry. Drawings and diagrams were made and submitted to a team of artists, architects, historians and scientists and linen was specially woven in Switzerland for the base. The ladies then set to work with specially spun and dyed thread to produce the finished article of 42 separate panels which showed great skill and captured the real feel of the country. The whole tapestry showed a subtlety of colour, great precision and was truly beautiful. All too soon it was closing time again and we still had the Hall of Invertebrates to view. The museum and its exhibits had become an obsession.

The next day we spent most of our time trying to find someone, anyone, on the black market who would take travellers' cheques. Everyone we approached, or who approached us, knew someone and we were sent off in every direction but most were a waste of time. We began to think it would be quicker to go to the bank. Zimbabwean prices were so cheap that even the official bank rate of exchange made everything affordable. We gave up with the black market, borrowed some cash from Peter for petrol and went with him to the Chipangal Wildlife Orphanage which was a private sanctuary set up to provide homes and care for orphaned and injured animals. Most of the animals could not be returned to the wild but there were breeding projects which included two leopard cubs who would be taken from their mother soon after birth and hand reared by the human keepers.

The Orphanage had rhino, antelope and a large enclosure

of bright and beautiful birds which housed flamingos and birds of prey alongside more ordinary ducks, pigeons, owls and budgerigars. A large cage contained little vervet monkeys and other varieties who played, somersaulted and chased each other all around. The carnivore area with lions, leopards and cheetahs was, by comparison, quite depressing as the cages seemed too small, with little to occupy them. We waited for feeding time when their boredom was broken by pulling and gnawing on great lumps of raw meat – a cow's head or whole chickens.

But, money was still a pre-occupation as we'd almost spent the Z$100 Peter lent us and we owed Simon and Belinda money for the game drives and beers we'd shared. So, we went in search of money changers. At the railway station Suliman, who we'd met previously, called a friend over who knew someone, somewhere and offered to take us there. I gave him my helmet, he hopped on Flossie's pillion seat and Charles drove off following directions. Twenty minutes later they were back – empty handed. So, with no other choice we finally gave up on the black market and went to the bank to cash US dollars and a eurocheque. Solvent again!

We spent the rest of the day settling our various debts and then Charles repaired punctured inner tubes and we went hunting for batteries for the torch and a foot pump – for future puncture repairs. When we got back to camp Charles tried the foot pump and it turned out to be almost useless. This, of course, did nothing to improve his already poor temper so I kept quiet while he muttered and grumbled as he checked Flossie's timing and tick over and thought out loud about repairing the foot pump or returning it. We decided to return it.

We were both getting very short-tempered with everything and everyone – including each other. Charles was fed up with all the minor errands we constantly seemed to have to do and the problems of getting cash. I was getting bored with our surroundings but very worried about what lay ahead in Botswana. We were still planning to go to Maun because it was the only way into the Okavango Delta which Charles was keen to see. We'd agreed that in Maun we would ask about the condition of the road from there to Ghanzi and Namibia. But, I couldn't imagine Charles turning back having got that close and everyone we'd spoken to said the Maun to Ghanzi to Namibia road was very bad with deep, soft sand – miles of it. Charles was not put off by any of this and I wondered what would put him off.

Charles did cheer up a bit when he'd got a new, working

foot pump and Peter showed us a gadget which used the compression of the engine to inflate a tyre. Peter couldn't easily use it on his bike because of the design of the engine but it worked well on Flossie so he donated it to us. I kept myself busy cleaning out and re-organising the panniers. The bottom of each one was suffering from being damp and wet a couple of times so I lined them both with old supermarket carrier bags to keep the green dust and mould gathering in the bottom from covering everything else.

It rained that night and by the time we were up Simon and Belinda were in the final throes of sorting and packing to say their goodbyes to the Land Rover and Paul was also ready to leave for South Africa on a tent and tyre buying trip before coming back for more tourism. We said our goodbyes to each other with promises of leaving notes in camp sites etc. on our travels. We didn't know if, or where, we might meet again but, probably, in the UK.

We left and drove towards the Botswana border. We were through the Zimbabwean customs and immigration in under 15 minutes and no-one questioned our currency declaration form which we'd agreed to lie about and say we'd lost. The only slight, potential, problem was that when we'd gone to Zambia for the day the immigration officer on the border who stamped us back into Zimbabwe had given us until 5th January and not until 5th February as on the previous stamp. We said this was, obviously, a mistake and the officer carefully amended the dates and stamped us out. Goodness knows what the point of amending the date was given that we were leaving but, no doubt, it was important to him in some way.

Across the border we faced the Botswanan formalities. Before we could go any further we had to dip all our shoes in a chemical. Zimbabwe had had an outbreak of foot and mouth and Botswana was keen to protect its herds. All luggage and every vehicle was also being searched. Charles came back from the immigration office and said they were unhelpful and unfriendly and insisted on seeing me in person. The search of Flossie had been done and milk powder and a tin of meat had been confiscated as dairy products. Charles then drove Flossie through a dip of chemical to disinfect her tyres and her underside was sprayed. All the shoes in our luggage also had to be dipped or sprayed.

In the immigration office I was asked how much money I had on me. I said "none." This was not the right answer so I explained that Charles had all our money. The official wanted to see Charles and I pointed out he'd already been through and sent me in while he waited outside. But, the official insisted on seeing Charles and listened disdainfully to our declaration of having 'only' £500. He insisted on seeing our credit cards and then gave me a 30 day visa. If the rest of Botswana was like the border and officials 30 days would be ample!

To add insult we then had to buy vehicle insurance and despite only having a 30 day visa we had to buy the 'minimum' which was for six months. Fortunately, it wasn't expensive and they gave us change in Botswanan Pula which saved the next, potential, hassle of getting local money. We finally entered Botswana in the late afternoon and the sky was overcast. We hoped to get to Francistown for the night before it rained and the road was good and fast with little traffic. The familiar scenery of scrubland and a few primitive buildings was much like Zimbabwe. As we drove the sky grew darker and we smelt the rain before it actually fell although, by then, we had turned off to a camp site in the grounds of a hotel.

Botswana was not as cheap as Zimbabwe and almost on a par with European prices so we decided to have a good dinner on a credit card and revert to camp cooking in future. This was the first dinner we had shared together without other company since before Christmas. We had an early night.

Our first task the next day was the bank. It was very crowded but, unusually, there was a long queue of locals at the foreign exchange desk. We waited in line for half an hour and decided to cash plenty of money if this queuing was 'normal'. Loaded with local Pula we headed for the supermarket to find an almost dazzling array of European goods squeezed in beside good quality, local produce. We stocked up for lunch and dinner and bought some store cupboard items and then to the bakery for bread.

At the camp site we relaxed until we heard the distant rumble of a bike – two bikes. We caught a glimpse through the trees and thought we recognised the combination of sounds as Rene and Olivia. It was and we waved them over. We compared notes about recent travels and plans. Rene was very surprised to hear what we had heard about the Maun/Ghanzi road as he thought it must be a good road because it was only one of two from northern Botswana to Namibia. Sadly, we knew Africa would never be that logical or organised! In conversation and poring over maps it became obvious, to me, that Olivia was very nervous of going off-road despite Charles and Rene's insistence "it can't be that bad." I thought of little else but the road and my fear had become something I could almost touch.

The more I heard Rene talking of the roads ahead the more I believed he had no concept of what it might be like for us. I understood he wanted to do some off-road riding and see the desert but he didn't seem to grasp the basic fact that there was nothing, nothing, between the few centres of civilisation on the northern edge of the Kalahari Desert. The road conditions meant it wasn't always possible to get from one town to the next in the daylight hours and we knew Rene was dead set against bush camping or staying in local accommodation which might not be "very nice". I hoped we'd meet him after Botswana to hear how he'd got on with it all.

We decided to all travel together for a while and the road from Francistown to Nata Lodge was good, straight tarmac until the entrance to the Lodge which was deep sand and all three bikes snaked through it. The road to the camp site behind the Lodge was no better and I got off to walk with Charles' jacket and helmet. I watched Flossie and the other two bikes struggle their way through and all three riders had their feet down to steady themselves. I couldn't imagine nearly 300 miles of this – I would be a nervous wreck!

Once we'd settled in we headed for the bar as it rained. We heard that rain fell regularly in the late afternoon at this time of year and we got chatting to a local, white Botswanan who knew the road from here to Maun. He told us it was 180 miles or so and only 40 miles of it was tarmac. The rest was dirt or sand. The road from Maun to Ghanzi was sand and rutted and he seemed doubtful we could do it on a bike. Charles said he was still determined to go to Maun and ask again and the local suggested we try the Caprivi Strip as an alternative route. Everyone we talked to had a different description, a different view on the condition of the roads. We talked with Rene and Olivia over the map and agreed that Maun to Ghanzi to Windhoek in Namibia was the shortest available route. I felt depressed and frightened.

The next day we relaxed over breakfast together and then got ready to leave for Maun. A Japanese road worker we saw at a junction came to chat and told us there was 24 miles of gravel (a good dirt road), 45 miles of tarmac and then another 24 miles of gravel before the rest turned to sand. When we got to the sand it was not too deep and we were in Maun by late afternoon. Maun was a lot bigger and bustling than we expected but the recent wet weather had left the roads wet and puddled and all three bikes were covered in sticky blobs of sand which set like cement. Flossie was a mess and everything (shoes, trousers, panniers) was covered in the sand. The last few hundred yards to the camp site was very pot-holed sand with deep puddles of water. I watched Charles take Flossie through with the bottom of the panniers underwater as she struggled through a particularly deep puddle. Olivia chose that particular time and place to fall off and although she wasn't hurt she was soaked.

We brewed some tea and began cleaning up. We dusted sand off everything and shook it out of everything and everywhere. The only diversion to this was a monkey who scooped up Rene's toilet bag and rushed up a tree with it to inspect the contents. He threw razor blades, malaria pills, toothbrushes and soap down to us in disgust and having found nothing edible swung off through the treetops and left the bag perched high in the branches. This seemed typical of Botswana. So far, we'd found the people to be surly, unfriendly, sullen and unsmiling. There was also a significant litter problem with tin cans and paper waste scattered everywhere with old car shells rusting at the roadside. Botswana was the first African country we'd come across where cold, soft drinks and beer were sold in cans and it seemed to be causing a real disposal problem – they just couldn't deal with the volumes of waste.

The next day we had an errand to do. Back in Bulawayo we had met a chap who had written a book about his travels, over 17 years, with a good friend called Bernie. Bernie was now living and working in Maun and we'd been asked to deliver a copy of the book as we were passing. We found Bernie in Maun without too much difficulty and handed over the book and the author's good wishes. Bernie asked where we were headed and said he knew the road to Ghanzi. He thought we would get through on a bike but added we would have to go slowly. He said there were 40 or so miles of tarmac and then rough but graded sand to Ghanzi. Ghanzi to the border was 120 miles of soft, rutted, narrow sand track with a high bank on either side and a hump in the middle created by four-wheeled traffic. He thought our main problem would be negotiating the sand and getting out of the way of faster or oncoming traffic. Great! We shared all this good news with Rene and Olivia but Rene was still convinced he could get to Ghanzi in one day and the rest would be OK.

I was fed up. I wanted to go home. I wanted to sit in a comfortable chair without ants and flies and mosquitoes. I wanted to sit on a clean toilet and cook in a kitchen. Several small mishaps added to my bad mood. The milk spilt in the rucksack and covered everything and the washing up liquid spilt in the pannier and Charles dropped the cooking oil on the ground and we lost a lot before he could grab it upright. We'd both got an impressive amount of bites and scratches on our ankles and lower legs. Despite all this, perhaps because of it, we decided to book ourselves onto a safari into the Delta – where there would be even more ants, flies and mosquitoes.

We packed everything we were taking with us: tent, cotton sleeping bag liners and one sleeping bag along with clean underwear, basic toiletries, cooking equipment, food and a simple medical kit. We had to travel light and everything else would be packed into the panniers, locked onto Flossie and left in the secure vehicle compound. I walked to the departure point with the loose bags while Charles rode Flossie to the compound. Flossie had a flat front tyre but it wasn't far to go and we'd solve that problem when we got back.

Once Charles was happy that Flossie was stored and safe we climbed aboard a four-wheel drive pick-up. Our fellow passengers were an Australian called Richard and a German couple – Peter and Ima. All three had been travelling together for a few days and although Richard would only be in the Delta for one night Peter and Ima would be there for three. They were all on month long holidays and we chatted happily as we bounced along a rough, sandy track to the mooring point of a motor boat.

On board the motor boat we sped off into a narrow channel with reeds and swamp on both sides. After half an hour we arrived at a small, basic African village boiling under a hot sun. The village was where we would take to the water in the makoros which were a local form of dug-out canoe. Several villagers chattered together about who would take who and they gathered their kit of blanket, cooking pot, cup and food. While this was going on we wandered around the village. The village was all in shade and people sat outside their simple huts built from mud and straw. We were invited to look inside one hut and although it was very dark inside we could see the sparse furnishings. Life was lived outside.

It didn't take too long for everyone to be ready and we settled ourselves in the makoros. We sat in the bottom of the boat. Charles was at the front, me in the middle on a bed of straw and we used our bags as backrests. The 'poler' stood behind me and pushed us gently up the river with his long pole while we relaxed and enjoyed the slowly passing scene. The river changed in width as we went along and reeds and rushes pushed through the water's edge and, in places, brushed the sides of the boat. Lily pads and flowers floated calmly on the surface.

The river was peaceful and a scene of complete tranquillity and we watched the colourful and varied birdlife until the makoros pulled into the bank and the polers indicated we could swim to cool off. The three men stripped to their underpants and dived in but Ima and I were content to just paddle in the cool, clean water. We made another short stop for lunch and then pulled into the riverside camp. We unloaded the makoros and walked a short way up a narrow path to a clearing in the deep shade of broad spreading trees. The polers poked a smouldering fire into life and we pitched the tents. We rested through the heat of the afternoon and I fell asleep until Charles woke me to say we were going for a walk. We all trekked off onto the hot, dusty plain through rough grass which rubbed our legs and scratched our ankles. We didn't see much game even though the polers seemed to be able to identify animals we could barely see in the distance.

The next day was cool and bright and we were soon ready to set off in the makoros again and within half an hour had stopped to start another walk. We set off and foolishly believed we wouldn't be going far or for too long. We had begun to loathe walking safaris as hot, tiring and not much chance of seeing anything interesting. But, to be fair, I don't suppose we really wanted to come across big game when we were on foot. Three hot, sticky hours after we set off we were back at camp and gulped down great mouthfuls of water. We'd seen giraffe, wildebeest, zebra and various antelopes but had decided that, overall, game walking was the most tedious form of viewing game and vowed not to go anywhere on foot for the rest of the day. The highlight of the walk had been when the three polers found a large monitor lizard lying in the grass. They were discussing how best to catch it to eat that evening when Peter touched its tail and it shot off, quick as a flash, through the grass and up a tree with the three polers in hot pursuit. It looked as though they'd be eating fish again that night!

Back at the camp we had a swim, saw Richard off and took a siesta in the shade. I lay on the cool grass and gazed contentedly up into the overhead branches. I watched the breeze rustle the leaves and felt it cool the air. Small, fluffy white clouds drifted lazily across a small gap of blue in the green canopy and it was almost hypnotic. I fell asleep thinking of people, places and events I had long forgotten. This was all very pleasant until Charles disturbed my reverie to say we were off again. We checked what was planned before agreeing to move but the polers said we were going in the boats and "no get out". So, off we went. Poling along the river was gentle and quiet and we saw lots of birds which included the huge grey heron, the largest in Africa, with an amazing wingspan of six feet. We saw a large herd of impala but otherwise just drifted along enjoying the serene beauty all around us.

The next day we were due to return and although we'd

enjoyed the experience we agreed it was long enough. We were quite grubby and looking forward to hot showers and cold beers. But, having packed everything up we were told to leave it in a pile as we were off again for a 'short walk'. We saw a group of giraffe but the most interesting event was meeting a group of Australians from a tour truck. They told us their makoros had been 'rushed' by a hippo the previous day. It had been quite frightening but the funniest thing was that at first sight of the hippo the trusty guides and polers had cried out and leapt from the makoros and run to shore. They were so keen to reach the bank they seemed to walk on the water and left the Australians staring after them until they too decided to make a dash for shore. It seemed the polers were not familiar with "women and children first" or captains going down with their craft and were more of the "every man for himself" persuasion which meant "RUN!".

Two hours of hot, dusty walking later I swore I would never walk anywhere ever again.

We returned to the village where we'd started in the makoros, paid off the polers and headed back to Flossie and the camp site via the motor boat and four-wheel drive. My feet and ankles were ingrained with dust and a mass of bites, cuts, scratches and grazes. I needed a shower and clean clothes. We started to wonder if Simon and Belinda would catch us up here and decided to ask at reception to see if they had arrived. At that very moment we saw Simon and Belinda walking towards us. They had hitched a ride in a pick-up. We were very tired but seeing old friends livened us up and we all retired to the bar and to eat – too tired to consider cooking for ourselves.

We were rudely awoken too early the next morning by a tour truck of Australians. They seemed to have to do everything at the top of their voices – anyone in the loo or taking a shower would not be excluded from the conversation or activities on and around the truck. The morning didn't get any better as we faced a pile of washing, a tyre to repair and foul tasting tea due to the water. There were monkey droppings all over the tent and one of the zippers was sticking and threatening to give up which would leave us exposed to mosquitoes.

Charles had blown up Flossie's flat front tyre and decided that as it was not deflating very fast he would postpone making a decision on what to do with it although he had plugged it with a screw glued in as a temporary repair. The short ride on Flossie from the vehicle compound to the tent showed that the dry sand road was considerably harder to ride on than the wet sand road. I just want to get on with the road to Namibia now

– get it behind us and think of other things. The next day we were packed and ready to go but had to pump Flossie's front tyre up as it had gone flat overnight. We said goodbye to Simon and Belinda and set off. First stop was to fill up with fuel and then enjoy the 40 miles of tarmac before the dirt road and 140 miles of whatever lay beyond. I was resigned to it now. No going back.

What did lie beyond the tarmac and dirt road was far worse than we'd been led to believe. The road was, for a while, quite firm in places and we could follow a good track although there were several sections of soft, deep sand which tested Flossie and us. Sometimes, all three of us would be left sprawled on the ground and sometimes we'd just snake along the track wildly until Charles finally lost control of her and we'd fall over. Heaving Flossie back upright again was tiring but, to a point, we coped. I spared a thought for Olivia and wondered how she had managed.

We stopped regularly for a drink of water and averaged about 20 miles an hour. After 96 miles of this (about halfway we hoped) we stopped for a drink and ate bread and cheese and some tinned fruit. As we sat quietly we heard a distant engine approaching. It sounded like a bike. A bike came into view. Another bike followed. I'm not sure who of us was more surprised to come across other bikes and they pulled over. The bikes were identical and ridden by two Swedish lads in identical motocross boots, trousers and t-shirts. They had come from Namibia and left Ghanzi three hours earlier. We exchanged information about the road each of us had travelled and they said they'd found the road quite good with stretches of washboard surfaces and some sand. They asked us about other bikes we'd met and when we mentioned Rene and Olivia they said they'd heard of them and that Olivia "had some problems". Oh dear!

Having stopped it was difficult to get going again and although we thought we might just make Ghanzi that day my enthusiasm for the whole venture was wearing out. Almost immediately we set off we found a patch of very soft sand and struggled to stay upright and on Flossie. The soft sand continued and Charles paddled his way through with both feet on the ground. In this way he could keep Flossie upright and moving forward. We were eventually stopped by a foot and mouth control fence but could see the 'road' the other side was soft, deep sand banked high between four-wheel tracks. This was going to be far too soft and deep for Flossie's tyres to get a grip and it went in a straight line for as far as we could see. We fell constantly. Flossie struggled her way along with Charles fighting with her for every inch of it. A couple of times he stopped her and turned the engine off in what felt like despair. I hung on grimly behind him.

It was depressing and depressingly slow with long stretches of deep, soft sand which we skated and snaked over using the whole width of the road as Flossie swung violently from side to side. The afternoon wore on and we got more tired and had very little drinking water left. By late afternoon we had had several moments when Flossie seemed completely out of control. We stopped, sat on the sand beside her and didn't speak a word for nearly thirty minutes. My heart was thumping and my hands shook. I'd had enough.

But, with no alternative, we pressed on and saw a wind pump in the distance. As we got nearer we decided to stop and fill up our water because unless the road rapidly improved (unlikely) we knew we would not make Ghanzi before nightfall. We had neither daylight hours nor energy to get there. At the wind pump there was no obvious water but there were some cows so we knew there must be some, somewhere. We followed the sound of trickling water and found a pipe feeding a drinking trough. I climbed over the rail, crossed the pen and hung bodily over the rail of the trough and could just about get our water container sufficiently under the trickle of water to fill it up. It took nearly a quarter of an hour to fill the container and we dropped a couple of purifying tablets in before setting off again. We agreed we could only go a little further that day.

Our slow, haphazard progress continued but and we were too tired to cope with Flossie's wild careering movements and so all began to falter and fall more often. I was more than ready to stop and although Charles said he was looking for somewhere suitable I insisted we'd found it. It all looked the same! But, we did agree on a small clearing behind some bushes and unloaded Flossie before bringing her off the road and to the bushes. We sat down on the panniers and had a long drink of water. We brewed two large mugs of tea with lots of sugar and then used our non-drinking water to soak our flannels and bathe our faces and necks. The water container had been sitting in the sun all day and that and the heat of the engine had raised the contents to a very pleasant, warm temperature for washing. In the quiet of the desert in our makeshift camp we both stripped off and used the rest of the warm water to freshen ourselves up and everything felt much better. We didn't feel very hungry so finished off the bread and cheese and tinned fruit, pitched the tent, secured everything and went to bed.

We'd travelled 130 miles that day. Most of it had been tortuous and we still had 50 miles more to do before Ghanzi. The scenery had been unchanging sand and thorn scrub but we'd hardly had time or inclination to care. The only change we'd noticed was in the colour of the sand which only served to suggest how deep it was going to be.

We were up at daylight, drank some tea and set off. It took a few attempts to get Flossie going smoothly and I was very tense and nervous on the back. The road was still very sandy and it wasn't long before our first fall. On one of our crashes the day before we'd bent the right hand pannier frame and it was now much closer to the swinging arm and suspension unit. On one of today's crashes we landed heavily on the left hand side and the pannier broke. The lid, hinge and back panel split.

The miles crept slowly and unsteadily under Flossie's wheels and I wondered how we could carry on to Ghanzi and how I would find the courage to go on after Ghanzi. One more fall and we landed badly and Charles scraped his shins on Flossie as she went over. He yelled out. Falling over and off on the sand was tiring but didn't generally hurt and as Flossie's panniers and frame were so wide she rarely fell completely onto her side but there was always the risk of trapping a foot or ankle underneath. Scraped shins seemed not too bad by comparison.

Charles checked Flossie over, declared her fit to go and got back on. This latest incident and near miss was, however, too much for me. "Come on, get on", Charles said.

"No."

"What?"

"I'm not getting on." I burst into tears.

"What are you going to do then?"

"Nothing," I said, sitting down. "I'm going to sit here."

We'd been riding for nearly two hours without a break and the latest crash was one too many for me. Charles tried to reason with me but I didn't move. I sat there with tears trickling down my face. Charles pointed out the hard surface was in sight and promised we would stop there. I told him I'd walk and set off. The hard surface turned out to be bumpy with a little loose sand and it was uncomfortable but infinitely better than the soft sand. The miles rolled slowly on and after what seemed forever we saw a sign for Ghanzi and then a few houses and then the town itself. We turned off and pulled up outside the smart looking Kalahari Arms Hotel.

Charles stripped off down to his underpants and dived into the pool. I found my swimming costume and followed. After our swim we pitched the tent, cleaned up Charles' scraped shins and looked Flossie over. The pannier was damaged but repairable. We took stock of where we'd fought so hard to get to. The hotel and all the buildings were crude and dismal. The general store was stocked, sparsely, with various tinned, dried and packet goods but nothing fresh. Not surprising really – I wouldn't travel that road just to deliver fruit and vegetables.

The weather was hot, very hot and although there was a breeze it was like sitting in front of a fan heater. The white clouds in the sky built up gradually throughout the afternoon to become grey and threatening and then a short, light shower of rain. I didn't care – the road was behind us and ahead was Namibia. A solitary donkey walked down the main street as we drank a cold beer and reflected. We had travelled 180 miles on sand to get here which seemed to be nowhere in particular.

We asked in reception about Rene and Olivia and were told they had arrived, stayed two days and left. It was good to know they had made it too.

The night was windy and the tent rattled and thrashed but we were warm and in a well-shaded spot so could lie-in the next day. A trip to the bank took almost all morning and then we found a local museum selling souvenirs of local crafts and displays of local artefacts and tools representing the lifestyle of the local bushmen. Back at camp I set about washing our travel clothes while Charles repaired the pannier. It was blistering hot but in the late afternoon the sky clouded and the breeze was strong enough to blow sand around and into everything. A few spots of rain fell and we took refuge in the tent just before it rained heavily and we wondered what effect the rain would have on the road ahead...

FEBRUARY 1992

BOTSWANA TO SOUTH AFRICA

SCRAPES, BUMPS, MISHAPS AND TEARS

The evening rain only lasted a half hour or so and as the wind dropped it became a warm night. We were up early and under a cool, cloudy sky we packed up, pumped up the front tyre and headed out for breakfast and petrol and west to Mamuno and Namibia.

The road was fairly hard and gravel for quite long stretches with corrugations in places and, always, just enough sand to keep our attention. We trundled along and by the time we stopped for a drink we'd covered 20 of the 120 miles to the border. The 20 miles had taken us an hour and in another hour we'd travelled another 20 miles. We continued in this slow, steady way until Kalkfontein which was, we guessed, just about half way.

Kalkfontein was a tiny hamlet with a general dealer, post office, several watering holes and holding pens for livestock – cattle as far as we could see. Most of the local population moved around on horseback and whilst I knew nothing about horses I could see they were fine looking animals and some had leggy foals skittering at their heels. We stopped for a short break to admire the scenery and relax.

On the road again, the first stretch was quite sandy and soft and despite a couple of falls we made fairly steady progress to another collection of huts and a sign telling us we were at Karakolas. We carried on and after 104 slow miles we reached Xanages where we were expecting to find the start of the final 20 miles of bad, soft sand. We stopped for a drink and looked ahead. The road split into two 'carriageways' – one east and one west divided by a wide, high bank of sand. Each 'carriageway' was itself just wide enough for a vehicle with two tyre tracks running through the sand and a ridge between them with high banks of sand and thorn bushes on the nearside verge. Great! And, 20 miles to go.

We set off and immediately fell off – quite heavily. We got going again but fell several more times and although we found a hard patch of sand it was only for a mile or so and back on the soft sand Flossie was on her side again. Flossie took a lot of punishment and seemed heavier every time we had to pick her up. Charles was getting exhausted from the effort of riding and lifting and getting angry – with Flossie, the sand and life in general. I was exhausted and frightened. My mind was constantly running through too many "what if?" situations – and no good answers.

A local vehicle came up behind us when we'd got Flossie stuck sideways across the track and as there was no room for them to pass we had to sort ourselves out and ride on with them right behind us until they got fed up enough to risk passing at a point where they could cross to the other track.

We fell off a dozen times in all on that perilous stretch and once Charles saved Flossie only to get his foot stuck under the left-hand pannier. I struggled to get off but couldn't lift her alone although we managed to manoeuvre her enough so we could both get a grip and lifted her just enough for Charles to get his foot out. Fortunately, there was no serious damage – it wasn't twisted, sprained or broken. Charles always insisted we pick Flossie up as soon as possible because on her side there was the risk of oil or fuel leaking and we didn't need any more problems but this time we left her lying on her side in the sand and struggled up the bank to recover our nerve. My heart was pumping wildly and I couldn't catch my breath. My hands shook. How much further?

We steadied ourselves, picked up Flossie and gave her a quick check and set off again. But, that wasn't the last time we abandoned her on her side and retreated, panting and exhausted, to fling off gloves, jackets and helmets and wonder how we could go on. The answer to that was, of course, that we had no choice. We watched a pick-up carrying a group of happy Africans go past, waited until they were long gone and then set off again on our own slow and unsteady progress. We were doing quite well too when we came up behind the pick-up blocking our path. The passengers had retreated to the sparse shade while several men stood around looking at the punctured tyre. We couldn't get round them on either side and couldn't cross the high, soft central reservation so had to wait for them to repair the puncture. It soon became apparent they had no jack to remove the wheel, no tyre levers to remove the tyre and no patch to put on the tyre. We supplied a patch and tyre levers and while I sat in the shade Charles helped them repair the tyre and get it back onto the wheel and back on the truck.

On our way again we were still hoping to make the border crossing that day. The pick-up driver had told us it was three miles to the border which closed at 5.00 p.m. but we thought there was a slim chance of us making it. The road continued to be soft, sandy and treacherous but the long stop of repairing the tyre had calmed us both down and our progress was slightly less precarious. It wasn't long before we finally left the 'carriageway' arrangement onto a wider, flatter track. The track was no less sandy but Charles had room to manoeuvre and after a while we reached the border post – it was 11 minutes to five. Just before the border a sign told us "You are now leaving the Ghanzi District. Have a safe journey!". The irony was not lost on us but, at least, they'd had the tact not to wish us a "safe journey" as we entered the Ghanzi District.

However, the day was not done with us yet and the border post was on the point of closing. Charles pleaded with the officials to speed us through and we hastily scribbled on the departure form answering all sorts of tedious questions before running back to Flossie. An official wanted an engine number which seemed ludicrous but he insisted. Finally, we were through and on a fairly good gravel road for the two miles to the Namibian border. We reached that border post just as the flag was being ceremoniously lowered – it was 5.00 p.m.

Before we could get off Flossie the flag lowering official was back inside the building and had locked the door. We knocked and knocked and he did come to the door and after pleading and smiling and unashamed flattery he agreed to let us through. We filled in the arrival forms – more silly questions. Charles declared our money as £180 which was a mistake as it left me nothing to declare except £2. This was obviously not enough money. "Oh no," I said "that should be £200." The official rolled his eyes, tutted and carefully told me that I hadn't written it properly. "Silly me, that's the way we write it in England." He corrected my 'mistake' and we were through. Namibia! It was 5.30 p.m.

Once clear of the border we stopped for a much needed drink. We were low on water, again, but so thirsty and tense we both felt sick. The road ahead now was fairly hard gravel with some corrugations and with 70 miles to Gobabis we hoped to get there before dark. As we rode we watched the sun rapidly sinking in font of us and setting over Gobabis. Finally, tarmac and we knew it couldn't be far to the town.

Gobabis was modern and neat and quiet and we stopped at a petrol station to ask about hotels. At the Central Hotel we were welcomed despite our very smelly and dirty appearance. Charles drove Flossie into the car park surrounded by rooms and parked her right outside our room which was brightly decorated in sunshine yellow and navy blue with curtains and bedding to match. There was carpet on the floor and a sparkling bathroom with a huge bath and large fluffy towels. We'd arrived in heaven! Before sorting ourselves out Flossie was a priority and we made a damage assessment which revealed we'd lost a piece of wood that helped to keep the pannier in place in its frame, torn a mattress bag and dented the front mudguard. I had cut my heel in one of our falls and everything we had was dusty, dirty and covered with, or full of, sand. We shook the worst of the sand out of the luggage, our shoes and socks and I ran a bath.

While Charles was in the bath I phoned home. It was the 1st February and my mum's birthday. Mum sounded very bright and cheerful but misheard 'Namibia' and thought we were in Libya (geography was never her strong subject) and said she knew we wouldn't be home until March – not a bad guess, maybe. Clean and in clean clothes we headed for the bar and a long, cold beer. It was late before we sank, exhausted, into the soft, clean sheets. What a day!

We were awake early the next day and were stiff, weary and thirsty but keen to move onto Windhoek, the capital of Namibia.

Windhoek was a very quiet, calm city in the early afternoon of our arrival and our guidebook suggested three camp sites: one a few miles out of town, another about 10 miles out and a third even further at 15 miles away. The middle distance one sounded the best so we set off for it but couldn't find it. The closest camp site was closed and the third was three miles inside a park which didn't admit bikes. The owner suggested we leave Flossie at the gate and enter on foot but we couldn't camp without her and wouldn't leave her so headed back to town to look for cheap hotels. It was now late afternoon and, still recovering from the previous day, we were getting tired so while Charles stayed with Flossie I found a phone box and phoned a few hotels for prices. I only managed to get through to one and a thick German accented man gave me a price – expensive.

Charles had, however, got into conversation with a portly Englishman who'd stopped his car for a chat. He'd been in Namibia for 20 years and was sorry he couldn't offer us accommodation but gave us a phone number and told us the camp site 10 miles out of town was still there and gave us clear directions. So, we decided to give it another go before dark. We set off but despite asking a policeman we still couldn't find it. We pulled into a lorry repair yard and found a woman watering the garden of one of a few small houses. The woman told us which signs to follow and we went quite a distance off road following them and down a long sandy (more bloody sand!) road until we found a collection of buildings. The woman who appeared told us there were no camping facilities – just rooms priced even more expensively than the hotel. So, back down the sandy road to the tarmac, the town and the hotel where a toothless German brusquely confirmed the price and handed us a key. We didn't bother to shower or change our clothes but headed out for a beer and food and then bed. We were tired and disillusioned with Windhoek.

Our disillusionment continued next morning when we tried to get a map and other information from the tourist office. The maps were huge, poster size (apparently that is what most people use them for) and totally unsuitable for folding up and using on Flossie. There was no information about accommodation although the Wildlife Office just across the road would help and, coincidentally, they also sold expensive safaris. Next stop was the BMW dealer – Motorcycle Centre – and the General Manager asked us about Flossie and the journey, had met the two Swedish bikers we'd crossed with and was waiting for parts for Rene's Husqvarna. We also found out Olivia was limping.

The General Manager offered us the use of his pressure washer (a man and a machine) to clean Flossie up properly so we could decide what work she needed to have done. Flossie certainly looked better when the clinging sand was washed off and Charles spent the rest of the day working on her. He changed the front brake pads (actually adapting the only ones Mike could supply), changed the gearbox oil, topped up the engine oil, cleaned the carburettors and repaired the crack in the front mudguard mounting. The pannier still needed fixing but could wait. Mike generously donated his workshop facilities and we promised to come back the next day for Rene's part and take it to him in Swakopmund.

The next day Rene's part was waiting and Mike only delayed us to take a photo of us for his workshop and showroom 'wall of fame'. We were headed west to the Atlantic Coast which would mean we would have touched the west and east coast of the continent. We'd touched the north and hoped to complete the set before too long by touching the southernmost coast in South Africa.

The day was hot and like riding with a fan heater on the handlebars. The scenery was unchanging thorn scrub with distant mountains until mid-afternoon when, quite suddenly, it changed to desert with bright yellow sand and very little else. The temperature dropped and became cooler and we rolled into town on the second reserve of petrol towards the seafront and then to find Rene.

Olivia beckoned us down a long drive between two bungalows to a third behind them. Their tent was pitched at the end of the drive and they explained that when they'd arrived in Swakopmund they had been hailed by a German couple and invited to camp at their home. The couple had been in Namibia for two years and were planning to drive home to Germany the next month. At least, the man planned to do so and had built a strange three-wheeled contraption with the front forks of a Honda CX500 and the rather luxurious back seat from, probably, a VW Beetle. This was transport for himself and the family dog to drive to Germany although he confessed to being happy if he got as far as Kenya. His young wife would fly back with their toddler.

Rene and Olivia shared their story of the road from Maun to Ghanzi and they'd done more or less the same as we had: bush camping, two nights in Ghanzi and then a night at the Central Hotel in Gobabis. Rene had the grace to admit the road was worse than he'd thought and finally seemed to appreciate how bad an African road could be and how little a map could provide. The German man they were staying with had invited them to stay because he wanted to find out about the road from here to Kenya and we wondered how Rene could keep up the pretence of having done all of it.

We planned to stay at the Rest Camp and booked into what they called a 'holiday bungalow' which was a small, concrete hut with a shower, loo, basin and two small bedrooms with bunk beds in each as well as a kitchen with a fridge and hot plate, sink, table and chairs. It was simple and clean but tired and very 1950's. It reminded me of the English holiday camps of my childhood. The receptionist told us we couldn't drive Flossie in the camp and the manager of Motorcycle Centre had told us about the strong anti-motorcycling feeling here because, a few years ago, the country attracted a lot of young Afrikaans on bikes who tore up the place and terrorised everyone with noise and speed. Local attitudes were changing but a lot of places still had their "NO MOTORCYCLES" signs in place to, at least, give them the option to refuse access. Luckily, the receptionist took pity on us and seemed to think we looked responsible and respectable so allowed us to take Flossie to the bungalow "very slowly, please" and Charles spent some happy hours looking at her fuel taps and carburettors as he was not happy with her running.

The next day we met Rene and Olivia and drove out to Khomas Hochland which was famous for its lunar landscape – a flat, barren desert. The road was quite good gravel but bumpy and loose in places and although it probably wasn't that bad it quickly unnerved me again. We only stopped briefly to look at the strange, quiet landscape and then headed back to the beauty of tarmac although Rene continued off road beside us and dodged around boulders and flew over humps of sand at great speed. He was, obviously, a very good rider and had said he didn't fall once on the road from Ghanzi which must have been quite something to see – man and machine in perfect harmony. Rene had been asking a lot of questions about our trip from Kenya. He wanted to know about the food, people, black market and petrol and although he said it was for their 'next trip' we strongly suspected it was to satisfy the curiosity of their German host. Rene also thought he would bring a credit card next time which would be "useful". Well, yes it would be - we'd used ours to pay for his parts at Motorcycle Centre.

Back at our bungalow Charles spent some more time trying to get Flossie's engine to tick over nicely. He admitted he was 'garage sick' which was a revelation and, perhaps, a sign he too was getting ready to go home. Charles also admitted to going "all to pieces" when he saw a dirt road and it was strangely comforting to know it wasn't only me who felt that way.

The Namibian coast was much like any other sandy coastline but the sea was magnificent. The waves rolled in and huge breakers pounded the rock and sent spray up high in the air or rushing up the beach in a flurry of white foam. But, we've never been beach lovers and had a bus to catch. The bus took us out to the Rossing Uranium mine and the tour started promptly at 8.00 a.m. We went 24 miles to Arandis which was a desert town built for the workers of the mine. The town was built on tribal trust land and self-sufficient with good, low cost housing, free water and electricity, schools, a medical centre, shops and sports facilities. There were various day activity centres for the wives and children and the wives were encouraged to learn crafts such as sewing and knitting and sell their handiwork at local markets. Everything was well-designed and neat and some of the unskilled labour force would have enjoyed a better standard of living than they could expect anywhere else.

The mine itself was an open cast one of vast dimensions. Everything was huge and we were very impressed. The whole tour was a public relations exercise but at 5 Rand a head it was good value. After our tour Charles was keen to get back to Flossie and her engine in another attempt to improve things. He then disappeared for over an hour and told me he'd found the two German brothers on BMW bikes that we'd met in Lilongwe. They had come here via the infamous Maun-Ghanzi-

Gobabis route but the younger brother had had to put his bike on a truck for the last 60 miles because the frame had broken. Their bikes were less than a year old but looked 10 years old and although they constantly fussed about having the right tyres they paid little attention to the mechanical condition of the bikes.

The brothers were planning to be in Cape Town before the end of the month but wanted Charles to go out and 'play' in the dunes with them on the bikes. As long as I didn't have to join in and Charles didn't damage himself or Flossie I was happy and the three of them spent a few happy hours fooling around in the dunes. Flossie got stuck in deep sand a few times and it took a lot pushing and pulling to get her moving again. I watched the large storks which glided and floated gently along the ridge just skimming the sand and using all their skills to find the best currents of air. Whilst watching the birds I missed the excitement of the older brother getting really stuck in a deep V-shaped gully. It took all three riders a lot of time and energy to get the bike out and back up to the ridge again and just as they did so the younger brother rode off and next we heard was a yell and turned to see the bike in mid air. Bike and rider landed very heavily. The rider was dazed and the bike frame was bent which put an end to the afternoon and our stay at the bungalow.

The next day we took the coastal road out of town. The road turned to dirt and the morning got hotter as we rode along. The landscape was boring, the road got rougher, we got hotter and I felt miserable. A short, angry exchange of words between us did nothing to improve matters and although the scenery became a little more interesting the road got looser and bumpier. Charles had earlier told me off for being miserable and over-critical of Namibia (poor roads, expensive and intolerant of motorcycles) but now he was less optimistic and lost his temper with it all.

We drove on and decided to skip Walrusbaii and stop overnight in another town called Solitaire. The town was aptly named and only had a closed down petrol station, bottle store and small hotel so we just re-filled our water containers and left. Progress was painfully slow and the several short stretches of sand road did nothing for our mood until we saw a sign for a Rest Camp a few miles off the road. The bungalows were very expensive and we fell once on the sand back to the road – such as it was. We bumped along hot, tired, depressed and with a raging thirst. In fact, Flossie had a thirst too and was on her petrol reserve. We weren't sure we'd get to the next camp which was at Sessriem.

We had no choice but to push on to Sessriem but the road unrolled further and further into the distance and we wondered if we'd missed a turning. A local man at the roadside pointed excitedly down the road when we said the word Sessriem but he didn't speak any English so all we could be sure of was that we had probably not missed the turning. Before too much longer we found a turning marking eight miles to the Rest Camp but the sun was now very low which made it difficult to see the road surface and sandy parts and it was blowing a gale – a hot one! Flossie went onto her second reserve.

We rode on and I couldn't imagine we wouldn't get to the camp on the dwindling petrol but my faith was only based on not being able to imagine not getting there after such a day. Charles later admitted he thought we might only have to walk a mile or two when the petrol did run out. But, thankfully, I was right and as we drove through the gates and pulled into a parking place Flossie coughed and her engine stopped. No petrol. We paid for our camping and although the warden told us we couldn't take Flossie any further and not to Sossusvlei (the huge sand dunes we'd come to see) he did agree not to look when we took her into the camp site. We bought four cold beers and four cans of soft drinks from their fridge and sank one can of each immediately. Charles went off to the petrol pumps to fill the jerry can so that Flossie could quench her thirst too.

As I waited with Flossie I could see Charles in conversation with a car driver and pointing back to us. As they came over I tried to look happy and friendly in the hope they would give us a lift to the dunes in their hire car. I didn't need to pretend for long though as I quickly saw it was a French/Spanish couple (Thierry and Rosie) we'd met earlier in our travels who were hitching a ride with Simon and Belinda. They would, of course, give us a lift. We'd been given the pitch next to theirs and as we sorted ourselves out in a high wind blowing sand Thierry recommended cooking in the shelter of the men's shower block. He was cooking chips – what else would a Frenchman cook on a camp stove, in a shower block in the desert?

We had an early start the next day and headed out to the dunes. Only 4-wheel drive vehicles were allowed right to the dunes so we had to leave the car and walk the last part which took about an hour on the soft sand. As we walked we admired the gemsbok as although we'd seen a few yesterday we hadn't been in the mood to appreciate these attractively coloured animals. Chatting to Rosie as we walked the conversation turned to jobs and home and Rosie was surprised to find out our ages (Charles and I were mid 30's). Rosie had thought I was in my twenties and that Charles might be early 30's. This cheered me up because Olivia had remarked, more than once, that it was good people "of your age" could make an overland trip. Olivia had actually made it sound miraculous that we, at our age, could get as far as the garden gate!

The walking was hot and difficult but from the foot of the dunes to the ridge only took another hour and we could sit on the top with a magnificent view of the path we'd followed and the many dunes stretching into the distance. Thierry compared the dunes to the Sahara and we compared them to the Pyla dunes we'd seen on the west coast of France. We sat for a while just admiring the view but then decided we should get back before the morning got too hot. Going back down the dune was a lot quicker than the climb up but any hope of hitching a ride back to the car were dashed when a minibus ignored us and set off half-empty. By now, we had all but finished our water supply and the walk was hot and tortuous. The sun beat down, the flies buzzed around our faces and the sand was hot on our feet in sandals. I fell way behind the others. My lips were dry, my head ached, my hands were swollen, my toes burned, my heart was beating too fast and I was breathing fast and heavily. My legs kept going by force of will until the car came into sight and we all gulped down the water we'd left in it.

Back at the camp we passed the afternoon doing nothing much and the small amount of washing I did dried almost instantly in the fan heater breeze. It was usual for the breeze to pick up in the late afternoon and it was quite unpleasant by early evening as it blew sand into everything. During the night the breeze was a howling gale and I lay awake for some time watching the tent poles buckle and twist under the strain. By morning everything was whisper still again and there was just the sound of campers packing up.

Our next destination was Mattahohe and then a tarmac road to Luderitz. The first hour of riding was slow and bumpy with a couple of nasty stretches where Flossie fought for grip and direction and Charles fought to maintain our balance. The sky was cloudy and dull and we didn't stop for 40 miles. The scenery changed to mountainous landscape and the road surface improved. We made good progress on hard, smooth mud and stopped briefly on a cool, windy plateau thinking we might be in Mattahohe by midday. But, the overcast sky had obviously brought heavy earlier rain to the plateau and there were large puddles at the roadside and right across the road. The wet surface was slippery but we only found this out when we hit the first puddle and slid down onto a pannier. Upright again, we rode more carefully and tried to find the driest path but skidded and snaked through most of them.

We approached one patch which only looked damp but it was actually very wet and we were going too fast. Flossie skidded wildly as her tyres fought for grip. They fought for grip and failed to find it. We fell heavily and both landed on the ground with Flossie completely on her side rather than just leaning on her pannier as usual. Charles had landed particularly heavily on his shoulder and was yelling but we got to our feet and struggled to get Flossie onto hers as well.

Flossie's handlebars and mirror had touched down but apart from a burst water bottle (quickly discarded) on the front carrier rack and a bent water carrier (quickly straightened) on the crash bar there was no apparent damage. Flossie started first time. Damage to Charles was, however, a little more serious. He had hurt his shoulder – perhaps strained or pulled a muscle and we took some time to gather ourselves before going on. A police vehicle which had passed us earlier re-appeared to check on us and warned us of a few very deep stretches of water ahead. They offered to follow us to help if required but we preferred to be able to do it at our own pace so persuaded them to leave us to it. There were several deep patches of water which spread across the whole width of the road. Charles took Flossie through these while I negotiated them on foot. We all got wet feet but there were no more falls and we eventually found drier road which became smooth mud and then tarmac and we got to Mattahohe without further mishap.

Our overnight stop was, hopefully, going to be in a bungalow somewhere beyond Hardap Dam as we were keen to avoid Charles having to sleep on the ground in the tent. We found a very smart recreational resort with a very imposing entrance but that, in the event, was all we saw of it. We had a long, strenuous, pleading conversation with a woman on the end of a phone in a distant office but she was adamant we couldn't come in with Flossie. It was hard to understand why Flossie raised such strong feelings – we thought she was lovely!

So, we pressed on to Mariental but both hotels were full and although they phoned around there was nothing and they could only suggest we try Asab. Asab was 60 miles further on a day when we'd had more than enough riding and when we found the hotel there was no-one on reception. Someone eventually appeared and gave me keys to take my pick of two rooms. Another man appeared and showed me the rooms but explained he was a guest himself and just keen to be helpful. I chose the better of the two rooms and asked about parking and, again, the guest explained there was parking at the rear of the hotel and then introduced me to the owner. The owner had actually been standing outside the hotel when we'd arrived but had chosen to ignore us although he did now show us where to park Flossie. He added, almost as an aside, there would be no electricity after 10.00 p.m. He went onto say that the lights and fans would not work but if we got too hot in the room it would be OK for us to sleep in the car park "no extra charge"!!

We got ourselves settled and Charles discovered a graze on his leg which was bleeding. He looked in his camera bag for a plaster and found a 50 Rand note. The plasters were, in fact, in his money belt. So, the money was in the camera bag where he thought the plasters were and the plasters were in the money belt where the money should be – and I trusted my life to this man!

In the hotel restaurant we waited for someone to serve us and directed several potential guests to the bar in the hope there might be some staff there. We eventually got our dinner and went wearily to bed. Almost every day in Namibia had been difficult and expensive and we'd usually ended up driving further than intended. What a country.

Charles woke several times in the night trying to get his injured shoulder comfortable and loading Flossie the next day was a slow process as pain kept calling a half to proceedings. But, we eventually got going and were headed to Keetsmanhoop - 80 miles away. Our first stop in town was the bank and we were approached by a very elderly gentleman in a pin-stripe suit who took a great interest in Flossie, us and our trip. The gentleman recommended a local caravan park but we said we were hoping to go on to Goageb for the night. He shook his head and said that the hotel there was "no good" as it was "run by a black family" and he felt we should go on to Aus which was 60 miles on dirt road.

In Goageb we found the only hotel but it was closed and being used as offices for a road construction crew moved in to tarmac the 60 miles to Aus. Two Englishmen came over and said they remembered us from the visit to the Rossing mine and were on holiday driving down to Cape Town from their jobs at the mine. They said the gravel road to Aus was very good (I've heard that before) but that a hotel in Bethanien was only 20 miles on the tarmac road.

We decided to give Bethanien a try and found the hotel. I went in through a door with the hotel sign above it. I found myself in a bar with a barman and one customer. The barman told me to go out and through the next door for the hotel. I did and found myself in the empty hotel reception. A voice called through from the bar next door (where I'd just come from) and I walked through to talk to the same barman in the same bar where I'd been 10 seconds before. It then turned out that the barman was the owner of the hotel and the hotel was full. Grrrr!

I asked if there was anywhere else to stay and was told "Yes. Of course – Aus." He also advised that we should always phone ahead to hotels.

Back with Charles and Flossie I gave him the somewhat amazing news that this hotel in the middle of nowhere in particular was full which meant we had to go on to Aus. I suggested we phone ahead to, at least, make sure they had a room. Back in the bar I asked if they had a phone so I could call the hotel in Aus and was directed to the post office. I had some coins but when I asked the operator if it would take the combination I had she told me not to worry and "just speak for a few minutes". The man at the hotel in Aus said he had plenty of rooms and seemed a bit surprised I should even be asking but agreed to keep a room for us as we didn't expect to get there until early evening.

The gravel road to Aus was actually fairly good and quite

smooth most of the way and Flossie kept up a steady speed across the flat, endless landscape. The last 10 miles were a bit more difficult as the road was very dusty and the wind blew strongly and pushed Flossie sideways with each gust. Back on the tarmac for a short distance and we turned off to what seemed to be the centre of town although it was just a street with a few buildings, hotel, post office, petrol station and a car breakers' yard. The landlady of the hotel was very apologetic our room had no bath but it was spacious and pleasant and the bathroom and toilet were just along the corridor. It was all spotlessly clean and the parking for Flossie was guarded by an aging Staffordshire Bull Terrier and her two very excitable, identical puppies.

Another day of travelling in Namibia ended with so many trials, circumstances and events you wouldn't expect to come together in one day. Our guide book had said that Namibia was famous for its hospitality and that Namibians welcomed visitors and threw open their homes to them. Our experience was that they stared openly and silently or ignored us completely. They answered questions with a simple "yes" or "no" and rarely offered any information.

Our plan for tomorrow was to pump up Flossie's tyres to road pressures, re-fuel and travel the 80 miles of tarmac to

Luderitz. We planned to arrive by midday, get settled and enjoy a celebration dinner at Luderitz's famous seafood restaurant as tomorrow was not only Valentine's Day but marked 10 months on the road. We were hopeful but recent experience suggested that anything could, and probably would, happen.

We rode along steadily and as we got nearer Luderitz and the Atlantic coast we felt the air cool and the breeze picked up. The road itself was like a black ribbon stretched through the flat yellow desert and there were large groups of ostriches by the road. We pulled into Luderitz and as we paused at a railway crossing, Flossie's engine stalled and when Charles tried to re-start the whole electrical system was dead. We pushed her across the junction and into the kerbside. We took the rear luggage off so that we could remove the seat and check the battery connections and investigate matters. The seat wouldn't come off! Charles pulled, pushed, tugged, yanked and swore but it was 10 minutes before he wriggled it free of its fastening. It had never got stuck before and while it's fair to say the fall on Tuesday may have damaged the fixing why does it happen now? What had I been saying earlier about anything can, and probably will, happen?!

The battery connections appeared to be fine so Charles

checked the dashboard bulb which showed the battery warning light. This also seemed OK and after further technical 'poking about' Charles decided the voltage regulator was probably blown but that if we got the battery re-charged we could get to the camp site and sort ourselves, and this new problem, out. Charles removed the battery and went off to find a garage. When he'd been gone about 10 minutes a pick-up stopped beside me and the driver came and asked what was wrong. I explained Charles had gone to get the battery charged. The man said he had an old BMW and that Werner always fixed it for him and that if we wanted to contact Werner we should go to his electrical shop down the street and ask his wife there to phone Werner. The driver's name was Gunther. He left adding that he had a yard where we could store Flossie if necessary because "the people here will take anything". Charles soon returned and I told him about Gunther but Charles said Gunther had found him at the garage which had no charging facilities and put the battery on charge at his lock-up yard beside the service station. We were to return at 1.00 p.m. to collect it and Gunther would also phone Mike of Motorcycle Centre in Windhoek for us. We put Flossie back together again and Charles rolled her down the slight hill (thank goodness for that) to a small coffee shop.

Over a cup of coffee our conversation randomly turned to our future and whether we wanted children together. I didn't know and Charles didn't either but we agreed to let fate decide and see what happened. It was likely we would be "fairly settled" for the next couple of years and would adjust our plans as circumstances dictated. So, in a non-descript café on Bismarck Street in Luderitz on the windswept Namibian coast of the African continent with a broken motorcycle we made a life changing decision. But, that decision concerned the future and for now the present needed dealing with and we had to get mobile again. We waited outside Gunther's shop until he came and gave Charles a lift to collect the battery. With her fully charged battery Flossie started at the touch of the button. We agreed it was too windy for the tent so Gunther suggested we go off to the holiday bungalows and return later to call Mike in Windhoek.

The bungalows were on the windy seafront with fishing boats bobbing at anchor amongst the white capped waves. The receptionist was ungracious and confused about what was available, for how long and for how much but we finally managed to agree on a price and that we would stay in Bungalow 27. At this point she seemed to have to take a phone call and gestured that we could take our own key off the rack.

We found Bungalow 27 and parked Flossie outside. The bungalow was a small rondavel and looked a bit like a prison cell with its small window and metal door. Inside were two metal beds, a sink, table and chairs and a hotplate. When we'd unloaded Flossie we went back to Gunther's shop and his wife (Marian) phoned Mike for us. He had to check the availability of the part so we headed off to the supermarket but Gunther found us there and said the part was available and we should come back to the shop and confirm we would buy it. Back at the shop Marian said the part was on its way and might be here tomorrow. We were to pay her and she would sort it out with Mike. With everything settled we headed back to our rondavel where Charles tinkered with the broken regulator to convince himself it was the part we needed and then we cooked dinner and enjoyed a good bottle of South African red wine. Lying in bed we counted the sides of the rondavel – 11. This seemed very odd and we fell asleep wondering about it and listening to the howling and whistling of the wind outside.

The wind eventually dropped in the night and the dawn of 14th February which marked 10 months on the road was pleasantly still. We were planning tourism today and an excursion to a mining ghost town five miles out of town. We had to get a permit and meet a guide at 9.30 a.m. the next day.

We also checked out which camp sites in the Fish River Canyon were open and were told Ai-Ais was closed until the end of March but that the other one was open so we could make some plans around it. During the morning we had several local chores to do and the wind rose until, by midday, it was blowing strongly again and whipping the sea up. Apparently, it is typical for this time of year due to the high temperatures in the desert and was the reason for camping at Ai-Ais being closed. In the afternoon we went to Gunther's shop, collected the part we needed for Flossie and fitted it. Unfortunately, it made no difference except we were 285 Rand lighter and still had a broken Flossie.

Gunther offered us the use of his test equipment and offered to charge the battery again overnight so at least we would have transport around town. Back at the rondavel Charles began, again, to work out what was wrong with Flossie – we were both depressed. Eventually, thanks to Gunther's test equipment, Charles found that Flossie's problem was the alternator – an even more expensive part to replace. We discussed the possibilities of getting it fixed locally or going on without it and getting the battery charged every few days. At Gunther's house we put the battery on charge to leave it overnight while Gunther explained there was no-one locally who could re-condition an alternator and we arranged to talk to Mike again. We would have the use of Flossie the next day to get to the mine, could remove the alternator in the afternoon, using Gunther's workshop and tools, and he would take it to Windhoek on Sunday for us.

The next day we phoned Mike who would arrange shipping of the part and then headed out to Kolmanskuppe with just enough time to skid to a halt beside the dozen or so people gathered there for the tour.

Kolmanskuppe was a collection of semi-derelict buildings which used to be a prosperous, thriving town with hospital, school, post office, houses and a social life. It was now a ghost town in the desert. The story of the town began when a German came to Namibia early in the 1900's for his health. He was asthmatic and the dry, desert climate suited him and his large house in the desert suited him even more. He told the local workers who were clearing sand from the railway track to "Bring me anything interesting you find. Any plant or animal or object you think is interesting – bring it to show me." One day a worker took the German a diamond and so the diamond rush began. People, apparently, just walked around the desert and found diamonds lying around and photographs of the time show people crouching or lying on the ground searching for diamonds. And, they found them - five million carats in five years. The local hotel in Luderitz became a stock exchange for diamonds and when money ran out waitresses were paid in diamonds. The story continued that eight companies began seriously mining the diamonds in what had been 'forbidden territory' and brought in heavy plant and machinery for the work. After the First World War Consolidated Diamond Mines bought out the smaller companies and ran the mine. In the 1930s there was a slump and the discovery of an even bigger diamond area to the south drew people away from Kolmanskuppe until, in 1956, the last inhabitants left and the town stood empty.

The empty buildings were soon ransacked of anything useful: doors, window frames, floorboards, fittings and tiles were taken by the locals. The constant wind blew sand into the buildings and piled it up and around the walls and against the doors. Some buildings eroded and cracked badly until the Consolidated Diamond Mine Company called in experts to see what could be made of the town. The answer was to restore it, prevent further deterioration and let the public in.

The ghost town became a tourist attraction. The former inhabitants had obviously lived well and the town's shop had been refurbished to the style of the day and the shelves boasted displays of caviar, champagne, oysters and all sorts of luxury goods. The largest building was the casino which dominated the town and had been the centre of their social life with a bar, dining area and private dining and sitting rooms for the local VIPs. There was also a skittle alley and a magnificent hall used for dances, meetings and a stage for visiting troupes from Germany as well as a projection room to show the latest films. The tour officially ended in the main street and we were encouraged to wander around on our own "with care" because not all the buildings were sound. Charles and I walked out to the edge of town where the grandest houses stood for the mine manager and architect and were amazed to see the toilet fittings still mostly in place, a beautifully tiled bathroom floor and huge concrete bath.

After the tour we headed back to Luderitz and Gunther to find our part was on a flight from Windhoek to us. We arranged to collect it from the airport the next day and would, again, pay Marian who would arrange payment to Mike and ship back the regulator we didn't need with the broken alternator to be re-conditioned.

At midday the next day we drove out to the airport and were nearly blown away in the high wind sweeping across the open desert. The airport itself was just a narrow stretch of tarmac runway and a quiet, empty building with a desk, weighing scales and some chairs. There was a man sweeping sand out of the building (a full-time job, no doubt) and a girl and a desk. These two people formed the airport staff. Slowly, passengers arrived and then a plane landed. The girl raised her voice slightly to announce the arrival of the flight and that passengers for Cape Town could board. They began to drift out to the waiting plane but we didn't hang around. We signed for our parcel and headed back along the windswept road with the sand being picked up and whipped across the road and catching our cheeks and faces as it did so. Charles fitted the new part and Flossie was fully functioning again and although she could have done with a little attention Charles was reluctant to do anything more than necessary with the sand blowing everywhere. He settled for putting a rubber bung repair in the front tyre. Although we were slightly cheered up that Flossie was back on form we went to bed in what now seemed like a very depressing room.

By now, we were quite low on funds so had to visit the bank. I queued at a teller's desk only to be told I had to go to the 'Enquiries' desk. I didn't have an enquiry but I had to go there first. I queued and was told they didn't accept our credit card and was referred to another bank where I started the whole process again. At the Enquiries Desk it became apparent that the sole purpose of it and the staff of three was to fill in the form for the customer to give to the teller. A lot of the customers in the queue could not write, couldn't even make a 'mark' and used a thumbprint as a signature.

Once we'd got our cash we paid our bills with Marian, thanked her for her help and were on the road by 11.00 a.m. We were glad to be leaving and we trundled along on the windy road out of town. The gravel section was slow going, bumpy and uncertain in places and I wondered how much more of these roads I could take – not much more.

In Keetsmanhoop we headed straight for the caravan park which was quite shaded but the ground was rock solid – like concrete. The only grassy area was lush but in full sun, wet from sprinklers and right outside the toilet block. Charles swore freely as he tried to get the tent pegs into the hard ground. I was on the verge of tears and once I found solitude in the ladies' loos I had a good sob. I hated the country and felt jinxed in it.

Tears over and a good night's sleep and we went in search of a tube for the front tyre. The rubber bung in the thorn hole we acquired in Maun had worked well and then a woodscrew and some glue had done the job but Flossie badly needed a proper repair. While Charles sorted this out I phoned ahead to the Grunau Hotel in Grunau and booked a room for two nights. Our plan was to use the tarmac road south for 100 miles to Grunau, stay a night to visit Fish River Canyon and spend a second night in Grunau before heading south to South Africa – our final destination.

Driving the 100 miles with the certainty of a hotel at the end of it was quite a novel feeling even though the road was boring and hot with unchanging, limitless scenery for most of the way. We arrived at the hotel and it took some time to find anyone to book us in but the elderly gentleman we eventually found offered us a cold drink and showed polite, if confused, interest in us.

The gravel road to Fish River Canyon was quite good although the scenery was unchanging desert scrub past the resort of Ai Ais which looked very pleasant - but closed for another month. At Hobas Camp we paid an entry fee for the final six miles to the canyon viewpoint. The canyon is the second biggest (Grand Canyon in the USA being the largest) but our first impression was of it looking very similar to the Rossing's open mine at Skakopmund. The Fish River itself was just a muddy puddle at the bottom of the canyon. I wasn't exactly disappointed but the Victoria Falls had to be the most spectacular of our sightseeing. We headed back to Grunau – a round trip of nearly 200 miles – and as we left the dirt road for the tarmac I felt a small surge of joy and relief. From now on we would be heading south to Cape Town and there would be no more dirt roads. Tomorrow we would head south. South to South Africa. It would be the 20th February –10 months since leaving home.

The border formalities into South Africa were easier than expected and we headed straight for Springbok where we planned to spend the night. We found some camping in the grounds of a motel but it was blistering hot and we took refuge in the laundry room which was the only shade. Over a cup of tea we decided it was rather nice not to have had to fiddle around with currency at the border but that we didn't really feel we'd crossed a border. The scenery had changed a little and become slightly greener and the border itself had been marked by the Orange River running through a ribbon of vegetation. It had been quite a while since we'd seen anything other than a baked, dry and cracked riverbed.

Our next stop was Clanwilliam and the ride was unbearably hot. We must have missed a sign to a camp site and when confronted with a dirt road we decided to re-think things. We had gone on to reserve and didn't fancy a long, hot ride on a dirt road - possibly the wrong road. We headed back to town and got better directions to a nearby camp site at a dam. We ignored the 'No Motorcycles' sign and drove down to the lake's edge and parked Flossie under a large, shady tree. The receptionist told us that February is the hottest month of the year here and the last two weeks of it are the hottest in February. Apparently, 40°C is not unusual. So, our plan was to be up early, pack and get on the road.

We were up early and packed but Flossie's front tyre had gone flat overnight which meant we had another puncture. Both Flossie's tyres were almost bald and we were planning to buy new in Cape Town but had yet to get that far. On the road heading south the temperature rose and we made a brief pit stop to shake out the air filter which was full of sand and it wasn't long before Table Mountain came into view even though we were still 40 miles north of Cape Town itself. As Charles navigated Flossie through the road system of the outskirts of Cape Town my focus was the mountain, towering skyscrapers, modern office blocks, neat city streets and flower beds with a riot of well-kept colour in them. We had seen nothing like this for quite some time.

For want of anywhere better to go we followed signs to The Waterfront and found a busy dock area recently defunct and undergoing a re-birth with shops, bars and restaurants . The information office had none to offer and the tourist office had closed two minutes before we got there. We decided to head out to Muizenberg which was a coast resort and sure to have camping. We hoped to see signs for 'Observatory' which we'd been told was a suburb with a Mrs. Roche-style camp site.

We drove to Muizenberg and beyond to Fish Hoek before we saw any signs for camping and it then turned out to be for caravans only. I went to the office to find out if we could camp "just for one night" and when I got back to Charles and Flossie we were approached by a smiling, middle-aged lady who asked if we needed any help. The lady (Jean) knew a camp site in Muizenberg and gave us very clear directions but insisted we couldn't go until we had joined her and her sister for a cup of tea and some cake. How very English! Our polite little gathering was joined by another couple and they were all very interested in our journey. Jean had spent some time backpacking in Europe and promised not to take her eyes off Flossie while we went for a wander along the beach. We spent a happy afternoon in their easy company and by the time we left we felt quite at home. We found the Muizenberg camp site and were greeted by a cheerful, black gatemen as though he'd been waiting all his life to meet us. The camp site was neat with green grass and lots of shade. There was a clean, well-fitted shower and toilet block and every site was numbered with its own barbeque, or braai, as they called it. It seemed a very happy, relaxed place.

Bright and early the next morning Charles started servicing Flossie – he couldn't wait to get his hands on her and sort out some of her problems. Flossie was not running smoothly and had lots of minor leaks. Charles was very keen to get Flossie home, cleaned and properly serviced but that would have to wait. During the morning we got into conversation with a couple (Keith and Micheline) in a nearby caravan who had been watching us with obvious interest before coming to say "hello". They lived in Cape Town and had just come out for the weekend and invited us to their caravan for coffee. Coffee turned into lunch and it was early evening before we finally got back to our tent and had been invited to their home for a meal during the coming week.

On Monday morning the camp site had emptied out as the weekenders had returned home and we had to find some motorcycle tyre dealers. We were offered a good deal for tyres and fitting on Metzeler tyres and although another dealer made a better offer on Michelin tyres we opted for the Metzelers as they will be getting us home and be used in

England. Charles also phoned home to quite a cool reception from his mum who wanted to know what we'd be doing next and implied there was no point going home as there were "no jobs". Oh well!

The weather seemed to be equally cool towards us and the night was again wet and very windy. The tent poles bent and flexed under the strain and the fly sheet flapped and fluttered. The clothes on my side of the tent got quite wet as the outer tent blew against the inner and we had breakfast in the tent listening to the wind and rain blow and sweep around us. As if this wasn't all depressing enough when it did stop raining and we decided to go to Cape Town we found Flossie's front tyre was flat and would not pump up. Then, it started to rain again.

When we eventually got to Cape Town we went in search of air freight for Flossie. Although our original plan had been to sell her here and use the funds for our own air fares home we just couldn't do it. After so many months, miles and adventures together we couldn't leave her behind but had to find a reasonable way of getting her home. The first two quotes for sea freight were around the R1,500 level and we would be without her for a month. There would also be a UK customs handling fee but no-one here knew how much that would be.

We asked about air freight. While Charles pumped money

into a coin box phone I scribbled down information: R3.10 per kilo and R27.50 for administration for a flight booked a week ahead. The air freighters would put us in touch with a crate maker but we would have to make contact with them and an agent in Johannesburg.

If we decided to fly Flossie home we would have to do our tourism in Cape Town and go to Johannesburg. Flying Flossie to Luxemburg seemed the cheapest (and, therefore, best option) and the drive home from there would be an appropriate, if cold, end to our journey.

The decision to fly Flossie home was made and we contacted Sonia in Johannesburg who was the agent who would sort everything out for us. Sonia agreed to give us an 'all-in' cost for the freight and arrange for the crate to be custom-built. Sonia's price came in at R1,970 plus R45 for insurance which we agreed and booked space on a flight for the 18th March.

Next, we sorted out our own travel by booking flights with Zambian Airways for the same day. We would leave Johannesburg mid-morning, arrive in Lusaka, Zambia at midday and fly out with South African Airways early evening to arrive, via Rome, in Frankfurt early in the morning. Flossie would be in Luxemburg by then and we would catch a train from Frankfurt to Luxemburg to collect her and drive home through France.

So, progress and a plan. We would leave Cape Town in plenty of time to get Flossie ready for her trip although I wasn't looking forward to being without her or to the night flight and train journey to re-unite with her. But, first we had to buy wine and chocolates for our hosts for dinner this evening. We showered and tidied ourselves up as best we could and followed the written directions we had to the home of Keith and Micheline.

Keith greeted us and introduced Micheline's brother and sister-in-law and we settled down to chat until Micheline's sister and her husband arrived. The house was new and neat and furnished in a very modern, elegant way. The kitchen was ultra-modern and spotless with a seating area to one side which was described as a 'family room' whilst the lounge itself had a black leather suite and marble coffee table. The dining table was laid for dinner. The whole effect was very 'designer' and created a glossy magazine look. Dinner itself was an excellent meal and wine flowed freely. In fact, one whole wall of the dining room was dedicated to a floor-to-ceiling wine rack which was all carefully selected and fully-stocked. If we'd known we might not have dared to bring wine as we hadn't known what we were buying and the wine we all consumed barely made a dent in the wall. Our hosts were very disappointed we were not spending more time in Cape Town and insisted there was so much we should see and do. It was difficult to explain that we were travel weary and ready to make our way home.

Part of the plans to get home were to write to Charles' mum and ask her to re-insure Flossie, get some road tax for her and send everything to Luxembourg for us. We also sent her a letter to release some money from our savings to fund everything. We were, at that stage, non-committal about when we would be home and just mentioned it would be "next month". I'm sure she, and my mum, would have speculated about what we were up to but if she was cross about our deliberate vagueness and being asked to do our errands we would certainly know about it soon enough!

Charles tightened Flossie's heads and set the tappets to try and improve her running and then we went off to Simonstown to a pretty marina with lots of little boats bobbing about in it. We had lunch there and carried on to Cape Point Nature Reserve where we parked and walked up a short, steep hill to the viewpoint. We looked south to the blue ocean stretching off towards Antarctica. The coastline was rocky and the sea was rough and we stood against the wind looking to the point where, they say, two oceans meet – the Atlantic Ocean meets the Indian Ocean. We asked someone to take our photograph, for posterity, and then walked back down to Flossie to buy a commemorative postcard for home. The card showed Cape Point and I wrote the date and time, our names and Flossie's registration and the shop gave it a special stamp before sending it on its way to England.

The coastline here was very rocky and ragged and the sea pounded the shore. The occasional beaches could be seen as white, bleached sand but generally the coastline was impressive rather than inviting. Evenings in the camp site were quite cool when the sun dipped behind the mountain looming over it but we were quite sheltered from the breeze and cooked on our own braai every evening. On our first evening we had seen a tiny kitten and although he took a long time to pluck up courage to approach a bowl of milk he had become much bolder and came closer. Our new neighbours tossed scraps of food to him and came over to chat to us after we'd all eaten. The couple were German on an extended holiday in South Africa. He had been here many times on business but wanted to explore more of the country and although he wanted to bring their motorbikes she had refused and so they were in a camper van which they intended to sell here when they left.

As February drew to a close the 29th dawned and the weather looked promising enough for us to go to Table Mountain. The drive into Cape Town gave us a clear, spectacular view of the city and the mountain and we parked Flossie at the lower cableway station. As the cable car climbed higher there was a chill in the air but the view from the top was magnificent of the city, the surrounding hills, the suburbs stretched into the distance, the white strip of beach and the sea beyond.

We walked along the mountain top path to Maclear Beacon which was the highest point. It was a good hour of walking but mostly flat and we were quickly out of sight of the tourists and buildings. The air was cool and clear and after a short rest at the Beacon we realised it was nearly 4.00 p.m. and we'd better head back. As we walked the weather got colder and windier and cloud began to drift across the mountain's flat top and obscured all the views below. We quickened our pace and although we drifted off the route slightly we could just see the buildings of the cableway station and hear the tourists there who complained it was cold.

On the journey down the mountain the cable car broke

through the cloud and we saw, again, the city sprawled out below us and several hikers and climbers making their way up on foot. By the time we got to the lower cable way station it was definitely too cold to linger and by the time we got back to Flossie the cable way had been closed.

We headed for the waterfront development we'd seen on our first day for a beer and dinner. After several beers and wine I felt quite drunk and, apparently, told Charles about it several times. On the cold ride back to the tent I had to concentrate very hard on what I was doing and the seeds of a magazine article or story on pillion riding came to my mind. It sounded rather good in my head – I wondered if anything would come of it.

MARCH 1992
SOUTH AFRICA AND BACK

The weather was definitely cooler and we were both wearing a t-shirt and long sleeves for most of the day. We had obviously acclimatised to the hot African climate and couldn't adjust quickly to the Mediterranean weather of Cape Town and seemed to feel the cold more than most people. With thoughts of home we wondered how we would cope with Europe in March.

And, with home in mind we had a list of things to do. First was a visit to the BMW dealer. We needed some parts and wanted them to inspect our 'white power' shock absorber and declare it leaking so that we could claim a new one under guarantee when we were back in the UK. We were given a neatly typed statement with all the relevant facts and set off to the travel agent for our flight tickets. Next, we phoned the air freighters and confirmed we wanted space on the Johannesburg to Luxembourg fight on 18th March and would be in Johannesburg on 11th. The last stop on the list for the day was to get Flossie's new tyres fitted. All that done we decided to get in touch with some local friends of UK friends who lived in Franschoek. Our UK friends had urged us to get in touch (if we got this far) and so we did and had a fairly friendly chat. The friends of friends were Robin and Daphne and Robin said we must "be sure to drop in for a drink".

With nothing much else to occupy us we decided to take a ride along the coast away from Cape Town. This stretch of coast was windswept, pounded by waves and uninhabited. The road went on with no buildings except for a camp site and recreation park which seemed to be exclusively for South Africa's black population. Under a grey sky and in a chill wind we turned back to Muizenberg. The night was not as cold as previous nights and when we woke next morning the day was bright and warm with a cloudless blue sky and no breeze. We decided the weather had taken pity on us for our last day in Cape Town.

Four small cats finished the last of our milk as we packed up. The milk was sour but the cats seemed to enjoy it. We couldn't use the sour milk for our tea and couldn't make tea as the new gas cylinder we'd fitted to our stove had been poorly fitted and leaked all night. This had happened before to the cheap stove we'd had to buy after the theft of the first one in Malawi.

In fact, everything was beginning to get an 'end of trip' feel to it. My t-shirts were becoming scruffy with holes, the zips on the tent had almost given up and would soon be useless and the stove had leaked gas more than once. Then, on the way to town for another gas cylinder we noticed Flossie had an oil leak. Charles spent some time trying to find the reason and decided he'd have to take the oil filter cover off and re-seat the seal. We drove to a local garage, parked in a side street opposite and with the aid of copious amounts of paper towel from the garage Charles set to work. First, we had to tip Flossie over onto her side to prevent her losing too much oil. We leaned her hard over so her pannier rested on the kerb and within about half an hour the job was done. Flossie hadn't lost too much oil so we were soon ready to set off again.

Before we could get going though we were approached by a young man who asked if we "go to camps" on our bike. I explained we had come from England on Flossie and he was clearly astounded.

"Shit! How did you do that?"

"We just did."

"Shit! But, how did you cross the sea?"

"On a ferry."

"Shit! And you came all the way?"

"Yes."

"Shit! Shit, you're lucky you didn't get shot. Shit."

Funnily enough, the likelihood of getting shot had not been high on our list of concerns. It was odd to have this new set of questions and this young man was not the first in South Africa to ask how we'd crossed the sea. All the way down through Africa there had been two questions everyone always asked "How fast does it go?" and "How much does it cost?" If we asked directions and asked how far, how long a journey would take the answer would always be "On this," indicating Flossie, "two minutes." Always two minutes - whether it was two miles or 20 miles to travel. Clearly, Flossie was a very impressive sight for the Africans and now having impressed this young man with her and our amazing abilities we moved on.

We went along the coast and only paused to check Flossie's oil leak. The leak seemed to have stopped but her engine was running badly. We were, however, soon in Stellenbosch and found a camp site on the low slopes of a hill. It was green but looked rather empty and run down. We decided to try and find another and at traffic lights in town a car behind hooted and the driver called to us. We wondered what he wanted and he pulled alongside and asked us to his home for a cold drink. We followed him to a tiny studio flat and answered his questions about our journey while we drank cold fruit juice. It was clear he couldn't help with accommodation though so we left to find a camp site.

Stellenbosch boasted lots of vineyards and wineries and wine tasting tours and it seemed rude not to give at least one a try. The scenery was very pretty and very French and as we waited for the tour to begin we sat and admired the view under a clear blue sky in warm sunshine. The room where the wine was matured was kept at 12°C which seemed very cool and it was unpleasant to think Europe was going to be much colder. Back in the sunshine we had a French-style picnic lunch with chicken, cold meats, salad, paté, cheese and bread with fruit and a cool drink with coffee to follow. It was expensive but so different from anything we'd had for quite a long time. Delicious! After lunch we found a phone and called Robin again to ask if it would really be OK to drop in. He seemed a bit cool and less sure but suggested we drop in at tea-time as they were going out to dinner. We felt very awkward. We understood completely though – they didn't know us at all and might have wondered what we wanted from them.

Through pretty scenery on a warm sunny day we got to Franschoek only to find there was no camping in the town but two sites just outside. The town was very French in everything and obviously in a wealthy wine area. Wealthy actually verged on the pretentious although the camp site was run down so we decided to head out to Robin and Daphne's house and see what we could find on the way. The grand imposing entrance to Robin and Daphne's house unnerved us as we drove up a long, steeply sweeping brick driveway to come, eventually, to the huge white frontage of the house. I was ready to turn and run but a big dog appeared and his barking gave us away until Robin and then Daphne appeared and welcomed us with warm smiles. They insisted we go round the house to the patio and sit by the pool for a cold beer.

Robin and Daphne had plans to go out that evening with gathered family and guests and so, one by one, they disappeared and re-emerged ready for dinner. In the comings and goings Daphne asked us where we were staying and we said we were at the camp site. Daphne asked us to stay with them if we wouldn't mind fending for ourselves for dinner. We were shown to a beautiful guest bedroom with a gorgeous four poster bed. Daphne apologised it was so small until I pointed out that the bed itself was about the size of our entire tent. We were shown to the kitchen and Daphne found salmon in the freezer for us to cook – in a real kitchen!

By the time we returned to the patio several guests had arrived and we all sat drinking and watching the sun sink behind the mountains across the valley. The house had magnificent views and had been very carefully placed on its hillside location to maximise them. With the sun gone everyone left for their dinner party and Charles and I were left alone. We had a quick peek around the house and then started to cook. It was very strange to be in a kitchen and we couldn't get over the illogical feeling that we should be quiet. We made a quick check on Flossie before bed but were fairly sure she would be safe enough with the large, long-haired Ben (the Alsatian dog of earlier) prowling around outside to keep her company.

The next morning we lingered over breakfast and coffee on the patio talking to Robin and Daphne about the future of South Africa, how their domestic staff were organised and the story of how they built the house. The house was built in a traditional Cape H shape which gave the house lots of windows and sheltered outside areas so almost every room had a dual aspect for sun and shade and access to the outside: pool, garden or patio. But, before we knew it the sun was high in the sky at midday and we had to make a determined effort to leave the comfort of a home and company of our hosts.

We were headed, for the last time, south to Bredasdorp and Agulhas which was the southernmost town in Africa. A little way down a gravel track we found the southernmost point itself – Cape Agulhas. A plaque marked the spot with the words "The southernmost point of the Continent of Africa". This was really our final destination and we stood looking beyond the rocks to the pounding sea and the next landfall – the South Pole. There was a compass point erected at the site which indicated distances to major cities of the world. London was noted as 9,797 kilometres although we'd actually travelled over 18,000 miles. Johannesburg was just 750 miles and from now on everything and everywhere would be part of our journey home. Eveywhere from Cape Agulhas, for us, would be north.

The weather was cool and clear and the gentle, green rolling scenery stretched away to distant mountains with a shelf of cloud just below the peaks. The fields either side of the road were home for cows and sheep and ostriches in quite large groups with young ones with them. We stopped for a picnic lunch and carried on to the town of George. The camp site at George was pleasant enough but during the night we heard someone moving around outside the tent and shadows fell and moved over it. Charles got out to check what was happening but whoever it was had moved off and he saw no-one. We lay still in the tent and hardly dared breathe and shortly the noises started and we saw the shadows again. There was definitely someone outside. Charles got up and went out to the toilet and shower block but there was no-one there and no sign of anyone around. We tried to settle back and sleep but could still hear the noises of movement and when Charles got up quickly and put his head outside he saw something, or someone, duck away and into the bushes nearby. We tried, again, to settle and convince ourselves it was baboons but there didn't seem to be enough noise in the treetops and as we lay listening to the night noises we both clearly heard heavy breathing close to the tent and Charles glimpsed a man standing close and looking in through the mosquito net. Charles thought the man had something in his hand but when he called to him and got outside there was no sign of anyone, again.

By now we had given up the idea of a night's sleep and Charles decided to sit up all night on guard. We discussed the other option of packing up and moving on. Neither idea seemed very practical. Charles went off to look in the bushes and then found an area close to the second toilet block where there were other campers. I waited by the tent straining eyes and ears for any movement or noise. Charles came back and said there was some space in a pool of light and he would wait by the tent while I moved the loose items from the tent to the ladies' toilets. We then both carried the tent over with all the bedding and light things inside. I sorted out the tent while Charles bought Flossie and everything else over to me. We finally settled down at nearly three in the morning and although I got off to sleep I don't think Charles did again. Charles was convinced the night prowler was a weirdo whilst I thought he was a nervous thief whose heavy breathing when he got close gave him away.

After an eventful night we were up early and spoke to the camp manager. Her comment was that there were 'blacks' in the bushes around the camp which was not entirely fenced and that we "should have shot him." Easier said than done when we couldn't see him – and didn't have a gun.

Our route took us through Knysna in warm sunshine and through the very pretty Storm's River area and onto the cool, breezy coast at Jeffrey's Bay. We then turned inland for

Uitenhage to look for somewhere to stop for the night. We paused at a turn off the main road with a sign to a resort but almost immediately a car pulled up beside us and a white South African got out to ask if he could help. He told us the resort was "multi-racial" and explained this meant "black and white together". He seemed keen to put us off and went on that there was no restaurant and no shops at the resort. After a bit more discussion we found there were no camp sites around and that we were on the wrong road and that Port Elizabeth was the best option. We had hoped to avoid Port Elizabeth and looked out for camp sites all the way there. But, no luck and before we knew it another car stopped to help us and directed us to the resort area which was very popular with restaurants, bars, ice cream parlours, tourists and camp sites. The price for a tent included a bin liner and loo roll and we pitched the tent as close to a lamp post as possible in the hope of avoiding a repetition of last night's problems.

The next destination was Grahamstown but Flossie quickly went onto reserve and although we were sure we would find a petrol station we didn't and soon she was on her second reserve. We were still hopeful of finding petrol but we didn't and Flossie finally came to a stop in a lay-by 12 miles short of Grahamstown. Charles stood at the roadside with our petrol can and after two or three cars with white South Africans driving had passed him a car driven by a black South African stopped. He had no petrol to spare but offered Charles a lift to the nearest petrol station and I waited with Flossie. I sat just off the road for a while but when a large lorry pulled in I went and sat beside Flossie to be more visible – just as a precaution. After an hour Charles was back from a lift by another black South Africa and said that lots of white South Africans had ignored him trying to hitch. But, at least we now had enough petrol to get to Grahamstown and fill up Flossie's tank.

Beyond Grahamstown the road was scenic and wound through a mountain pass and we pressed on through a series of towns exactly like almost every town we'd seen in Kenya, Tanzania and Malawi. We hadn't seen this sort of road side town since Malawi and felt we'd been transported back a thousand miles north. The towns had vast areas of flat mud either side of the road which were busy with people buying, selling or getting on and off minibuses and taxis. The houses were poor but the places buzzed with activity. By the time we got to Queenstown we had decided to call it a day and pitched on a small patch of grass in a pleasant camp site.

We drove Flossie into town for gas and food but as we were at the checkout in the supermarket I heard a passer-by shout to us that someone had knocked our bike over. I turned and looked to see Flossie in the road on her side. We grabbed our shopping, helmets and change and rushed outside to where the driver of a car was apologising for what she'd done to Flossie. Charles gave the woman a fair amount of verbal abuse as he picked Flossie up but there seemed to be no damage, saved again by the panniers, and after a bit more abuse of the woman we left.

The days were hot and although it was a bit cooler when we were riding we began to feel cramped on Flossie. We arrived in Bloemfontein for a night's camping and then headed, once more, to Johannesburg. We only stopped to phone Sonia at the air freight company who confirmed prices and that there would be space on the flight for the 18th March. We took directions to her office and said we'd see her tomorrow.

Closer and closer to Johannesburg we could see the tall, glass skyscrapers of a modern city looming until we had to leave the motorway as motorcycles were not allowed on them. We found the city centre busy with traffic and people and followed signs to the post office. The post office was closed and Charles was bad-tempered and said that Flossie was going to break down "at any moment". But, Flossie didn't break down and we headed out to Kempton Park where we'd heard there was a caravan park and we could camp until our flights. We lost the signs though and after 10 minutes sitting in traffic and not sure we were going the right way we stopped at a petrol station and asked the pump attendant for directions. Johnson, as he introduced himself, was very keen to help and directed us by enthusiastically acting out every word with a hand waving, body weaving pantomime of left turns, right turns and "straight, straight, straight." This went on for a full five minutes with Charles leaning on the tank and nodding seriously whilst I was in a state of near collapse trying to suppress giggles. When Charles was sure he had got at least the gist of the directions and Johnson had worn himself out we headed off into the traffic fairly confident of finding the right road.

As it turned out the instructions were absolutely spot on and we soon saw the turning for Kempton Park. There were, however, no signs for a caravan park, no obvious centre and not many people on what seemed to be a large housing estate. We drove around for an hour and a half and asked directions several times whenever we saw anyone and although we got a long set of instructions we had ridden miles and seemed no closer to a caravan park. Eventually, it was dusk and as the sun set we found the right place and the manager. We explained we were short of cash and wanted to pay tomorrow which didn't go down too well until Charles offered his passport as security. This seemed acceptable and we were shown where to camp between a group of residential caravans with large awnings and patio furniture. After a difficult day of 300 miles we were, at last, in Johannesburg and had a week or two to sort ourselves out. No travelling for a while now.

No travelling did not mean no riding though and next day we went in search of a bank and Sonia to go through all the details of the air freight. It was agreed we would go to the crate builder on Monday morning and were given a final price. The price included several fees and charges we'd not known about and customs clearing of the carnet as well as a sum to the airline for 'dangerous goods'. This last item raised the matter of draining oil, petrol etc. Sonia seemed to think we might also have to remove the battery acid but would check this. We agreed to drop the carnet off on Monday en route to the crater and left quite happy that everything was in order and Flossie would be in safe hands. At least, we hoped she would be as we didn't buy any insurance.

Back at the camp site Charles took Flossie's pannier rails and front rack off and we began to think about what luggage would go in the crate with her and what we would keep with us. The next task was to get some more camping gas and thermal underwear in preparation for days without Flossie and riding in European weather.

Saturday, 14th March dawned and marked 11 months on the road for us. We made a trip to a supermarket to buy all the food we would need until Wednesday when we would fly out. Kempton Park had no public transport and the camp site was a long walk from the shops – a long way from anywhere, in fact. All the food we bought was tinned except for some fruit and bread.

We both kept busy with washing and sorting clothes and bedding and Charles made some repairs to his riding trousers which had lost a button and were torn at the bottom. We also had a chance to observe caravan park life. The vans were generally older than those we'd seen on the open road and the huge awnings gave the park the look of a shanty town. The vans were quite closely packed together and the ground and roadways were dusty and although we were told the vans were beautiful inside they can't have been very spacious. The biggest drawback, however, seemed to be the communal toilet facilities. Everyone went off to the shower and toilet block and it was common to see women and several small children trotting off in their night clothes with a basket or case for loo roll, towel, soap etc. We presumed the long term residents were on the lower end of the white South African social scale. No-one spoke to us.

On Sunday we sorted out the luggage and packed everything going with Flossie into her panniers. When we were satisfied we'd got it all sorted out we sat quietly reading. We heard a long, loud hissing noise. Charles stood and went to Flossie and knelt by the front tyre which was slowly going flat. Our spirits sank with the pressure in the tyre. The reason for the tyre going flat was a bit of a mystery and a disaster as we were due to deliver her to the craters tomorrow. Charles tried replacing the valve and pumped the tyre up but this did no good and he took the tyre off. This revealed a hole in the inner tube which Charles repaired with a patch. When he was happy the tube was inflated the tyre seated easily on the wheel but just as he picked it up to put it back on Flossie there was a hissing noise and it went flat again. The tyre had to come off again and we found the patch had split. By now the sun had set and we couldn't do any more in the gloom so went to bed with plans for an early start.

Charles was awake early and fixed the puncture by putting the old tube in again with a new repair. Fortunately, this did the trick and the wheel was back on Flossie before breakfast. We finished organising luggage into "Flossie's" and "ours" with fingers crossed we'd got it right. At the air freight office Sonia gave us the news we'd been dreading – we had to drain Flossie's battery acid for the flight. We explained we hadn't had to do this last time and that it would make Flossie immobile. Sonia agreed to take advice from two men in a back office who thought disconnecting the battery and isolating the terminals should be good enough. This is what we'd done before so we were happy.

Next, we discussed how we would clear Flossie's carnet through Customs when she had been crated because the lid would be sealed and no-one would be able to check her frame or engine number. The men decided to clear her through Customs before crating and went off to make out the airway bill. We then followed one of them to Customs at the airport and Flossie's frame number was checked by an official and the carnet was stamped. We were then led off to the craters and drove Flossie into their building. A dozen workers were cutting and moving timber and one came over to measure Flossie while Charles started stripping her down for travelling.

There was no sign of anyone with a pallet for the base of the crate but the boss told us they would do it all later and we should leave everything ready for them. While the workers went off for lunch we set to work bubble-wrapping Flossie's forks, screen, mudguard etc. Two workers helped Charles lift Flossie onto a temporary base so he could take the back wheel and spring out to make her sit lower. Once we'd done all we could we had to leave with just time to take a photograph of the man who would build the crate and pack everything. He quickly adjusted is overall, slicked down his close cropped curls with a damp hand and smiled at the camera. We promised him the photo if he took good care of Flossie.

The craters arranged a lift back to Kempton Park for us. We now had no vehicle, no panniers to sit on and no light from Flossie's battery. We were pedestrians. We missed her.

Tuesday, 17th March dawned for our final full day in Africa. We phoned Zambia Airways to confirm our flight and arranged for a taxi to get us to the airport the next day. We then phoned Sonia who told us the paperwork was still at the airport and the crate was not finished but promised someone would meet us at the airport early the next day with the paperwork. The craters had, however, confirmed the final crate size as slightly bigger than planned which had added 50 kilos and money to the bill. We knew she fitted into the dimensions we'd given them and after some bargaining they agreed to trim the crate down but it was still heavier/bigger than before. The final bill for Flossie was R1,573.85 plus R375 for her crate.

At 8.00 a.m on 18th March we waited for our taxi and arrived at an empty airport for security and check-in. Back outside the terminal building we waited for someone to find us with Flossie's paperwork and just as we were beginning to anticipate a last minute hitch a Mr. Patel from the craters arrived, smiling, with the news that Flossie was on her way. We thanked him, said goodbye and headed for passport control clutching the precious paperwork which would let us re-claim Flossie in Europe.

We took off promptly and I had a last look out the window at South Africa. It would really be my last look at Africa as it would be dark when we were in Lusaka. We flew over Bulawayo and Lake Kariba to Lusaka and were back on Zambian soil again. We settled down for our eight hour wait 'in transit' although it passed fairly quickly as we'd both saved a good book for the occasion. Once on board another aircraft we settled down for the night with the prospect of arriving early to a cold, European dawn. During our descent to Frankfurt the weather was described as grey and zero degrees Celsius. Welcome home to Europe!

We collected luggage, changed our last South African money to German Marks and drew some cash on our credit card. The ticket office for our train was efficiency itself and the clerk gave us a route and price and then a computer print out showing the route with arrival and departure times. We would have an hour's wait for a train to Koblenz, change there for Trier and then one further change to Luxembourg. The first train would leave at 8.03 a.m. and the two connections would be just a few minutes each to arrive at 11.27 a.m. precisely. German efficiency after the chaos of Africa was a joy.

In the coffee shop we fell into conversation with a man from the flight who had ridden down to South Africa on a bike very similar to Flossie. He had travelled part of the way with the two German brothers we'd met in Lilongwe and again in Namibia. He'd shipped his bike home – at least he hoped he had because he knew it hadn't left Cape Town yet.

On our own again Charles and I talked about our feelings to be on the way home. We couldn't decide whether we were happy or sad to be going home and were confused. The best I could say was that I didn't feel I was home yet but that the adventure was over. The travelling was done and I was just going home but in a travelling kind of way. It didn't really make sense.

Before too long it was time to board the train which was clean and modern and seemed to run on almost silent wheels. We hadn't as yet seen the light of day and it came as quite a shock to burst out of the underground station and tunnel and into daylight. A dull, leaden grey sky and leafless trees greeted us. It seemed oddly beautiful after the African sky and landscape we'd become used to seeing.

The train was a minute or so late into Koblenz so we had to get to the next one at a run but, fortunately, the ticket collector on the train had told us which one to head for which saved valuable time. As we rushed onto the next train and sank into our seats we realised we had finally taken our first breaths of the cool morning air.

Over an invisible border to Luxembourg and we noticed the signs changed from German to French and when we got off the train we changed our German Marks to Francs and followed a sign for tourist information. We picked up a map of the city and a list of hotel accommodation and stepped out into the familiar bustle of a European city. We found the post office and asked at poste restante expecting to find a letter from Charles's mum with Flossie's road tax and insurance. Nothing. The clerk seemed to think it may have gone to "the other post office". We decided we'd find a hotel and leave our bags to make city life easier.

The next post office wanted ID but we'd left ours at the hotel. Charles persuaded the clerk to tell us if there was anything and then we'd go back and get our ID. He found our letter and bent the rules "just this once", and just a little charge for the service, by accepting a credit card as proof of ID. We didn't care about the charge though as the letter had the documents we needed and a quick call to the Luxembourg office of the air freighters confirmed they had Flossie and we could go tomorrow to collect her. We would have her back by the weekend.

Although the afternoon temperatures rose to 13°C and we were warm in long sleeves and coats we knew that even with our additional layer of thermal underwear we would feel the cold when riding Flossie – especially if it was wet. But, undeterred by the prospect of the cold weather we took a bus to the airport and walked a short distance to the cargo terminal. We found the air freighter's office, collected the paperwork and agreed that for a reduced fee we could clear Flossie through Customs ourselves. We found a Customs Officer and showed him our road tax and insurance cover for Flossie and after a few minutes behind closed doors he handed everything back and Flossie was cleared. We soon saw her crate coming through the warehouse on a fork-lift truck. A warehouseman appeared with some tools to open the crate and revealed Flossie inside and wrapped in a large, black plastic sheet. The sides of the crate fell away, we tore off the plastic sheet and there was Flossie. I was so excited to see her again.

Once we'd got all the packing clear we could see some minor scrapes on her handlebar guards but all the loose parts were there and as Charles set about re-building her I re-organised and re-packed the luggage. Soon everything was ready to go and as we drove out of the warehouse just after midday the sun shone hesitantly through a grey sky. We'd had a small jerry can of petrol with us so the first stop was to fill her tank and bring the tyres up to road pressure before heading to Metz. We were soon in France, made good progress and were not too cold. With a couple of stops for food, drink and to stretch our legs we were in Epinal and decided to call it a day and stopped for the night.

The next day was a cool ride under a cloudy sky and I struggled to keep up with the speed of the passing scenery. There was so much to look at – compared to Africa. Our plan was to stop for a couple of days with Charles's brother and his wife in France so we stopped for some food and drink to take with us and just after lunch we rode into the courtyard of their home. They'd been there a year - the year since we'd left and, as before, there was snow on the grass verges.

During the next few days we caught up with all the family gossip and thought about our own futures. We were both nervous of returning to England and committing to life there. We were afraid of getting caught back up in the rat race we'd travelled to escape from. During our travels we had often thought of setting down new roots in a new country but had, for various reasons, dismissed all the countries we'd travelled through. The one idea which had stayed with us was France. We decided to head for home and make plans for house hunting in France. We both felt slightly silly in our clothes and Flossie was decked out for African travel so despite the cold, the snow thick on the ground and the roads being wet with slush we set off north again for England. We stopped frequently for hot drinks to warm up and found a cheap, motorway style hotel for the night in Macon.

The next morning we were ready for another day's ride but it seemed Flossie was not. Flossie wouldn't start. The alarm had been turned on all night and it, as well as the cold, had drained her battery. We tried bump starting her but I couldn't push fast enough to get up enough speed. Charles went off to see if there was a nearby garage but soon returned without having found one so I approached a man loading luggage into his car. I explained the problem and asked if he had any jump leads and although he didn't seem sure a bit of rummaging in the boot of his car and he found some. He manoeuvred his car into position beside Flossie and with the help of the leads and his battery Flossie burst effortlessly into life. Relief!

We were ready for another cold day riding and it began to snow. We were planning to get to Auxerre and hoping to get on the Sunday boat but both were beginning to look doubtful as we made so many stops to warm up. And, on Saturday we'd lost an hour overnight when the clocks changed. Heading to Rouen Flossie began to feel, and sound, very rough and I could feel bad vibrations on the back wheel. We'd known for a while that the shaft drive was suffering but suddenly it seemed very much worse. Fifteen miles or so from Rouen and Charles told me that we would have to get Flossie fixed in Rouen and may not even get that far. We had to find a BMW dealer to buy a special tool to take the shaft drive apart, find the problem and fix it. Parts might be required. It seemed a shame Flossie could not have hung on a bit longer before giving up on us but she had put up with an awful lot lately. As well as the shaft drive problem both her cylinders were throwing out oil. One had been in need of attention since Egypt and the steering had a 'notch' in it. It all meant we wouldn't get to the ferry today and maybe not tomorrow either.

We found a motorway chain hotel with no staff. This was a new innovation of the time with automatic check in, codes for access to rooms and the toilets and showers cleaned automatically. The shower cubicle was a large plastic-lined space with a plastic bench and behind a small screen was the shower itself. I stepped in and pressed the button. An immediate, powerful jet of temperature-controlled water shot across the cubicle and nearly took me with it. This surge lasted about a minute and then shut off until I pressed the button again. In this fashion I had a very fast, hot shower and when I emerged I rather felt I'd been 'processed' rather than had a shower. Was this the future?

We were sure that Charles' brother would have phoned their mum and told her we were on our way. We were just as sure that she, and my mum, would both be expecting to hear from us or, even, have us turn up on their doorstep. So, it seemed a good idea to phone home and explain our latest situation. I told my mum we were in northern France and hoped to get a ferry the next day but that we had broken down and it would be another day or two now. I told her we'd be keen to get to Charles' parents as our warm clothes and cat were there and we wanted both as quickly as possible. Charles phoned his mum but couldn't get through – she was probably, by then, talking to my mum who would have phoned with the news of hearing from us. When Charles did get through it was a rather difficult conversation. Charles' mum said our car (parked with them in our absence) needed a new battery and that she had agreed my mum would go and stay with them when we got home. We hadn't mentioned house hunting to my mum and Charles urged his mum not to make too many plans around us. It seemed we were not even home and our lives were being organised for us but was it really reasonable to think we could just go back, pick up some of the pieces of our former lives and go our own way?

However, warm clothes, the cat and mothers were in the future – first we had to get Flossie fixed and get a ferry to face it all. We found the BMW dealer by asking around and hoped desperately that Flossie would get us there. It began to rain and the vibration felt worse but we found the dealer and, to our relief, he was open. It was Monday and many, many businesses in France closed on Monday. To save lengthy explanations in our poor French we told the garage attendant we were on holiday and Flossie had a problem. Charles and the attendant (Roland) pushed her into the workshop and started to take her apart. Roland decided it was not the gearbox connection and went off for a test drive. He returned pushing Flossie and showed us that the back wheel was not really rotating at all. He carried on stripping her shaft drive and found the problem. The shaft drive universal joint was broken. In fact, it was smashed and had been rattling loose and caused damage inside. Roland phoned for a new part and told us it would arrive tomorrow. It was expensive at £300 but it meant we could be mobile again tomorrow and might make the night ferry from Dieppe.

Roland agreed to let us leave most of our luggage in his workshop and directed us to a small, cheap hotel just a few minutes' walk. It was midday and the cramped, cold room had a view across the dismal rooftops of Rouen. We had 24 hours to kill and it didn't look as though there was much to do on a wet, cold Monday in Rouen. We started a list of "things to do" when we got home. As the list lengthened we began to wonder whether our journey had been so hard!

When the list of "things to do" became too long and too depressing we went for a walk. We found a pretty, neat public garden with greenhouses of exotic plants and a small aviary of birds and a pond with some ducks. We mooched around a furniture shop and an electrical store and then bought 'The European' newspaper which was the only English language reading material we could find. We had a coffee and wandered back to our hotel in drizzling rain which turned to heavy rain and we dripped through the hotel reception to our room completely soaked.

The next day dawned bright with a blue sky and weak sunshine. We found Roland waiting for us in the garage and he said he would be going off shortly to get our part. We wandered off again into town to find a travel agent. We found one and that there was a sailing from Le Havre to Portsmouth that evening at 2300 hours. We were hopeful of catching this ferry.

Back at Roland's garage he had the part and was working to fit it. At 4.30 p.m. he took Flossie out for a test drive and declared that all was well. We loaded the luggage, paid the bill, thanked Roland and sped off towards Le Havre.

We drove through rain and sleet but got to the terminal at Le Havre in good time to book ourselves onto the overnight sailing. This would be the last night of our African trip and we celebrated our last evening with a rather good meal and some wine.

We reported to the dockside and boarded P&O's "Pride of

Hampshire" – next stop England.

Our African journey would end as it began – on a cross-channel ferry and as we left France I remembered that it was just as we left England that I wrote the first words in my journal. The journal was eight books ago and covered the 353 days, 50 weeks, of our journey. Then, the trip was just beginning and we didn't know what lay ahead. Now, it was all behind us as memories and the days ahead were as unknown and uncharted as the African trip had been then.

The journal pages began on board ship in the hours around midnight and so, appropriately, they finished…

THE BACK OF HIS HEAD

THE BACK OF HIS HEAD

20,000 MILES THROUGH AFRICA AS A PILLION RIDER

AFTERWORD AND ACKNOWLEDGEMENTS

This story of our journey was written from the journals I wrote as we travelled. The journals started with short, clipped sentences but soon developed in to a full record of every day. It became a labour of love to write it. On some days I didn't think we'd be doing anything and there would be nothing to write about. Usually, by the end of the day, there would be something to note and, often, there were pages of totally unexpected events to note down.

Most overland travellers sell their vehicles at the end of their journey (wherever that might be) or ride them home. We intended to sell Flossie in Cape Town but after so long with her she was a part of us and we couldn't part with her. We shipped her home. We still have her, ride her and have days out and holidays on her. Flossie is on her third official ID now: the original F702 VEL was replaced by a local Egyptian plate for travelling there and since we moved to France she has been imported and now has a French number plate.

Flossie carried us faithfully for every one of the 20,000 miles from 1,400 feet below sea level at the Dead Sea to 10,000 feet above sea level and the roadhead on Mount Kenya.

Some names in this story have been changed, others have not and some may recognise themselves.

Many, many others have made the journey we made and have made other, more challenging journeys. Modern overland travel is very different to ours. We did it with paper maps, large cameras with film in them, no internet, no mobile phones, no e-mail, no SatNav and no social media to constantly update and share. Life was simple.

When we got home we sent some 'thank yous' to those in Africa who had been so kind or helpful. We sent photographs we had taken to the school at the Kenyan border with Uganda where we bush-camped. We sent a poster of a BMW motorbike to Mohamed's son in Cairo. We sent the photo of the man who made Flossie's crate in Johannesburg to them. We kept in touch with some of our fellow travellers for a while and with others for many years. We are still in touch with some and count them as friends.

As we settled back into life in the UK we decided not to get another job, another mortgage and another house and to move to France. We married, moved to France and had two children and sometimes it seems travelling to Cape Town on a motorbike was the easy option but, that's another story!

Charles and I should thank his mum for minding our long-suffering cat and dealing with all the post and administration whilst we were away. My thanks to everyone who ever suggested I "should write a book", to one new acquaintance in particular for really giving me the impetus to do it and, most of all, to Charles - the love of my life and the back of the head I spend so many happy hours looking at....

Printed in Great Britain
by Amazon